ESSAYS
FROM THE
HERMIT'S LODGE

ALI KINTEH

First published in Great Britain in 2022
by Rogue Press Limited.

A CIP catalogue record for this book is available
from the British Library.

ISBN 978-0-9934609-3-7

Typeset in Centaur MT by
www.chandlerbookdesign.com

Printed in Great Britain by
Clays Ltd, St Ives plc

ACKNOWLEDGEMENTS

I AM ETERNALLY INDEBTED to my father and mother who fomented my love of books and the written word from an early age, and to my brothers and sisters, their respective spouses and their children. And to Kaiser, my perpetual luminosity, the love of my life.

To my brother Ousman for preserving our indelible, immarcescible bond since infanthood. **You** made this book happen! My infinite appreciation to Danielle Aumord, who first proposed that I produce blogs and essays to enhance my reputation as a writer. The enactment of her brainchild inevitably led to the creation of this book. My immeasurable gratitude to Crystal. What I owe you is beyond appraisal. My profoundest thanks to Kishan Ramsamy for his coediting of my book and his ceaseless support of this project.

To Debz Hobbs-Wyatt, who meticulously finetuned and edited the manuscript; Cyn, of *@create_and_evolve*, who designed and illustrated the marvelous book cover; Helen Oscar-John, one of the all-time greats I have ever known. Haylee Venus, founder of *Mek Ah Step* and co-founder of *Tahawal Theater Company*.

I am indebted to Nyima Chorr and her gracious family, Mazhar Muharrem, Leta Hussey (you often joked how one of your descendants will be flogging a signed copy of this book on *The Antiques Roadshow*), Auntie Maureen Defoe, Dee Nash,

Morina Oscar, John Chandler, Audrey Atkinson, Arslan Akhtar and Paul and Marline Jones. To Jackie Whicker, R.I.P. You will forever be remembered. Also, a special heartfelt thank you to the tender-hearted Nasrin Fokeerchand, Bijal *Queen Rani* Halai and the inimitable Bobby Lane.

To my author-siblings Tony Nesca, Nicole Nesca, C S Fuqua, Laura Kerr, Chrissi Seppe and Tony Prokash. Working on *Howls From The Underground* was an enjoyable experience. To my kind friends at Outcast Press for the generous publicity and solidarity online with Rogue Press. Thank you so much.

To my mother,

Yours was the hand that guided mine when I wrote my first word.
Yours was the voice that taught my tongue to speak.
Your vision gave sight to my imagination.
Your love generated feeling to my heart.

I dedicate this body of work to you, Mom. I love you very much.

Your firstborn.

"Although I am unmanifest, the unwise think that I am that form of my lower nature which is seen by mortal eyes; they know not my higher nature, imperishable and unsurpassed."

(Bhagavad Gita: 7: 24)

"Wilderness is not a luxury but a necessity of the human spirit, and as vital to our lives as water and good bread."

(Edward Abbey: Desert Solitaire)

"Happy the man and happy he alone. He who can call today his own. He, who is secure within, can say: 'Tomorrow, do thy worst! For I have lived today.'"

(Horace's Ode: To Maecenas)

ESSAYS FROM THE HERMIT'S LODGE

ABOUT ALI KINTEH

I'M JOE LAPTOP REALLY. Auteur. Author. Man of Letters. Inspired by Huginn (Thought) and Munnin (Memory). Seduced by the liberal arts. Semi-retired from human affairs. Enraptured by literature. Captivated by the camera lens. Obsessed with notions of order. Black coffee enthusiast. Awaiting the metempsychosis of Zarathustra. Prone to melancholy. Obviating deliberately from ovine congregation. Author of *The Nepenthe Park Chronicles* and *Essays From The Hermit's Lodge*.

PLIGHT OF THE ELUSIVE ANTIHERO

D URING THE MONTHS OF a sober October and a dismembered November, I spent many an evening reclining in splendid Dionysian isolation with an abiding Norteño cigar tucked sullenly between my lips. The odiferous scent is beguiling. The harmattan vapor fills my room. It's the little things that concentrates the mind the most. The great Persian philosopher-poet Omar Khayyam preferred the company *of a flagon of red wine, a book of verses, a lot of bread and a little idleness.* Those of us whose solitude requires that we are brooked from the hellscape of Neolithic incompetence, we cache our *sine qua non* in our small Elysium: Carte Noir coffee, Johnny Walker's bitter Black, Pinot Noir's Pompeian red, a buffet of musical genres on tap and a miscellany of books that exalts the intellect. The so-called lockdown induced a cathartic reimposition of priority and importance. I vivified myself with the books of dead women and men. The company of warm-blooded males and females were scarce. This social distancing caper has its proliferating returns. I am spared the corncrake shrills of the ultracrepidarian, and those who fuss and quibble on matters beneath and beyond them. *Where there is a person, there is a problem,* remarked a wry Joseph Stalin. *No person, no problem.* Though I quote the deceased Georgian tyrant by point of order, I am not, by any means, advocating his methods of problem solving.

Even if I possessed his means. People can go their way. I go mine. I am long spared the selective keening being agitated in online rabbit holes. There is much pettifogging in public on the banal and the puerile. Too much caterwauling concerning much-ado-about-nothing: disproportionate communal debating on provisional truths. This white noise rigmarole is an incurred affliction of our times. A malady wrought by decadence and destitution of real purpose. *The best lack all conviction, while the worst are full of passionate intensity,* wrote W.B. Yeats in his monumental piece, *The Second Coming.* I am confined to my room. Shag intrusions arrive by way of phone calls from Nicodemus by night. By day, he is a Tyrannosaurs Rex, among a host of Velociraptors, in a Canary Wharf tower overlooking the Thames River. To look upon him, you would not think it. But more on that captive bad boy later.

I cast my Acheronian-laden mind from the social curlicues of our times. The American author Saul Bellow wrote that *we privilege our own times.* Many of us, conspicuously, wallow in its benightedness. A supposed, second lockdown looms upon the worn horizon. The misbegotten contortions asked of the British people are calibrated to induce compliance and fear. The fatalism of the scoundrel, aped by state emissaries, reign unchecked in the rabbit holes of the airwaves and the mainstream. Their fevered and noisy blandishments, accompanied by a pervasive madness and nonsensical hysteria, are enough to make a cat laugh. I don't laugh often. Not these days especially. My phone pings whenever I am forwarded unhinged conspiracies regarding this coronavirus lark. I seldom waste a nanosecond on gormless memes and irrational nonsense. During the solitariness of a dismembered November evening, I wrote a 5,000 worded *cri de coeur* on the crude revaluation of the incalculable values that have been upended within my lifetime. I am not foredoomed, however, into thinking we are descending into a synthesis of doom and damnation. Our condition is entirely redeemable. We ought to forebear this whirlwind if we are to pull back from the precipice. To quote UK vocalist Seal from one of his

acclaimed songs: ... *We're never gonna survive, unless we get a little crazy.*
Touché! A little crazy, we must get.

As I pondered the tyrannical solipsism of our recent times, I
found myself harking to an ineffable phase of my distant past, when
narrative and fiction were the polymorphous, prime movers of my
lateral thought process. In a world that agued and shrived, narrative
and fiction beckoned me towards the counter precepts of meliorism
and nihilism. The paradigm of fiction and celluloid presupposes and
unentangles the components and contours that make us human. I
rejected the Manichean principle. That doctrinairism is murkier than
its simplicity supposes. The Mob find consensus in it. Many find
unanimity and purpose in the hollow timbers of received opinion,
which explains why rogue elephants, avenging angels and lone wolves,
of immeasurable understanding, operate their hardihood far from a
Ballardian dystopia. They keep their thoughts and deeds in purdah.
Not every thought or deed need be expressed publicly.

I had long considered the flailing problem of reward and
reputation in the face of a self-indulgent, perverse, reactionary
Mob, whether they be virtual or otherwise, prevaricating on paltry
matters as a major pastime. The imposition of a performative
morality covets applause and praise to thrive. A symbiosis palpably
exists therein. But should good deeds be governed by piety, intention
or optics? Should we even concern ourselves with its governance?
There are those who are so moved to help their brethren, like the
Good Samaritan who came to the swift aid of a poorly stricken soul
by the roadside. They facilitate for its own sake. Then they go about
their business without a murmur. Nor do they retain the need for
their good deeds to be videoed and rendered viral. But it begs the
question: if an individual, resembling the vainglory and wealth of
a Louis XIV of France, lifted one hundred thousand people from
poverty for the sole purpose of raising his already inflated status
in the eyes of the Mob, should we be seriously concerned of his
motives? Should we not simply applaud his charity? Would we call
his action *virtuous*, irrespective of motive? Or do we subscribe to the

ancient Chinese proverb that *virtue that strives to be virtuous is not virtue. Virtue that isn't aware of itself is true virtue.* Albert Einstein, meanwhile, preferred *silent vice to ostentatious virtue.* I repine that too.

I reappraised the most luminary harlequins I read in literature or watched on film, on whether they subscribed to these timeworn theories. The antiheroes, that came to mind, were antithetical to the people they protected. Herds, like cattle, are not bound by dialectic or reason. They are fettered by survival and self-preservation. These cinematic and literary protagonists moved indistinguishably by light of day. When they emerged from their repositories under the obscure night sky, they exhibited their brand of justice against those who sought unremitting power, high velocity chaos and interminable disorder. They used guile, guises and aliases. Others harbored their animus and amorality to stay the hand of wickedness and injustice. Their intentions were oft ambiguous. Their motives were often reciprocated with disdain and suspicion. They (if I could speak for them) could invoke the Machiavellian principle that *any man who tries to be good all the time is bound to come to ruin among the great number who are not good.* They kept their powder dry. *Praise the Lord. Now pass the ammunition.* They kept their carrots close and their sticks closer. *You can get further with a kind word and a gun than you can with just a kind word,* remarked Robert De Niro's Al Capone from the 1987 film, *The Untouchables.* Most of these characters were prone to cruel necessity. They exhibited a kernel of coldness. They were laconic and clinical. They possessed boundless mystification and resourcefulness. They did not subscribe to false virtues such as modesty and altruism. And they were not prepared to die on a cross.

Prometheus' story, however, is a rare exception of total goodliness. His tale is almost Christ-like. According to Aeschylus' *Prometheus Bound*, he molded man from clay. He taught man the facets of civilization, as Zeus, Father of the Greek gods, had instructed. But the Lord of Olympus prohibited man the knowledge of fire and the Titan disobeyed this injunction. Man required fire for the most obvious of reasons. Prometheus taught him its appliance by the most rudimentary of means. As punishment, Zeus instructed his son Hephaestus, and Kratus and Bia, children of the River Styx, to fetter him with unbreakable iron to the Caucasus Mountains. Furthermore, he commanded an eagle to devour Prometheus' liver by day. During the night, his liver would reinvigorate back into full form. The eagle returned the next morning to breakfast that same organ. His torment was revisited daily. Prometheus had the gift of foresight, something that eluded even the great Zeus himself. He foretold a scenario that could topple Zeus from his Olympus. Zeus offered to bargain for this information in return for his freedom. Prometheus refused to play ball. According to Hesiod's *Works And Days*, Zeus also took vengeance on man for obtaining and profiting from fire. He presented Prometheus' brother Epimetheus with the first woman Pandora as wife. She was granted special graces by the Olympian gods. She arrived with a jar, forever known as *Pandora's Box* owing to a mistranslation from the Dutch philosopher Erasmus. She kept the jar in her pantry. She was given a strict order not to open it. But, like Eve of the Garden of Eden, she was teemed by curiosity. All the ills that would plague human existence: *pain, pestilence, depression, misery, sickness, famine, terror, death* etc. escaped the jar after she disobeyed the instruction, and *the earth and sea became full of evils*. Elpis, otherwise known as *Hope*, was the last to escape the jug. For many, Hope is an anchor for optimism against a tidal wave of indiscriminate suffering. I consider her a placebo. Whilst Jesus Christ is revered for his sacrifice for mankind and, in some quarters worshipped as a god, Prometheus was never deified by a wholesome number. A plaintiff against the Titan may argue that, though his benefaction was well-intended and his penalty unjust, his deed was against the ordinance of divine Olympus. Christ, meanwhile, was an instrument of heaven. Another plaintiff may further contend Prometheus was fictitious. Christ was not. These are digressions within itself were I to address these points here, so I will not.

I will, however, make a digression of another sort: One lugubrious Wednesday, in mid sober October, I listened to an unwonted blather of churlish anecdotes on the *virtues* of perfidy and avarice. It was Mr. Tyrannosaurus himself, imbibing on Tunisian marijuana. I was bemused by his wanton réclame. He was without the humility of his midnight alter ego Nicodemus. He worked the hard yards. He was slave to the raptures of the body. He explained how he *washed clean* by sponsoring the destitute in poverty-stricken lands. He bragged about the thousands of Euros donated to refugees on the Syrian-Turkish border. He crowed about the provisions supplied to the good people of Bangladesh. Fuck the folks he was screwing over by day in business. These folks, he said, were as insidious as he. In the big city, you had to be unashamedly sanguivorous to prosper. He didn't mind admitting that. I had already been informed by his drinking pals that his blandishments were, at best, fabrications, and that I was listening to the voice of Jacob whilst the hands of Esau worked tirelessly in Asia Minor. I compared his disposition to Shakespeare's *Richard III* when he said... *And thus, I clothe my naked villainy with odd old ends stolen out of holy writ, and seem a saint, when most I play the devil!* Whether his munificence was true or not, I felt inspired to explore the conundrum of the antihero from the perspective of literature and film. Mr. Tyrannosaurus' fanfaronades were not my business. I longed to return to *The Hermit's Lodge* in splendid Dionysian isolation with a Norteño cigar and my Dell laptop.

After I eventually wrenched myself from his company, I returned to *The Hermit's Lodge*. I settled for a convalescent smoke, courtesy of Central America's finest export. My mind rekindled a plethora of Jolly Roger stories past told, and the harlequins and heretics that starred in them. Among the fabled symphonies etched in my mind's eye was *The Scarecrow of Romney Marsh*, an excrescence from the mind of British novelist Russell Thorndike, younger brother of legendary Shakespearean actress Sybil Thorndike. The hero of these pages was the Janus-faced Dr. Christopher Syn. The incarnation that introduced me to this protagonist was the 1963 Walt Disney film titled *Dr. Syn alias The Scarecrow of Romney Marsh*. Legendary American-Irish actor Patrick McGoohan played the elusive hero.

By day, the Reverend Doctor Christopher Syn was a run-of-the-mill 17th century parson. He granted comfort, sustenance and prayer to the parishioners of Dymchurch-Under-The-Wall, who were under the yoke of cruel levies imposed by His Majesty's Customs and Excise. By night, he was the imperious said Scarecrow, leader of motley bandits. He roamed the Kent-Suffolk marshes, smuggling tobacco and brandy from continental Europe. He wore an imposing basilisk scarecrow costume. He spoke with a chilling, rasping voice. His bloodcurdling cackle was reminiscent of the Devil's shrill. Thorndike wrote that he rode a black stallion named Gehenna, so named after a valley in Jerusalem where, according to the Book of Jeremiah, Judean kings sacrificed children by fire. Thorndike's books were inspired by the Hawkhurst Gang of the 18th century. They revolted against the Inland Revenue for fifteen years but they were eventually beaten. Their leaders, Arthur Gray and Thomas Kingsmill, were captured and executed. McGoohan's Dr. Syn, however, fared much better. Only his sexton Mipps (*nom de guerre* Hellspite) and the Squire's son John Banks (otherwise known as The Curlew) knew the identity of the Scarecrow. And it was gratifying to watch the final scene when, after the prisoners were freed, his battles won and his motley men having emigrated to the New World with their spoils of rebellion in tow, Dr. Syn sipped a hearty toast with Squire Thomas Banks in honor of the Scarecrow. (Squire Banks' eldest son had also been rescued from prison and put on the high sea to America by the Scarecrow, having been captured by the Press Gang on charge of desertion). The noble Dr. Syn required no reward for his goodness, save for his scant personal satisfaction for a job well done. Even as I watched as a boy, I remember feeling particularly heartened by that self-congratulatory sherry-sipping scene.

Zorro and *The Scarlet Pimpernel* are cut from the same cloth as *The Scarecrow*. Zorro (Fox, in Spanish) flashed his rapier in the Pueblo of Los Angeles, Spanish California. He was the creation of American pulp writer, Johnston McCulley. His guile and cunning meant he easily outwitted the pursuing authorities. Zorro was a staunch defender of the downtrodden and oppressed. He called upon a band of loyalists who dared not reveal his identity. *The Scarlet Pimpernel*, the creation of author Emma Orczy, was the *nom de guerre* and calling card of Sir Percy Blakeney, a decadent fop who lived during the Reign of Terror in 18th century Paris. His social endeavors, as a wit and raconteur, delighted the aristocracy (or what was left of them). He was also an audacious swordsman who rescued French nobles condemned to the guillotine. Like *Zorro* and *The Scarecrow*, he possessed a retinue of loyalists, whom he could call upon. Orczy also wrote a splendid novel *Beau Brocade*, based on a fictional Dick Turpin-type highwayman. Brocade was once Captain Jack Bathurst of His Majesty's White Dragoons who, having fallen from Royal Grace, bore a price of hundred guineas for his head. I should hasten to mention *The Crimson Pirate*, a motion picture swashbuckling 1952 sea caper, starring Burt Lancaster, as the valiant Captain Vallo. Nick Cravat played his mute lieutenant, Ojo. Vallo's seafaring factotums harnessed the seas of the Caribbean blue and pillaged the king's frigates. Vallo's fecundity of mind and permeating energy enabled him to finally outgun the villain of the film, Baron Gruda. And of course, Robin of Locksley, better known as Robin Hood, is in keeping with these buccaneering types. What has been written of him are plenty. But the fables are mostly in agreement that he was a resident of Sherwood Forest, Nottingham. He rode with a band of Merry Men clad in lincoln green. He robbed from the rich. He gave those spoils to the poor. He constantly bamboozled the Sheriff of Nottingham and evaded his noose. He was loyal to his king, Richard the Lionheart, but hunted and ate the King's Deer. The trope of the gentleman outlaw is concordant with the ancient Chinese proverbial that *a gentleman does not fight. But were he to do so, he would win.*

In Confucianism, the gentleman *Junzi* is terse in speech but robust in action. He seeks fulfillment within himself. He possesses no need to seek meaning outside himself. This discipline is in keeping with the Clint Eastwood *Man With No Name* persona, whom he played in classic Westerns: *A Fistful Of Dollars, A Few Dollars More* and *The Good, The Bad And The Ugly*. Eastwood's character seldom betrays motive. He is called Joe and Blondie. His true name is unknown. He is a wanderer. He scarcely wastes words. He is clinical with his pistol. His desert-brown eyes scan the badlands of uncultivated America. He is a *Ronin* (a wave man) without retinue. In *High Plains Drifter*, Eastwood plays an enigmatic, menacing stranger who comes to the willful aid of an old mining town, whose inhabitants are in fear of a triumvirate of soon-to-be released convicts. The town seeks his help after he shoots dead the mercenaries hired to rid them of the aforementioned convicts. His price is high. The Stranger discovers quickly that the townsfolk are both corrupt and cowardly. They yield to his every whim. He becomes the sole occupant of an entire hotel. He appoints a local barber as both sheriff and mayor. He rapes a woman who slaps a cigar from his mouth. He sleeps with the hotelier's wife in her husband's bed. The town's inhabitants are ill-equipped to deal with him, and the gunmanship of the three convicts when they finally return. And it is the Stranger who slays the unholy trinity by use of the bullwhip and pistol. *I never did know your name*, says the Stranger's appointed mayor. *Yes, you do*, he answers cryptically. He then rides into the yeasty wilderness, as countless lone wolves have done, before and after him.

Eastwood's final Western released in 1992, *Unforgiven*, is his most acclaimed of the genre. William Munny's cinematic exit on his pale horse, as the one-time retired assassin, is in the ferocious rain, not with the rosy sunset as a backdrop. He leaves Big Whiskey, having slain the unfeeling Sheriff Lil Bill Daggett and several of his minions. His presumptive biographer W. W. Beauchamp (Saul Rubinek) observes studiously as he leaves town. The denouement was written for him by scripture two thousand years ago: *And I looked, and behold a pale horse: and his name that sat on him was Death, and Hell followed with him.* (Revelation: Chapter 6 Verse 8). An earlier iteration of Death riding a pale horse is seen in the 1985 Eastwood film *Pale Rider*. An enigmatic preacher appears as an answer to the prayer of young Megan Wheeler. She asks God for one miracle after her dog is killed during a raid on her village by vagabonds. The Preacher brings death and pestilence to the wrongdoers, as scribed in the Good Book. And there is the mysterious gunslinger Shane, played by Alan Ladd in the enduring 1953 motion picture, *Shane*. Shane, like the arcane prophets and hell's angels before him, emerges from the boondocks. His past is obscure. Of his proficiency with a pistol, there is no doubt. Young Joey Starrett warms to him and loves him whilst he worked on his parents' homestead. Like Megan, Joey's family and folks are plagued by bad men who want them evicted from their lands. And like Eastwood's Preacher, Shane brings death and hell to those bad men. The final scene between Shane and young Joey is one of the most touching farewells recorded on film.

Guile and cunning were the hallmarks of Odysseus, the Sacker of Cities. Whilst Achilles and Ajax are universally recognized as the greatest warriors among the invading Greeks, it is difficult to envisage how mighty Troy would have fallen had Odysseus not partaken of the Trojan War. It was he who convinced Achilles (and after Achilles was slain, his son Neoptolemus) to join the Greeks since it was foretold that Troy could not fall without their participation. It was he that conceived and orchestrated the theft of the Palladium, or the Luck of Troy. It was his stratagem that devised the plot of the Wooden Horse that hastened the destruction of Troy. His *nostos* to Ithaca is one the most famous narratives of all human history. That decade long voyage home saw him encounter the Lotus Eaters, Aeolus the Keeper of the Winds, the Cyclops Polyphemus, the Laestrygonians, the witch Circe, the Sirens, Scylla the six-headed monster, the whirlpool Charybdis, and the nymph Calypso. He bore the enmity of the Sun God Helios for slaying his sacred cattle and the hostility of Poseidon, God of the Sea, for blinding his son, the Cyclops Polyphemus. After returning to Ithaca, he slays the 108 suitors that sought the hand of his loyal wife Penelope. The Homeric and Ulyssean virtues are incompatible with the cardinal rectitude of the Abrahamic and Central Asian faiths. Shrewdness, deception, cunning and fibbing ensure Odysseus wins decisively. His protector, the goddess Pallas Athena, praises his duplicity in the *Odyssey*. ... *Even if a god were to encounter you, he would need to be wily and devious to outdo you in cunning... Since you* (Odysseus) *are far best of all mortal men for stratagems and fables, and I* (Pallas Athena), *among all the divinities, am famed for my wisdom and subtlety...* For the record, Dante was unimpressed with the deeds of Odysseus, having studied him solely through Latin texts, in particular Cicero's *De Finibus* and Virgil's *Aeneid*. Ulysses (Odysseus' Latin name) is condemned as *scelerum inventor* (deviser of crimes) and *dirus* (dreadful). In his epic poem *Inferno*, Dante casts him in the Eighth Circle of Hell as a *false counselor*. You cannot please everybody!

I doubt fiction has, in its sempiternal cauldron, forged a more insurmountable bad ass figure than John Milton's Satan in *Paradise Lost*. He is the Evening Star. He shines refulgent in the darkness. He dared to instigate a *coup d'état* against the Lord God Himself, who created him from the smokeless fires of Samum. Legend had it that Satan had been Head of the Celestial Choir and lead tenor at the Heavenly Hacienda. The Michael Bublé of his day. But he resented his herbert existence. He was bored of the tautology: the quixotic gowns, the tireless servitude, the tedious carol singing, the obstreperous repetition of *hallelujah* for ten billion years. He was certainly a sadist but equally a savant. He spearheaded an army of disaffected angels. *Non serviam* was emblazoned upon their banneret. They charged towards the Pearly Gates. They were intercepted there by the Archangel Michael and the Seraphim. The cosmic war raged for three Xanadu days. Then Jesus Christ entered the battlefield and, singlehandedly, defeated entire legions of devils, demons, hellions, imps and ifrits. The Apostate Angel himself was soundly whopped. He and his factotums were cast *nine times the Space that measures Day and Night* into Pandemonium, capital city of Hell. *He,* according to Milton, *with his horrid crew lay vanquisht, rowling in the fiery Gulfe, confounded though immortal. But his doom reserv'd him to more wrath, for now the thought both of lost happiness and lasting pain torments him.*

In the terrors of Tartarus, Satan reenergizes his forces with his bellicosity. I cannot fail to be impressed by his eloquence in the deepest, darkest bosom of an unplumbed, swirling firestorm in front of a Motley Crew of Cruels, soaped with abject lassitude. He delivers a speech that, in my humble view, dwarfs Shakespeare's Henry V's famous declamation (bathed by Laurence Olivier's valiant light) at the battle of Agincourt. *The mind is its own place, and in itself can make a Heav'n of Hell, a Hell of Heav'n. What matter where, if I be still the same, and what I should be, all but less than he whom Thunder hath made greater? Here at least, we shall be free. Th'Almighty hath not built here for his envy, will not drive us hence: Here we may regain secure, and in my choyce, to reign is worth ambition though in Hell. Better to reign in Hell than serve in Heav'n.* His lieutenants Belial, Mammon and Moloch counsel on whether to take up force of arms once more, or simply settle for their lot and mine the pits of hell. The Lord of the Flies, and Satan's second-in-command, Beelzebub proposes a third way: a new front in the war to corrupt God's new green earth and his vicegerents, Adam and Eve. His legions accept his plan. They could hardly otherwise reject it. No devil dares volunteer to put this scheme into motion so Satan offers himself for the job.

Long is the way and hard, that out of Hell leads up to light. Satan, *the proud aspirer,* braves the perils of Abaddon. He meets his daughter, Sin. She guards the gates of Hell. Above her waist, she is all-woman. Below her girdle, she is serpent-tailed. She was birthed from his head in much the same way Pallas Athena sprung from the head of her father Zeus. And since mortal sin is conceived in the mind, it was only natural, for want of a better word, she emerged from there. Satan had lusted after Sin when he had been Celestial Choirmaster. He raped her and she begot Death, who was *fierce as ten furies, terrible as Hell.* Death, in turn, raped his mother and she begot the monsters that feasted upon her duodenums, jejunums and bowels, barking and shrieking as they did. Death was stirred to intercept the Devil but was on the verge of defeat, had not mother intervened and introduced father to son. Satan informed them of his plans and promised that they would all rule over God's new creation - Sin and Death would be a constant among the sons of Adam, daughters of Eve. Sin permits him to fly through the gates of Hell. Chaos, and his consort Night, directs him towards Earth. But *to cut a long story short*, to quote Spandau Ballet, Satan achieves his objective by convincing Eve to eat the fruit from the Forbidden Tree. Eve and Adam are expelled from Eden. Satan returns to Hell in triumph. Though he and his acolytes morph into serpents whilst they celebrate, they return to preside over the corruption of the entire earth with their allies, Sin and Death. In the 1997 film, *The Devil's Advocate*, Al Pacino's character, incidentally so-named John Milton but revealing himself later as Satan, delivers a thunderbolt line worthy of a moment's contemplation: *Who, in their right mind, could possibly deny that the 20th century was entirely mine?* If you, dear reader, believe in the physical existence of an actual Prince of Darkness, you might want to consider, in the tide of Coronavirus infections, whether he be clear favorite for claiming the 21st century too. The wicked, truly, do not rest.

Neither does the elusive antihero. In the 1968 film *The Thomas Crown Affair*, Steve McQueen's Thomas Crown masterminds an elaborate robbery involving five men who know not his identity. The heist unfolds seamlessly. More than $2.6 million is stolen. He retrieves the entire amount disposed in a waste bin left by the getaway driver. He distributes to the men their share of the money through Swiss Bank accounts. He returns to his abode without a scratch on his back. In the solace of his home, he celebrates with a glass of whiskey and a delectable cigar. He laughs and jigs to himself. He craves no kudos nor spotlight. He requires no pat on the back or outward praise. This is also true of the Special Forces. They complete their classified mission by virtue of silence and surprise. They return to their base quietly. They uncork their favorite poison. They sing Queen's *We are the champions*. They might dare to smoke Gurkha Black Dragon cigars! But their gallantry will be neither confirmed nor denied by Her Majesty's government. The public will not know of their successes or scars. A large part of the magnetism that pulled me towards a Simon Templar type (The Saint no less), or a Robert McCall of *The Equalizer* fame, a James Bond or even Paul Kersey of the Death Wish films, was their clandestine ruthlessness with which they pursued with maximum prejudice. *Conceal me for what I am and be my aid*, uttered the resourceful Viola in William Shakespeare's *Twelfth Night. For such disguise as haply shall become the form of my intent.* Consider how Superman conceals his identity, how the masked Batman comes out at night. Superman sought refuge in his *Fortress Of Solitude.* Batman lay low in his Batcave. They applied their supernatural powers for the betterment of Planet Earth. They sought no reward for aiding mankind, except their own self-indemnification. Batman was so unyieldingly enigmatic that many residents of Gotham City were intimidated by his unpredictability and mystery. The Mob demand indiscretion, nakedness and revelation from their public figures. They mistrust what they cannot envisage. It didn't matter much that Batman was chief protector of their crime infested city. In their hour of need, they would shine the Bat Signal into the night sky and wait impatiently for his help. But even Batman himself was not unmindful of the caprice of public opinion. *You either die a hero or live long enough to see yourself become a villain,* he opined.

Loneliness is the coin opposite of solitude. Solitude is an oasis where one thrives in splendid isolation. One disenthralls himself from the world and shades himself from the teeth of philistine winds. His itineraries require nobody's permission. Loneliness is a desert where the wādī runs dry. Mirages befog the horizon and deludes the mind. The loner, meanwhile, is prone to profound sadness, lingering apathy and simmering rage. It is important not to conflate these two states of being. Those who have withdrawn from the world, not from choice, but from their feeling of inadequacies are pained by experience. In Albert Camus' *The Stranger*, we see a similar manifestation in the lead character Meursault. He is apathetic. His life finds no meaning. His indifference commits him to reckless murder. The murder leads to his own trial and extinction. The fact that he cannot grieve for his mother on the day of her funeral exhibits his dearth of human feeling. Camus later wrote *the hero of my book* (Meursault) *is condemned because he doesn't play the game.* As his end approaches, Meursault takes solace in life's absurdities. He reconciles with its senselessness. In the same vale we find Cross Damon, the lead character in Richard Wright's solemn novel *The Outsider.* His perpetual suffering in America injects the vulgarity and meaningless of being. He is considerably meek in the face of an unrelenting power. He is scalded and seared by racism. He finds no refuge in religion or ideology. He is an intellectual who doesn't know his mind or heart. His education has not liberated him. It has only served to puzzle and imprison him. He drinks liquor to ease the pain. After he is believed to be dead, he creates a new identity. However, his misfortune exacerbates. An unfortunate chain of events breeds a murderous inclination that culminates in the death of four people, by his own hand. Before he is executed by the State, he is asked about his life. *It was horrible,* he replies.

2020 was a year of palliatory, not curative solutions. Innumerable lives have been barnacled by covid. Winter has rung in December skies. A Fourth Tier of the so-called lockdown has been marked. The Third Tier was deemed insufficient to curb the mutating virus and its variant brethren. Like *The Three Mothers*, this disease has produced sighs, darkness and tears in abundance. I have even heard talk of a Tier Five. I can feel the modulated timber of town life suppurating in near silence whenever I walk through the town center, breathing God's air. The River Brain susurrations cuts crispier without the sound of children playing. Britain remains worn as we reach for the New Year. But we should not be shorn into compliance, conformity, submission and unpleasantness, even while the world is at its darkest and unfriendliest. As Sheikh Ilderim advised Judah Ben Hur when he spoke of their mutual friend Balthasar, in the 1959 epic film *Ben Hur: Balthasar is a good man. But until all men are like him, we must keep our swords bright. And our intention true.* The blackguards outnumber the Balthasar's among us. But we must still *keep our swords bright and our intention true.* If we are to return to some semblance of normality, we are inclined to rely on a modern-day Prometheus, burrowing away in some laboratory, conjuring an antidote that could deliver people from the mortal risk of pestilential harm. We may not know her face on sight. His name may not sit on our tongues. She may not possess the flamboyance of a Zorro, a Beau Brocade or a Scarecrow. They need not be rogue or outlaw. The door should remain ajar if they need be. *Maybe they could be heroes,* as David Bowie put it, *just for one day.* What is prescribed lawful is not necessarily right, as most are inclined to believe. Deeds rendered illegal forty years ago are safeguarded by Common Law today. These outliers of progress will be offered ribbons, buttons and titles. Their smiles emblazoned in media print. Their faces lit by paparazzi flashbulbs. Both State and Society have a marauding appetite for the flesh of *cause célèbres.* The permanent need for the independence of mind to question, scrutinize and challenge authority, even if they be a lone person in the tundra, is paramount for any freethinking milieu to thrive. Even if the penalty be ridicule. Even if the price be vindication after death. And like Satan, they reserve the right to declare themselves *non serviam.* This covid vortex is fleeting and ephemeral. Our principles should remain earnest and steadfast. *Do you not think,* to quote the 13th Governor of the State of Virginia, John Page, *that an angel rides in the whirlwind and directs this storm?*

December 22, 2020.

YUL BRYNNER:
THE KING AND I

I N THE FINAL SCENE of Cecil B. De Mille's 1956 Biblical motion
picture, *The Ten Commandments*, the Lord of Hosts for all intents
and purposes, holding aloft two tablets of imperishable stone, saw fit
to plagiarize the vaunted refrain of *Rameses II* in His final analysis: *So
let it be written. So let it be done.* It is somewhat germane that the master
villain in this visual wonder fest is subject to this peculiar *homage*.
Not that it would have displeased the leathery actor who portrayed
the Bronze Aged Pharaoh. For Yul Brynner was an Augustan actor
within the reels of real life, theater and film. His debonair grace and
distinctive radiance were replenished by his colossal and flamboyant
character roles. His pulchritude and personality redounded upon
those who crossed paths with him. His accent was extrinsic but
unambiguously self-assured. He would remain among the apogee
of Hollywood for almost forty years.

When I was a lamb, there were four terrestrial TV channels
and no 'pause and rewind' option on remote controls. My father
often watched sword-and-sandal matinée epics that lasted an entire
afternoon. These motion pictures depicted some of the greatest
fictions and figures in human history: *Spartacus, El Cid, Ben Hur,
The Robe, Alexander The Great, King of Kings, The Ten Commandments,
Doctor Zhivago, Lawrence Of Arabia, The Fall Of The Roman Empire, Samson*

And Delilah. Etc. Etc. Etc. These ineffaceable films were the best of the peplums. The dialogue was often cerebral. The accompanying ethereal soundtracks were exquisitely coated with elegance. The good were nonesuch and noble. The diabolically wicked were accursed with their cowardly plotting. They were verily damned in the end. Things were more or less exorbitant and elementary in the olden days when God, or the gods, spoke directly to Man.

I could rhapsodize on Yuliy Borisovich Briner unfettered all evening. For brevity's sake, I shall limit my meager words to a few thousand. For here was a man, positively secure within his own skin. He saw no need to seek his self beyond himself. When he was in Switzerland, he was as Swiss as a Rolex watch. In France, he was as Parisian as the Notre-Dame. In America, he was as American as John Wayne. His congruence among men was admirable. He demanded respect and accepted nothing less. His regal returns in *The King And I, The Ten Commandments, Anastasia, The Brothers Karamazov, Solomon And Sheba, The Magnificent Seven, Taras Bulba, Villa Rides!* and *Westworld* established him as one of the standout actors of his generation. His countenance, in some of his films, was like that of Percy Bysshe Shelley's *Ozymandias: ... whose frown and wrinkled lip, and sneer of cold command...* and Brynner would, of course, play Ozymandias on film. His gimlet-eyed stare and shaven head made him instantly recognizable. His mélange components were demonstrative of a man whose home could have bordered any one of the seven seas.

The bagatelles he told of his heritage were an obscuration. He claimed, among other things, that his birth name was Taidje Khan, that he was born of a *black Mongolian gypsy woman* who died giving birth to him on the island of Sakhalin which nested in the Sea of Okhotsk. His father was supposedly Japanese-Swiss. Or a Japanese prince in another version of the tale. His only son, Rock, wrote a demystifying book after his death titled: *Yul: The Man Who Would Be King.* His candid pen strokes included incroyable accounts of Brynner's corruption by fame, the revelation that he and his siblings were removed from their father's will, and that his fourth wife Kathy Hill inherited whatever was left behind. It was unfortunate to read these suppurating issues in any family. These cleavages between kin are ineluctably human.

The truth of his ancestry and early life were no less byzantine than the myth. He was a synthesis of Swiss-German-Russian-Buryat. He was born in the port-city of Vladivostok, Russia, on July 11, 1920. His mother Marousia and older sister Vera were both performers. They migrated to Paris, France, when he was still a boy. He played guitar while singing Roman and gypsy songs in Russian nightclubs to cosmopolitan audiences. You can listen to Brynner's attar-preened vocals signing in glorious Russian verve on YouTube, if you so choose to. He is accompanied by the acclaimed gypsy singer, Alyosha Dimitrievich. He became a trapeze acrobat in a French circus. A back injury compelled him into acting. Just as World War II was foreboding, he and his mother traveled to Harbin in north-eastern China. And while that part of the world was fomenting with internecine tumult by the threat of a Japanese invasion, they crossed the ocean aboard the *President Cleveland* bound for America.

He studied acting under the tutelage of Michael Chekov, nephew of the Russian playwright and short storyteller Anton Chekov. He embarked on short spells working on TV and radio. He was photographed nude by subversive photographer George Platt Lynes. He successfully auditioned for the part of *King Mongkut* of Siam in the theater production of *The King And I*. He is forever closely associated with that role. He won a *Tony Award* for his performances. When he starred in the *Rodgers and Hammerstein* film version alongside Deborah Kerr, he won the *Academy Award* for Best Actor. He stood magnificent in character, in crown, in costume. *Song Of The King.* He waltzed across the stage effortlessly with Ms. Kerr. *Shall We Dance?* The chemistry between them was *Something Wonderful* to behold. In the meanwhile, legendary American filmmaker, Cecil B. De Mille, was earnestly searching for an actor with peculiar qualities to play *Rameses* in the remake of his silent 1923 classic *The Ten Commandments.* When he stumbled upon Yul on stage playing *Mongkut*, he instinctively recognized his Pharaoh. *Getting To Know You.*

Brynner's performance, in only his third film, as the rarefied but perpetually brooding Rameses II was both resplendent and imposing. The haughty but hierarchical son of Sir Cedrick Hardwick's Sethi viewed Charlton Heston's Moses with acute suspicion from the outset. *I am the son of your body*, he told his father who dared suggest a rival to his birthright. *Who else can be your heir?* Moses was the obelisk that stood before the throne of Egypt and the throbbing heart of the Princess Nefretiri (Anne Baxter). Both rival brothers, as they were then, possessed chiseled pectorals and stout shoulders. Brynner was pressed to work on his muscle tone. He had been a little discombobulated by Heston's physique. Rameses was wilier than Moses, thanks to his alliance with Dathan (Edward G. Robinson), the scapegrace Hebrew overseer.

There existed a prophecy that obnubilated the House of Pharaoh; that a slaved Hebrew from the land of Goshen would deliver the Children of Israel from bondage in Egypt. And while a gallant Moses was encumbered by Royal Sethi into building a new city, the resourceful Rameses was tasked with finding whether the deliverer be myth or man. *If he's a myth, bring him to me in a bottle*, Sethi instructed. *If he's a man, bring him to me in chains.* Rameses responded with his envoi that served him well throughout this near four-hour epic: *So let it be written. So let it be done!* Having forewarned the nubile Nefretiri who betrothed herself to Moses, *you will be my wife. You will come to me whenever I call you...*, he delegated the task of finding the deliverer to the stoolpigeon Dathan whilst milling around on his chariot. *You have a rat's ears and a ferret's nose*, Rameses told him through wrinkled sneer. *Add to them the eyes of a weasel and find me this deliverer!* The deliverer of the Hebrew nation was, of course, Moses. And Dathan was able to deliver Moses unto Rameses ...*with the blood of the master builder* (Vincent Price's Baka) *red upon his hands.*

Rameses would, undoubtedly, have gained the upper hand over Moses after casting him into the wilderness of Shur, had the Lord of Hosts not intervened in the form of a Burning Bush. Moses was divinely emboldened to smite Rameses (who became Pharaoh upon Sethi's death) with his trusty staff (which transformed into a serpent at his bidding) and free God's people (the Children of Israel). He spurned the advances of the now Queen Nefertiri, *like a strumpet in the street*. Fetid blood spunked the Nile River. Darkness covered Egypt for three days. The obstinate Pharaoh yielded finally after the most dreaded plague, the Destroyer, took the lives of the firstborn males of Egypt, which included his only son and heir. Queen Nefertiri, who appeared more pissed having been rejected by Moses than the death of her firstborn, coerced her husband to gather his chariots and slaughter the Children of Israel in the desert. And while Moses parted the sea and barred Pharaoh's army with divine fire from the heavens, Rameses uttered probably the haughtiest line in all of cinema history: *Better to die in battle against a god than to live in shame!*

Brynner's cuthbert Rameses arguably outshone Heston's credible Moses in this timeless blockbuster. Both actors would star together in a mediocre affair called *The Buccaneers*, directed by Mexican-American icon Anthony Quinn. Brynner played the role of Jean Lafitte, the infamous French smuggler. Heston was General Andrew Jackson, future President of the United States. Before *The Buccaneers* and after *The Ten Commandments*, Brynner enjoyed a string of motion picture successes. He starred with Swedish superstar Ingrid Bergman as General Bounine in *Anastasia*, which was based on a play of the same name by French playwright Marcelle Maurette. This film marked Bergman's return to Hollywood. She had been blacklisted following an illicit affair with married film producer Roberto Rossellini, which resulted in a child out of wedlock. Bergman won an exultant Academy Award for Best Actress in the title role, which was, perhaps, some consolation for past troubles. And then Brynner played the eldest brother Dimitri in the film adaption of Fyodor Dostoevsky's august novel *The Brothers Karamazov*.

For *Solomon And Sheba*, Brynner accepted the role of the wisest of kings alongside sultry Italian goddess Gina Lollobrigida. He was hired upon the untimely demise of Tyrone Power, who was initially cast as Solomon. Neither Brynner nor Power's Solomon was the Solomon I read of in the Old Testament. Neither was Gina's Sheba. Their 1959 picture was far from their finest. Brynner's Solomon not only incurred the wrath of his older brother Adinojah (played by George Sanders) having denied him his birthright by becoming King of Israel but he brought the Sheban god Almaqah for worship before the god of his fathers. His concupiscence for the orgasmic Queen of Sheba blinded the Wisdom of Solomon. Not even the stern chastisement of a perpetually indignant Prophet Nathan could abate his desire. The film was not a petard for the careers of Brynner and Lollobrigida. It is memorable insofar as the habitually bald-headed Brynner wore a hairpiece for the role.

Not only was he central star of the Western classic *The Magnificent Seven*, he held main sway on the casting. He selected Steve McQueen to play Vin Tanner, the next supporting character to his Chris Adams. He clashed famously with McQueen, who exploited every tincture of screen time they shared together. They reconciled almost twenty years later when McQueen was dying from cancer. *Taras Bulba* produced another decent offering. Brynner was apparently comfortable playing percipient strongmen. Plainly, the film was a botched retelling of Nikolai Gogol's tragic novella. The ending culminated heroically for the Cossacks and a deserved death for Taras Bulba's apostate son Andriy, played by an attractive looking Tony Curtis. Lovestruck Andriy had fallen for a Polish woman. The Poles ruled his people, the Cossacks. His affection for his sweetheart compelled him to treacherously lead a Polish contingent in battle against his brethren. The story was, in some ways, an inverted version of *The Prodigal Son*. Taras Bulba chose to kill young Andriy after capturing him and defeating the Polish army. *I loved you as I loved the steppes*, he said, obviously overwhelmed with grief. *I gave you life. It is on me to take it away from you.* And with that, he shot his boy down.

In *Villa Rides!* Brynner was Pancho Villa, the romanticized hero of the Mexican Revolution. Supporting roles were prized to old friends Charles Bronson, Robert Mitchum and Herbert Lom. It was a decent film of old with Brynner resorting to type. His 1973 film *Westworld* is widely regarded as a cult classic and a prelude to the Terminator films. *Westworld* is a theme park constructed for wannabe cowboys longing for cathouses, the saloons of old, and the gun duels of the wild, wild west. Brynner portrayed a robot scalding gunslinger, who malfunctions after being reassimilated, and goes in pursuit of a mortified guest at a canter, after killing his friend in a duel.

Brynner's dexterous talents roamed into photography. He took pictures of fellow stars like Frank Sinatra, Ingrid Bergman, Richard Burton, Gina Lollobrigida, Elizabeth Taylor and Charlton Heston. He also took photos of his family, and of places he visited on behalf of the United Nations. After his death, his daughter Victoria published a collection of these photographs in book form titled: *Yul Brynner: A Photographic Journey*. Yul was immensely proud of his Romani heritage. He was named honorary President of the International Romani Union. And he lent his voice to the plight of refugees worldwide by becoming a United Nations consultant for refugees. In 1960, he published a book (which I have not yet read) titled: *Bring Forth The Children: A Journey To The Forgotten People Of Europe And The Middle East*. While Vietnam recovered from being bludgeoned by American fighter jets in the mid-1970s, he, and his third wife Jacqueline Thion de la Chaume, adopted two Vietnamese girls, Mia and Melody, as their own.

He spent his final years playing his most famous role: King Mongkut of Siam in *The King And I*. He lost his voice in his latter shows but never his luster. Rock, who eerily sounded like his father, spoke his lines for him. After doctors examined Yul's vocal cords, they discovered he had inoperable lung cancer. They gave him three months to live. He would defy death by surviving another two years. As death neared, he recorded a moving television commercial, warning the public of the perils of smoking.

My erstwhile colleague, Mrs. Jasmin Hewitt, gleefully looking towards her retirement this year, had the good fortune to watch Brynner perform one of his 4,625 appearances on stage as King Mongkut in London. I listened attentively to her retelling. Despite his sunset years, the impetuosity and brilliance of his stage presence bewitched the audience. His perorations and monologues merely confirmed the legend. His magisterial swagger was abundant in its self-belief. As the Russian dramatist Konstantin Stanislavski succinctly put it: *If you believe it, the audience will.* And who could believe otherwise, when one witnessed the undertones and overtures of such refulgence in one man?

February 4, 2018.

IN THIS AGE OF DISTRACTIONS, THERE ARE PLENTY DISTRACTIONS

I REMEMBER MY DO-NOTHING days as if they were yesterday. I defenestrated Father Time repeatedly. In my youth, I was bequeathed with plenty of Him. Like Frank Muir before me, I was educated in E10, not Eton. I had been sheltered from the cumulative frenzy of a whimsy world that was replete with serpentine dames and sharks in suits. Honorable men are dead. The world belonged to Superfluous Man. Contrary to popular belief, the meek were never destined to inherit the earth. *The Matthew Principle* was inordinately attuned to the natural order. *For unto everyone that hath* **shall be given, and he shall have in abundance: but from him that hath not, it shall be taken away, even that which he hath.** (Matthew 25:29). In other words, karma is a bitch goddess to the have-nots. Only a neophyte (which I was then) could solemnly believe in a drollery, otherwise known as a meritocracy. Having suddenly been exposed to these visceral vestiges, I was repulsed. I sought refuge from its conjecture. As a consequence, I became laden with ennui. I was a loner, a drifter, a flâneur, a gadabout, a college drop-out.

I had not yet descended to the Schopenhauerian theory that life was a whirlpool of perpetual suffering, that true fulfilment was unattainable, that it was better not to have existed. I had already bastardized a quotation from Albert Camus, which I thought apt for my inertia: *Don't walk behind me for I may not lead. Don't walk ahead of me for I may not follow. Don't walk beside me either. Just leave me alone.* I was Ali Kinteh, *contra mundum*. I spent days and weeks deconstructing putative myths that I was raised to believe in. I would sit with my PlayStation and play FIFA games, sometimes for a quarter of a day in one sitting. Winning the Premier League title on a console game perhaps had meaning, for the football club I followed often flirted with relegation. They were never likely to become champions of England anytime soon. If it could not happen in the real world, then one could make it happen in a virtual one. I could take cold comfort from that.

Please ponder the impotence and purposelessness of that enterprise: Thirty-eight fixtures per season. Each game lasting twelve minutes. After finishing a season, I'd move on to the next and bleed more time on this temporal plain. The vacuity of that perverse undertaking still haunts me as I write these words. I think back to the decimation of so many hours and minutes. I was scarcely employed. I worked temporary shifts for employment agencies like *Ambitions* and *Brook Street*. I shunned every form of permanency. When there was no shift work, I remained sandbagged in my bedroom watching *Perry Mason* and *TFI Friday*, *NYPD Blue* and *Goodnight Sweetheart*. By night, I listened to Rhod Sharp's habitual show *Up All Night* on *BBC Five Live*. I had a deep appreciation for his imperturbable radio broadcasts from the other side of the Atlantic pond. Former *BBC* presenter Stuart Hall also possessed that metrical rigor fused with Shakespearian allusions when delivering his football match reports from Goodison Park and elsewhere.

I stooped along *Torpor Street* for almost a year with zero zeal. I was twenty years old, if that. I was not entirely hedonistic. I read erratically. I was a scripturient who wrote nothing. I had no girlfriend or constant companion. My awkwardness in open society meant I was forever misread. I was treated like a goofball. That often depressed me. The meatheads I encountered were convoluted, vicious souls who cast aspersions with impunity. They were indecorous to virtue.

They wanted their pound of flesh. They were mostly remoras who lacked the predatory wherewithal of a shark. They calumniated and gossiped on red meat that floated their way. This caused me, in turn, to care less for the inference of strangers. I preferred introspection to their impudence. The *Bhagavad Gita* offered salutary counsel. *When you move amidst the world of sense, free from attachment and aversion alike, there comes the peace in which all sorrows end, and you live in the wisdom of the Self.* (Chapter 2: 64-65). I identified with Arjuna and his anguish. He had been ushered into conflict, against his will, against ex-friends and former associates. It caused him great pain. I took heed of Lord Krishna's exhortations. I took leave of the world.

And so it came to pass: I was able to slalom my way from this malaise. I became self-sufficient to a vantage point. I embraced the notion of being an outsider and an oddball. Difference was not wrong. Mindless conformity was daft. I desired neither acceptance nor permission from nobody. I considered it madness to seek accedence from maladaptive and protean fellows, who could gull without a shade. I would not be a factotum. Neither would I be anybody's disciple. Like Satan, I was *non serviam*. I was convinced, out of my own heightened self-belief, that I could enjoy the fillips of opportunity on these terms. If I were to lose, it would be on my terms. My conscience would be, more or less, intact. A. E Housman's seminal work *A Shropshire Lad* also resonated some truth for this Leyton lad (me), in particular, this poem *Now Hollow Fires Burn Out To Black*:

> *Now hollow fires burn out to black, and lights are guttering low.*
> *Square your shoulders, lift your pack, and leave your friends and go.*
>
> *O never fear, lads, naught's to dread. Look not left nor right:*
> *All the endless road you tread. There's nothing but the right.*

I shall take the liberty to quote the Athenian tragedian Aeschylus here, from his inclining play *Oresteia*, (for literature is an antidote and an ultimate form of catharsis), citing the lessons of a lifetime from the ascetic mouth of proud Agamemnon, king of all the Greeks, as his end drew near:

> *Wisdom comes through suffering. Trouble, with its memories of pain, drips in our hearts as we sleep.*
>
> *So men, against their will, learn to practise moderation, with a grace that comes to us from the gods.*

As I sidled back into the world from my self-imposed purdah, the obscurantists, masquerading as terrestrial revivalists, sought me out for indoctrination. Their charlatanry, guised in the amorphous burkha of religion, identitarianism and politics, preyed upon the docility and disaffections of the incipient youth. These were The Wonder Years, when the zeitgeist, pinioned to a grunge and Britpop soundtrack, were ambivalent to the genocides in Rwanda and Bosnia. Angry Young Men, brooding upon their meager lot in a fraught world, were a lusty wet dream to born-again merchants and those from The Party of Liberation, otherwise known as *Hizb-ut-Tahrir*. These were polite gentlemen who appeared sincere in their beliefs. The born-again Christian peddled soteriology. Hizb-ut-Tahrir sold Shariah. Foaming at the mouth, they argued that society had degraded to a trepidatious pit, where the lives of men and women were, in the Hobbesian view, *solitary, poor, nasty, brutish and short*, but divine exception would be made in my case if I supped plentifully and wholeheartedly on the insoluble nonsense that was being served as the main course meal.

Though some of the issues raised tolled some plangent bells (i.e., UK foreign policy, the depredation of society), I found their propositions unedifying and terrifying. I had long been contemptuous of monolithic groupthink. My individuation was sacred and non-negotiable. It was all I had. They had zero chance of recruiting me. I was like Groucho Marx: *I didn't want to belong to any club that would accept me as a member.* I would rather have lost myself by myself than to lose myself in transhumance, as part of an ovine flock led by malevolent shepherds that (unbeknown to their followers) harbored an insatiable desire for hogget. Tergiversators that decided to oscillate mid-journey bore the bullwhip reserved for apostates. I witnessed a few scars on backs since. And that has caused more harm upon their wellbeing than good, if only they had scrutinized the what-ifs in the first place. I observed closely as erstwhile associates became entranced by non-linear schools of thought. They behaved as if they were subjected to an invasion by the Body Snatchers. By the end of their reprogramming, they introjected the words of their shepherds. Their actions contorted the demagoguery of their master theorists. Their individuation had been stripped bare. They were deemed mortal dangers to themselves if their natural inclinations remained unchecked. So they removed their finespun raiments to put on the tunic of Nessus. They cut away pounds of their own flesh for the cause, cheerily (and eerily) waving aloft their scimitars. Indissoluble ideologies were inserted in tablet form by feint hands and slipped down passive throats, putting simple minds to sleep. They were diabolically intent on purging the world from sin.

During the nineties, I followed many a news story (thanks to the likes of Rhod Sharp) on charlatans the world over, dinning about their divinity during the tumult and scourge of the so-called *end of days.* Their own end of days was climatical in itself. Marshall Applewhite, Yahweh Ben Yahweh, David Koresh and Shoko Asahara, having all claimed to being the Messiah, promised their adherents first class tickets to the Resurrection. People were indomitably damned when they eventually delivered. It was said in the New Testament, Matthew 7:15: *Beware of false prophets, which come to you in sheep's clothing, but inwardly they are ravening wolves. Ye shall know them by their fruits!* I observed folks starved of meaning. They surrendered themselves to vulgar and toneless drivel. Their eyes-wide-shut acquiescence and lack of critical thought caused them to flock to imposters. They became instruments and playthings to these soothsayers. Needless to say, it would end neither well for prophet or puppet.

Growing up, as Bonnie Langford once chirruped merrily in a song, *isn't easy*. Growing up in today's climate is a considerably challenging chore for the contemporary youth. For as we wrestle with the malcontents of our lives, belligerent, nuanced and subtle, we must also contend with a myriad of infractions that kill purpose and neuter Old Father Time. Indeed, winsome sprees help numb the angst of a monotonous life. Social media masterfully lambent the embers of our solipsism. Their disseminations are designed to appeal adversely to our base instincts. Some of us discern unlettered posts and tweets, clips and memes from certain celebrities and *influencers* as if they were conceived from the brow of Athene. Canards ferry the superhighway seas, trending the salacious as well as the facetious. The Internet was as if it were, in the words of Samuel Taylor Coleridge: *water, water everywhere. Not a drop to drink.* I would search online for hours, and not find a potation that quenched. Many associates felt differently and embraced its amrita delectations. They encompassed its visceral delights. The dark prince Belphegor beguiles with ingenious quick get-rich schemes. The cambion Asmodeus incites lechery, lust and licentiousness. Cyberspace is the contemporaneous mother and father of all distraction, which is why my laptop is instantaneously unplugged from the Matrix the moment I am bound into the staid typing of essays and novels. Whenever I'm asked to consult *Google* as a research tool, my eyes roll inwards and fade to black. Clickbait and viral clips are harmful to my concentration, memory and focus, which is why I do not bite. These diversions do not neuter the hellacious pain. They increase it. Goethe wrote that *the hardest thing to see is what is in front of your eyes*. That is certainly true of what I've borne witness to online.

In the eighties, Neil Postman, one of the most prescient minds of the latter twentieth century, wrote a distinguished cynosure titled *Amusing Ourselves To Death: Public Discourse In The Age Of Showbusiness.*

Television, in the days of Reagan and Thatcher, had diabolically replaced typography as the main source of information and entertainment. The Internet has since infected our discourse to a pyrexic degree. In the foreword of his book, Postman compared both the Orwellian and Huxleyan dystopias. While society were mindful and fearful of Orwell's auguries, Huxley's prognostics lay siege to great sways of societies with barely a whimper. Postman wrote: *Contrary to common belief even among the educated, Huxley and Orwell did not prophesy the same thing. Orwell warns that we will be overcome by an externally imposed oppression. But in Huxley's vision, no Big Brother is required to deprive people of their autonomy, maturity and history. As he saw it, people will come to love their oppression, to adore the technologies that undo their capacities to think. What Orwell feared were those who would ban books. What Huxley feared was that there would be no reason to ban a book, for there would be no one who wanted to read one. Orwell feared those who would deprive us of information. Huxley feared those who would give us so much that we would be reduced to passivity and egoism. Orwell feared that the truth would be concealed from us. Huxley feared the truth would be drowned in a sea of irrelevance. Orwell feared we would become a captive culture. Huxley feared we would become a trivial culture, preoccupied with some equivalent of the feelies, the orgy porgy, and the centrifugal bumblepuppy. As Huxley remarked in Brave New World Revisited, the civil libertarians and rationalists who are ever on the alert to oppose tyranny "failed to take into account man's almost infinite appetite for distractions." In 1984, Orwell added, people are controlled by inflicting pain. In Brave New World, they are controlled by inflicting pleasure. In short, Orwell feared that what we fear will ruin us. Huxley feared that what we desire will ruin us.*

Towards the end of his life, Huxley, author of the classic fables *Brave New World* and *Point Counter Point* furnished his position in a speech to the Tavistock Group, California Medical School where he spoke of *placebos* and *scientific dictatorships*: *There will be,* he said, *in the next generation or so, a pharmacological method of making people love their servitude, and producing dictatorship without tears, so to speak, producing a kind of painless concentration camp for entire societies, so that people will in fact have their liberties taken away from them, but will rather enjoy it, because*

*they will be distracted from any desire to rebel by propaganda or brainwashing,
or brainwashing enhanced by pharmacological methods. And this seems to be
the final revolution.*

I am not a Luddite. I recognize the innumerable benefits of the
Internet and a social media platform as I appreciate the comforts
of, say, liquor. And I am not in the business of proselytizing. I
grapple enough with my own dichotomy. That, in itself, behooves
me to let others be. But I must add to this: I had to lose myself in
order to find my purpose. A period of inertia, seclusion, prison,
or working a dead-end job might be necessary to chisel character,
induce refraction, stimulate refinement, or provide containment
against one's self-subordination to someone else's will. But with
an entire gamut of snares and trappings to beguile, stun and kill
the critical mind, the victor can still claim a scalp when every
waking potential is rendered comatose. Now I have little time to
kill as I gallop reluctantly towards my Middle Ages. I, therefore,
shun those soft quantifiers used to ensure that adolescence can be
expediently prolonged right until death, if it is so willed. I have
little need for these tranquilizers, and the side effects they accrue.
And I pay no heed to charlatanry, vaticinating on subjects that are
simply unknowable. I would rather gaze through a telescope at the
awe of the heavens than to gaze gormlessly at some celebrity TV
bot droning on about contouring. But it took a lone walk across a
burning furnace to get to this point.

August 14, 2017.

AMITABH BACHCHAN: SHAHENSHAH

B RITAIN'S CHANNEL 4 COULD TAKE some credit for my aborning worldliness. At its nascency, their Reithian programming featured a renaissance of British-Asian, African-British and African-Caribbean talent. These newfangled prolusions delved into the entrails of the cultures and mores outside of my bed of feathers. They did not compartmentalize the heterogeneity of everyday woman and man toiling arbitrarily in the mother country. It was on *Channel 4* that I first watched Horace Ové's film *Pressure*. Incidentally, Ové was the first British filmmaker of African-Caribbean descent to direct a feature-length film. Sam Sevlon, author of *Moses Ascending*, *The Lonely Londoners* and *Brighter Sun*, cowrote the *Pressure* script. His writings are integral coming-of-age readings. *The Lonely Londoners*, for example, is an edifying book about migrants from the Caribbean, and how they acquired lodgings and work in a disobliging city. It was similar in tone to the oral narrations of my father. *Pressure* told the story of a young African-Caribbean man named Anthony who, having excelled academically, was rendered chronically unemployable in a society plagued with racial prejudice. He is betwixt two cultures. He rages against his Trinidadian heritage. He embraces his English identity. *So what's wrong with bacon and eggs, fish and chips and Gary Glitter?* he asks his Black Nationalist older brother, who scoffs at his preference for *white food. Pressure* was released in 1976. Any reference to the glam rocker Glitter, therefore, was unsuggestive of what he'd become commonly associated with. Like me, Anthony was the first of his family born in Britain. Like him, I was ridiculed blithely for my music preferences. Not everyone was keen on Duran Duran, David Bowie, Pink Floyd, Nirvana, Radiohead, R.E.M and Led Zeppelin. Not that it ever bothered me like it did the young Anthony! *Pressure*, though a full generation away before I sought employment, was a visceral window into the obliquity of an inequitable world. The film featured brief appearances from actors Norman Beaton and Ram John Holder. Both would star in a future *Channel 4* comedy classic, *Desmond's*. In another *Channel 4* showing *Black Joy*, starring Beaton and Floella Benjamin, an African-Caribbean narrative was characterized through humor and hubris. The lead characters betook sufferance and serendipity whilst they dallied and exerted themselves along Brixton High Street. The Kinteh household also favored a *Channel 4* comedy program *No Problem!* which starred Victor Romero and, the Lovers Rock singer, Janet Kay. They played two of the five Powell siblings living together in a council house in Willesden Green. The show was relatable. The writing was crisp. The characters of the siblings were distinctly constructed. The plotlines were light-hearted escapism. The episodes were written by playwrights Farrukh Dhondy and Mustapha Matura. Dhondy went on to script *Tandoori Nights* for *Channel 4*, which featured the late British-Asian actor Saeed Jaffrey. Jaffrey enjoyed an extensive career in both Bollywood and Hollywood motion pictures. I can recall Jaffrey being ubiquitous in several films I watched in close succession. *The Man Who Would Be King. Gandhi. The Courtesans Of Bombay. The Jewel In The Crown. A Passage To India. My Beautiful Laundrette. The Deceivers.* Thus far, I've only seen him in a single Bollywood incarnation, *Henna*, which starred the aesthetical Bollywood heartthrob Rishi Kapoor. But more on Mr. Kapoor later.

Indian cinema was popular at No. 1 Boscombe Avenue, Leyton E10. We preferred the films that pruned several genres under one umbrella — Shakespearian-like tragedy, martial arts style action, comedic drollery, sonorous musicals, heightened melodrama. These were known as *masala* movies. They were lengthy affairs. We didn't care. We sang the songs: *Meh hoon Don, Meh hoon Don. Meh hoon, meh hoon, meh hoon, meh hoon Don!* And *Anhoni ko honi kar dein, honi ko anhoni!* The English subtitles were a sufficient guide. My younger brother and I recreated the choreographed fight scenes the best we could. Some films even transcended the supernatural realm. *Nagin*, for instance, was a magnificent horror picture: A female serpent that could shapeshift into any woman she chooses. After her husband is unwittingly killed whilst in the physical form of a snake, she vows vengeance on the men she holds responsible. One after the other, she takes the physical human form of their partners. As they lay most vulnerable, she metamorphosed back into a snake, stinging them to death with her venom. After her initial slays lead to unwholesome demises, the surviving men seek the help of a *Babaji*. He provides them with phylacteries for protection. She befriends a goon to help her by providing a sob story. Whilst the goon provokes a fight with one of her husband's slayers (played by the prepossessing Kabir Bedi), he snatches the amulet from his neck. She eliminates Bedi's character within the flick of a switch. Literally. She kills *Babaji* too for attempting to thwart her vendetta. She threatens another of the fellows with the life of his daughter if he declines to remove his periapt. This was *Nagin's* most heart-wrenching scene: The tearful child sobbing for her father while the bloodthirsty snake coils herself around her helpless, frightened body. Her father did what any good father would. He surrendered his life by removing his phylactery. She flies across the room, sinks her fangs into his skull and he, too, lays dead from her poison. *Nagin* starred Reena Roy as the widowed shapeshifter. Sunil Dutt played the herpetologist Vijay who eventually outwits her in one of the most nail-biting finales you will ever see. But to better understand the provenance that gave rise to my appreciation for Indian cinematography, I ask that you kindly take a peep through my antelapsarian periscope. It is not that I wish to be filiopietistic. It is so that you may gander the home that forged me.

I came into consciousness in Leyton, east London. My father migrated to England before Windrush. I am the third of his eight children, the second of five sons. My mother was several years younger than he. They married in the mid-seventies. I am firstborn of their six children. My parents are from The Gambia, the smallest nation on mainland Africa. They were devout Muslims, of prominent Mandinka, Wolof and Fula extractions. Some among my forefathers were scriveners. They recorded their own histories as well as their knowledge of alchemy, herbalism, Koranic sciences and astrology. Their Mandinka writings in the Arabic script are hundreds of years old. They are kept by family custodians in Jassong, the birthplace of my father. My parents shared with us stories of our antecedents. My father's recent forebears emerged from the towns of Oualata and Nema in the Hodh Ech Chargui region, eastern Mauritania. My mother's forefather was born in Fouta Djallon, modern day Guinea. Nationality is as fluid as the river running through many lands, yet each have a legitimate claim to that river. My mother was a lacquered student at the Lycee John F. Kennedy School in Dakar, Senegal. Her extricating mind had been further polished by the writings of Birigo Diop, Camara Lye and Leopold Senghor, the first President of Senegal. She'd been further enlightened by the works of Ousmane Sembene, inarguably one of Africa's greatest cinematographers. She was bound to study medicine in Moscow, capital of the Soviet Union, when her father (whom I'm named after) received a proposal from my father for her hand in marriage. Her plane to Sheremetyevo International was irrevocably canceled in favor of a flight to London Gatwick.

We lived in a large house containing fifteen rooms. My three brothers, two sisters and I slept in our own bedrooms. We weren't rich; my parents did their utmost. Leyton itself was like a Stanley Gibbons album. A confraternity co-existed amongst us all. Most of the time. It wasn't Eden. It wasn't John Steinbeck's *East of Eden* either, but it was enough. The African-Roman poet Terence, from his play *Heauton Timorumenos* (The Self-Tormentor) wrote the immortal line *homo sum, humani nihil a me alienum puto.* (I am human. Nothing human is alien to me). I was nurtured into this thinking by the didacticism of my parents and the cultural multiformity of the neighborhood. This seabed of treasures provided the unbridled elasticity to aviate the realms of self-determinism, and not confine oneself to a meager category or label on a government tick box. My identities are multiple, indefinable, and interchangeable. The French poet Stéphane Mallarmé wrote that *to define is to kill. To suggest is to create.* Within the pages of *The Picture Of Dorian Gray,* Anglo-Irish wit Oscar Wilde inserted the line: *To define is to limit.* They both couldn't have been more correct. As we immerse ourselves in this 21st century Albion, a solipsistic energy rages to ingratiate tribes into pens so that their respective cooing, mooing and clucking are adumbrated. If anyone coos when they ought to cluck, they can expect to be clipped by the prefects in their pen. Or shooed in their place by an overly zealous farmhand. Or pecked to pieces by their own stock. Or shunned by a rival strain. This is a *Sign O The Times!*

Many of our neighbors were indigenous to the vast Indian sub-continent. The Indus Valley is one of the bedrocks of human civilization. It lies in this territory. The Ganges River flows through this region. The Himalayas guards its northern frontier like an impenetrable granite citadel that even Gog and Magog themselves could not breach. It was in these lands that the *Mahabharata, Rigveda* and *Ramayana* were written in Sanskrit by some of the finest scribes that ever breathed. The *Panchatantra* and *Bhagavad Gita* were mettle that aided me at a nadir where I thought was no return. I imagined I was Arjuna being counseled by Krishna. The Taj Mahal, Humayun's Tomb, The Jantar Mantar and the Golden Temple were whittled by mortal hands of residual endeavor. To the south lies the remnants of an enchanting Buddhist temple at Polonnaruwa and the ancient fortress of Sigiriya (The Lion Rock) built fifteen hundred years ago. From these territories, you will find Hindus and Sikhs, Christians and Muslims, Jains and Jews, Buddhists and secularists. You will discover Dravidians, Gujaratis, Punjabis, Sylhetis, Bengals, and various branches of Indo-Aryans that populate Central Asia. *O Mankind!* says The Koran in chapter 49 verse 13. *We created you from male and female. And We made you into nations and tribes, that ye may know one other. Verily, the most honored of you in the sight of God is (he who is) the most righteous among you.*

India, herself, had long held a simpatico, pluralist tradition of *Sarva Dharma Sama Bhava* (All religions are possible). As is the capricious tide of human nature, she has deviated from this aspiration, most notably during the Indian Partition of 1947 which caused not just Pakistan, but the deaths and displacement of millions of people. As a child, I remember being impressed that the Indian sub-continent had a population larger than the entire African continent. Here lived more than two thousand ethnic groups that spoke more than four hundred languages. A lazy glance at an entire sway of people gives the false depiction that they possess collective traits that renders them deleterious or exceptional by their corresponding groups. While a people can be analogous culturally, binding and blinding their perceptions to constructs and customs, could cause one to be suppositious in one's engagement with a single individual. To think, then, that some stumpy mandarin or a chia seed porridge-eating nanomachine crudely decided that a heterogenous tapestry of British peoples originating from Africa and Asia could be condensed under the acronym BAME (Black, Asian, Minority Ethnic) is frankly insulting, to say the least, and further demonstrates the exigent need to put whole peoples into sober categories and under simplistic labels.

My peers, of Indian sub-continent heritage, were first and second generation British-born. We played in each other's gardens. We dined in each other's homes. We watched *Dungeons And Dragons* on each other's television sets. Our parents lent movies that were keyholes into our respective heritages. My mother lent Ousman Sembene's *Xala* and *Camp de Thiaroye*. We received Nargis' *Mother India* and Amitabh Bachchan's *Shaan* in return. *Channel 4* provided a further boost to my education with weekend matinée showings featuring the cinema of India. At that time, India produced more films annually than any country on earth, and approximately twice more than Hollywood. Their motion pictures were exported as far afield as West Africa. And so Amitabh Bachchan, India's biggest film star of the 1970s, was already known to my mother in Dakar, Senegal. My family were particularly close to an Anglo-Pakistani family who lived on Abbotts Park Road, Leyton. Their patriarch was a friend to my father. They prayed together at the local mosque. Their daughter Farzana and I were in the same school year. And it was Farzana's oldest brother Muhammed who phoned our home just after midday one Saturday to inform us that *Amar, Akbar and Anthony* was being shown on *Channel 4*. Someone plucked out a VHS cassette and recorded it. I have watched the video one hundred times since.

Amar, Akbar and Anthony bespoke a kaleidoscope of genres. Its undertones narrate an alternative story of India, without the bloody partition, internecine sectarianism and religious feuds. Three brothers are separated from their parents on Indian Independence Day. Their father Kishanlal is pursued by a marsupial gangster named Robert, who reneged on a promise to take care of his family having spent time in prison as his fall guy. Robert had killed in a hit-and-run accident. Kishanlal had been in his employ. Kishanlal's wife Bharati found life unbearable with her husband incarcerated. Her suicide attempt fails. She loses her sight as a consequence. Kishanlal, after his release from jail, had left his sons by the Mahatma Gandhi statue in Borivali Park so that he could ward off Robert's goons unhindered. When he returns, his sons are gone. They had all been found separately by three strangers. The eldest son Amar is found by a Hindu policeman. The middle son Anthony is discovered by a Christian priest. The youngest Akbar is adopted by a Muslim tailor. Both Kishanlal and Bharati believe that each other, as well as their children, are dead.

Fast forward twenty-two years, and the film catapults the biggest male dreamboats of 1970s Indian cinema before our eyes. The larrikin Anthony Gonsalves is played by Amitabh Bachchan.

Rishi Kapoor is the considerate musician, Akbar Ilahabadi. Vinod Khanna is the belligerent, slim-mustachioed Inspector Amar Khanna. The cast list includes Parveen Babi, Nirupa Roy and Pran Krishan Sikand. These actors reunited with Bachchan in several blockbusters. In this film, Babi co-starred as the divine Jenny — his love interest. Roy and Sikand play his parents, Bharati and Kishanlal. *Amar, Akbar and Anthony* contained romance and raillery. The songs are captivatingly reminiscent of those of *Fiddler On The Roof* and *Guys And Dolls*. I would not classify the acting itself as melodramatic, yet there are stunt scenes and supernatural interventions too. When Bharati is pursued by Robert and his underling towards the temple of Sai Baba of Shirdi, the *fakir* sends a cobra to foil their hunt. She enters his temple safely. He restores her sight. There are fight scenes, common at the time, pseudo emulating the arts of Bruce Lee and Yi-Min Li. I was most moved by two scenes in particular: Khanna reuniting with Kishanlal, having dug up the toy gun his father had given him when he was a child; And Anthony Gonsalves' stupendous monologue to the stature of Christ Jesus, having found his adopted father's slain body in church sanctuary. He vows to become villainous and vile if the murderer is not made known to him. This film served as an exordium to the magnificence of Amitabh Bachchan. *Amar, Akbar and Anthony*, in effect, is an allegory of India. The three brothers represent her three largest religions, yet they are one family. When the blind Bharati requires blood after been injured in a car accident, her sons, unbeknown to her and themselves unbeknown that they are brothers, donate their blood that returns her health. Bharati herself is the idealized personification of sacred Mother India.

The propinquity of Bachchan's film character roles are mnemonic because of the overcast, irate weather served. Their lives often begin in exiguity. They are either foundlings or outsiders, fallen into badinage and tragedy. The kismet often beggared have the rising odds stacked against him, whether he be righteous or rogue. As he matures, he must contend against the devils in the vault. His characters are guided by visceral, uncompromised truth. Whilst he is compelled to enforce villainy and devilry, his audience roots for him. He is often fueled by fury. He commingles raw will, by which he mostly overcomes his foes. Otherwise, he dies trying. Bachchan was described as *the angry young man* of India's 1970s cinema. Judging solely on the woeful plight of his characters, that ire is justified. His characters are often wronged, even in childhood. That same injustice, intimidation, contempt, disgust, rage, festers as the child becomes a man. The man, often stricken by strife, piques into transgression. It does not extinguish with the passing of time. *Every time fatality comes before will, I am suspicious* wrote Andre Malraux in his depressingly exhilarating novel, *Man's Fate*. No such suspicions can be harbored against Bachchan in Bollywood. He is resolved against fatality. Bachchan's characters embodied the Everyman, his rigidity distilled with a soupçon of madeleine tenderness. At the core of Vijay Khanna (Zanjeer), Vijay Verma (Deewaar), Jai (Sholay), Anthony Gonzalves (Amar Akbar Anthony), Don/Vijay (Don), Natwarlal (Mr. Natwarlal) and Inspector Vijay Srivastav/ Shahshenshah (Shahshenshah), buried therein is a seed of goodness and goodwill that perpetuates in every soul, no matter how forlorn and perturbed. In *Zanjeer*, he is Inspector Vijay Khanna, a solitary soul rendered an orphan in childhood by the murder of his parents. He is forced to confront the criminal underworld in his town. The trauma of his boyhood regularly rears itself. In *Sholay*, he is Jai on a Seven Samurai-like mission to capture a vagabond chief named Gabbar Singh who had terrorized a local populace. In *Don*, he is Don, a slick murderous gangster hunted by the police. He shrewdly evades their traps. When he is killed after a shootout with the cops, Bachchan becomes Vijay, a homeless itinerant, whose physical likeness resembles Don. The police ask Vijay to masquerade as Don so that he could help them bring down the criminal organization. In *Shahenshah*, a film written by his wife Jaya, Bachchan plays not only a cowardly and corruptible cop Vijay Srivastav but he is the titular paladin, out to avenge the shame and suicide of his father.

For whilst his name lit the welkin like a comet, his counterparts in Hollywood were also playing roles made turbulent by tyrannous circumstances. American counterculture had heralded a subversive *looking glass* through the camera lens. Convention was being uprooted by iconoclasm. Realism wrestled with idealism. Incantatory, brooding images shot by the French *Nouvelle Vague* contrasted the quick-tempoed, ejaculatory scenes featuring highly-strung antiheroes such as Brando and Bachchan. Character roles seldom had the patience to filibuster like James Stewart's Jeff Smith in the 1939 Hollywood motion picture, *Mr. Smith Goes To Washington*. They held up banks and fought the law like Warren Beatty and Faye Dunaway in 1969's *Bonnie And Clyde*. They hewed enough grievance to keep the masses on side. They fought back against the inveteracy of the establishment. Protean actors like James Caan of *The Gambler* and of *The Killer Elite*, Al Pacino of *Serpico* and *Dog Day Afternoon*, Robert De Niro of *Taxi Driver* and *The Deer Hunter*, Gene Hackman of *The French Connection* and *The Conversation*, Donald Sutherland of *Klute* and *Don't Look Now*, Jon Voight of *Deliverance* and *The Odessa File* were of Bachchan's needlepoint. British actors Laurence Harvey, Albert Finney, Richard Harris, Richard Burton, Michael Caine and Oliver Reed were of that same vexatious embroidery as far as some of their character roles were concerned.

Deewaar, released in 1976, is a *meisterstuck* of cinema, fraught with bedazzlement and affectivity. It is incontrovertibly one of my top ten great movies of all time. This film disports a brooding depiction of a Cain and Abel tale. This lamenting jeremiad centers on brothers Vijay (Bachchan) and Ravi (Shashi Kapoor). They are sons of trade unionist conciliator, Mr. Verma. When the workers threaten a strike, he is called to negotiate with their gluttonous bosses. He arrives in foreboding monsoon weather to discover these barons aren't wont for bargaining. They threaten to kill his wife and sons if he doesn't submit to their demands. He signs the papers that betray the workers who, unaware that he acted under severe duress, vilify and assault him. Their conjecture bought to mind one of my heroes, the indomitable Irish revolutionary, Michael Collins. He was sent among a contingent to negotiate Irish independence from Great Britain. British Prime Minister Lloyd George demanded their signatures on the Treaty in less than twenty-four hours, otherwise Ireland, he threatened, would face *an immediate and terrible war*. The old British bulldog got what he craved. Collins was left to rue that, by inking the Treaty, he had signed his death warrant. Less than nine months later, he was assassinated in an ambush. Mr. Verma, unfortunately, possessed the cowardice of his convictions. His idealism led to naught, save the contempt of disenfranchised laborers and avaricious nabobs. He abandons his family to destitution, traveling the railways for years without destination. His wife and sons feel the brunt of his faithlessness. Eldest son Vijay is branded with a tattoo on his arm: *My father is a thief*. His wife is forced to leave for Bombay. She and her sons sleep beneath a bridge by night. Eventually, she finds work as a laborer on a construction site. Her wages could only afford to send one of her sons to school. Vijay champions Ravi for an education whilst he becomes a boot polisher. He is acutely wounded by his father's disgrace and his mother's struggle. He refuses to worship at Lord Shiva's temple, preferring to wait outside whilst his mother and brother prayed. Ravi, being younger, is apparently unladen with his brother's hurt.

Throughout the film, Vijay's smoldering eyes betray his subterranean spleen. Even Alankar Joshi, who plays Vijay as a boy, seethes with perpetual fury, throwing a rock into the face of the supervisor who boors his mother at work. With the alleged sin of his father tattooed to his wrist, and the perpetual sorrow of his mother furrowed in his brow, he becomes an atrabilious man. He works on the docks. He befriends an avuncular man who gifts him with a 786 amulet, numerically conflated into a verse of the Holy Koran: In the name of Allaah, Most Gracious, Most Merciful. He believes this to be a lucky charm. The dock workers are extorted into giving a sum of their wages to a hoodlum mob. In one of the memorable scenes in Deewaar, Vijay locks himself in a warehouse with the hoodlums and kung-fu kicks the shit out of them.

Vijay succumbs to the temptations of working for a kingpin against his rival kingfish by robbing his wares. He buys his mother a home she built with her own hands as a laborer. Ravi, meanwhile, trains and becomes a police officer. He is promptly tasked with arresting the kingpin that employs Vijay. In the most compelling dialogue of the film, Ravi tells his brother that a wall (*Deewaar*) exists between them. He demands the names of his criminal associates. Vijay refuses to betray his associates. Finally, they argue over their mother. Mother chooses to leave with Ravi who finds a humbler abode. Vijay is grieved by his mother's decision. What grieved me most about *Deewaar* was the lack of reciprocity from Ravi and his mother upon Vijay. Though they love Vijay, they pay no heed to binding his wounds. Irrespective of their sufferance, there is an expectance that there ought to be no deviance. Especially onto pirate waters. Ravi was fortunate insofar as he was granted a good hand. He had waddled off to school and obtained a good education. His fiancé's father career guidance opened a door into the police force. His new job exhibits a coldness within him. He shoots a boy for the crime of stealing bread. He is remorseful and visits the boy's family, presenting them with a gift of food. The boy's mother is understandably angry when he confesses to shooting her lad. The father acknowledges his son's wrongdoing and tells Ravi he did what was right. This enables him to pursue his big brother.

It is the love of another, Anita, played by Parveen Babi, that provisionally binds Vijay's wounds. After she becomes pregnant with his child, he vows to renounce his criminality. Anita, however, is brutally slain by his criminal nemesis. She dies tragically in his arms. Vijay slays her killers, including their head honcho whom he throws off the balcony from a top floor porch. The police arrive as he escapes. Ravi relentlessly pursues him, repeatedly warning he would shoot if he declined surrender. Vijay loses his 786 amulet during the chase. Seconds later, Ravi fires his pistol. Perhaps Vijay believed his brother would not shoot, which was a reason why he kept running. But brothers had committed fratricide before: Romulus upon Remus, Cain upon Abel, Arjuna upon Karna. Michael Corleone felt compelled to order the death of older brother Fredo. Set saw necessity to murder and mutilate the flesh of his brother Osiris. However, I could not envisage Vijay ever pulling the trigger on Ravi had their roles were reversed. While their mother lay comatose in a hospital bed, Ravi crawled the premises with police. Should Vijay dare visit her, he'd be arrested. One can be cold to the world in pursuit of righteousness and sterility and be blind to nuance and mitigation. In one of the masterful scenes in the film, Vijay removes his shoes to walk into the temple he once vowed never to step foot in. He dispels with any reverent invocation or prayer. He communes angrily with Lord Shiva for the life of his mother. He asks nothing for himself. And Shiva would know his heart and sincerity better than any cockalorum who hastens to be offended on his behalf. His mother's health is restored. When she wakes from her coma, she calls his name. And so it was somewhat poetic that when Vijay dies, he does so in her arms in the temple, under Shiva's eternal gaze.

While Bachchan was at the peak of his monologuist powers in *Deewaar, Sholay, Amar Akbar and Anthony* and *Don*, it is important to note that India dwelt in a nadir of bedlam and babel. A State of Emergency had been imposed by Prime Minister Indira Gandhi. The national government infiltrated the judiciary. Opposition figureheads were detained. Newspapers were censored. Civil rights violations were conducted in plain sight. Forced sterilizations were imposed forcibly for the purpose of birth control. Unions were curbed. Dissenters were imprisoned. After unanchoring herself from Great Britain, India sailed upon an expedient tide. Pakistan and East Pakistan were cleaved from her body. She forcibly swallowed Goa and Hyderabad. *Operation Smiling Buddha* rendered India among a crop of elite nations that possessed nuclear weapons. Though Prime Minister Gandhi behaved as a *de facto* tyrant from her abode at No. 1 Safdarjung Road, New Delhi, Bachchan was not unmindful of the deteriorating social conditions of everyday people. His character roles betook the ire of the Everyman; the justifiable indignation against authoritarianism, secular as well as supernatural. He evidently felt he could improve the people's lot by running for Parliament. So, like Glenda Jackson, John Gavin and Arnold Schwarzenegger, he broke from acting and became a politician. He partook in the 1984 elections. He secured one of the largest victory margins in Indian election history, winning more than two-thirds of votes for the Allahabad constituency. After three years, the constraints of politics wore thick. Malicious allegations threatened to stick. He resigned his seat after three years. He returned to the Bollywood scene to critical acclaim with the film *Shahshenshah* (King of Kings).

Bachchan's glittering film career has extended six decades. How he endured the foofaraw into his personal life, I'll never know. A harpy friend of mine described fame as *a foretaste of paradise*. She has ineluctable designs to succeed in celebrity hell by way of a fist full of YouTube dollars. *Nishabd*, co-starring the late British-American ingenue Jiah Khan, is the most recent Bachchan film I've seen. His character becomes infatuated with his daughter's best friend. The disintegration of relations with his family follows a plotline similar to Kevin Spacey's *American Beauty* and Tom Skerritt's *Poison Ivy*. His tethered incendiarism has not diminished with time.

Some of us, raised in Leyton, became young angry ants once we stooped to the realization that our world was adumbrated with mistruths and ill-will; that authority, belied by calumny and cynicism, was projected by overweening men and women who intrigue and were masters of mischaracterization, division and subdivision; that fate itself was unjust and inequitable; that the concept of karma itself was a controvertible truth. (We ought to do good for goodness sake, and not for fantastical rewards in a virtual Second Coming or Third Renewal). Our lives are mitigated by vicissitudes and failures but, in the words of Samuel Beckett, we must simply *fail better* the next time round. Development and maturity are carved from err and indiscretion. Bachchan's films, as well as the miscellaneous variety offered by virtue of *Channel 4*'s Overton window, admonished me of a time to come: of an existential war of attrition waged within and beyond the self. Their programming projected a cornucopia of foreboding and sobering stories that illustrated a refulgent world in all its imperfections. Some lessons, served whilst I was a preadolescent, naturally escaped unheeded. But they hadn't fled my prevailing consciousness.

May 07, 2021.

ON DARCUS HOWE'S CONSTANCY

L EIGHTON RHETT RADFORD HOWE will be laid to rest today at the West London Crematorium, Kensal Green. But the racial causes, for which the man more commonly known as Darcus Howe waged in support of, have yet to find resolution in this increasingly fractious world. Contentions over race are perennially fraught and froward with divisible layers and indiscernible lines, smudged by the nuanced and the nebulous. Constructive examinations on race are deemed tiresome or, at the very least, confected by panoplies of voices with vested interests. But these are matters for our generation of Britons to contend with. Mr. Darcus Howe's work is complete.

Mr. Howe was never a man to seek haven in the false security of unanimity. He spoke on matters most folks dared think, let alone speak on. Conformity, conjecture and consensus, especially in these unscrupulous times, are exemplars over truth. These exemplars seemed never to have bothered Mr. Howe. He was nobody's servitor. He was unanchored to parliamentary politics. He spoke with a pacific voice. He wielded an unpacific stick. It was put to him in a 1975 Thames Television interview that he demeaned his fellow brethren when he dared describe their public sector jobs as *shit work*. Mr. Howe answered frankly. Many African-Caribbean workers had been contemptibly exploited by tinhorn supervisors. They were mercilessly abused by self-caricaturing, self-loathing customers. Their resourcefulness bridled the pretence that they loved their work. Their children, having been nurtured in Great Britain's underbelly, would not be so tepid. They were not unmindful of their parents' skirmishes in the workplace. They would discountenance such bane discourtesies from society and sundry. They would attenuate discrimination and racism stridently. Now some of that generation would have coiled behind their settees in embarrassment for their loathing of the disagreeable. Some may have clinched a proud fist at the wooden-clad television set to hear a belligerent young Caribbean man articulate so brazenly before the national gaze. But Mr. Howe had always been unequivocally plain speaking.

I was among the unborn when Darcus Howe fought his bitterest battles against his *bête noir* among the ruling classes. He had arrived by sea from his native Moruga, Trinidad and Tobago, to the port of Southampton, England, in 1961. He intended on becoming a barrister. He was but eighteen years old. The 1960s, arguably the most radical (and sappiest) decade of the twentieth century, heralded many civil insurrections against the transgressions of racial, social and gender inequalities. Mr. Howe was appalled by the penurious treatment of the burgeoning Asian, Caribbean and African communities living under Rachmanism and racism. This was, after all, the London of Michael X and Colin MacInnes, nevermind Carnaby Street and Jean Shrimpton. Dyke and Dryden hair products, not Vidal Sassoon. The England of David Oluwale and John Profumo, backdraught of The Rolling Stones and The Beatles. *She loves you. Yeah. Yeah. Yeah.* Mr. Howe soon veered into journalism. He was then steered into political activism by the stilled influence of his great uncle, the powerhouse writer C.L.R James. C.L.R James' body of work is an illuminating tower of erudition. His 1936 book *Minty Alley* was the first novel by a West Indian author to be published in Britain. His tomes titled *World Revolution* (on the incarnadine tug-of-war between Stalinism and Trotskyism during the interwar decades of the twenties and thirties) and *The Black Jacobins* (on the Haitian

Revolution) are catalytic reads. His 1963 book *Beyond A Boundary* is held in august regard among bibliophiles and sport adherents as the greatest book ever written about cricket. No doubt, therefore, that Darcus Howe was repurposed by a distinguished sage who saw the promise of his pugilism.

He befriended dub poets Linton Kwesi Johnson and Barbara Beese, activist Althea Jones-Lecointe, writer Farrukh Dhondy and Frank Critchlow, owner of the Mangrove Restaurant. He co-founded the British Black Panther Party. That movement later collapsed when its members turned on themselves. The Mangrove Restaurant, itself, was not simply a prosaic place for sustenance. The venue served as a social club and an activist hub for radical dissenters and firebrand intellectuals. Though it was the bedrock of the African-Caribbean community in Notting Hill, patronage was exclusive. The brightest thespians and thinkers congregated around its tables. They conversed the issues of the day. They advocated panaceas to the question of the racial problem. Bob Marley, Jimi Hendrix, Vanessa Redgrave, Diana Ross, Tariq Ali, Sammy Davis Jr and the luckless John Profumo (with Christine Keeler for company) were all waited on at the Mangrove. The police, however, were disturbed by the politics of Critchlow and Howe. They conducted twelve forensic raids on the restaurant in the hope of finding drugs, or any hint of illegality therein. They walked away empty-handed after every incursion. They claimed the Mangrove was a haunt of criminals, prostitutes and ponces. On August 9, 1970, their rudimentary prejudice knew no bounds. In response to the coniferous Metropolitan police, Critchlow and Howe organized a march outside their local police station with staunch community support. The march descended into conflict. Barbara Beese, Rupert Boyce, Frank Critchlow, Rhodan Gordon, Darcus Howe, Anthony Innis, Althea Jones-Lecointe, Rothwell Kentish and Godfrey Millet were arrested on spurious charges. They were collectively known as the Mangrove Nine. After an epic trial lasting fifty-five days at the Old Bailey, the Mangrove Nine were acquitted. Judge Clarke, who presided over the affair, admitted that the trial had regrettably shown evidence of racial hatred on both sides. This objective admission by the judiciary was considered by some as an equitable concession for the times. It would supersede the MacPherson Report by twenty-nine years.

Mr. Howe's later activism helped secure decent housing for the Bangladeshi community of Tower Hamlets. He supported worker rights and industrial action against the big businesses of Port-of-Spain, Trinidad. His basal organizational skills effectuated a demonstration of some twenty thousand strong after thirteen African-Caribbean youths were killed as a result of a suspicious fire at a house party in New Cross in 1981. He began his journalistic credentials with *The Hustler*. He became editor for grassroots newspaper *Race Today*. He wrote articles for *The News Statesman*, *The Observer* and *The Evening Standard*. His programs for *Channel 4* such as *Black On Black*, *Who You Callin A Nigger* and *Is This My Country?* were orchestrated to prick consciences, egos and ignorance.

My abiding memory of Mr. Howe was of the avuncular, curmudgeonly host of *Channel 4*'s *The Devil's Advocate*. He would stand imperiously at the podium, dressed in dark clothing, sporting a brambled beard. Guests included Nigel Benn, Chris Eubank, Imran Khan and La Toya Jackson (accompanied by her then-husband and manager Jack Gordon). He was not placatory. Neither was he propitiative. His inferences were deliberately impertinent. His unmerciful, rhetorical fisticuffs wounded discussants with distended pride. He challenged the divinity of Ethiopian emperor Haile Selassie before an indignant Rastafarian audience. La Toya Jackson was so enraged by his perversity that she called him the devil. But he played the act of *Advocatus Diaboli* unencumbered, and to the point. His show was part of a halcyon period for *Channel 4* when the then new station was at the forefront of avant-garde television. *Courtesans of Bombay*, *Right to Reply*, *After Dark*, *Brass Eye*, *The Word*, *Queer As Folk* and their notorious banned season of 1991 made the rest of British television seem, in comparison, antiquated and barren. Save for BBC's *Omnibus*, I hasten to stress. And Melvin Bragg's

The South Bank Show over on ITV. But I digress... The Channel gradually descended into the exploitatory field of mainstream television in pursuit of cheap ratings. They steadily deserted their intrinsic principles and hosted rubbish like *Big Brother, Hollyoaks* and *American Football*. But that is a subject for another essay.

Mr. Howe's later work titled Who You Callin' A Nigger? explored the maladaptation and anomies of multiculturalism. When he began his activism forty years ago, communities migrating from Africa, the Caribbean and the Indian sub-continent identified solely as Black people. They were offspring of Empire. They were rendered united by their contentions with the vestiges of slavery and colonialism in Britain. These same communities had become disparate and distinctive by the dawn of the twenty-first century. They were no longer a monolithic grouping. Their economic conditions differed wildly. They were invariably inclined towards their co-religionists and cultures of origin. They displayed gratuitous prejudice towards other ethnic folks. Mr. Howe, then in his mid-sixties, lost none of his pugnacity with his irreverent line of inquiry. A later battle with prostate cancer left his lambent zeal undimmed. After the 2011 London riots, a BBC newsbot, during a live broadcast, felt the brunt of his rage after having accused him of being a rioter in the past.

Mr. Howe's consequential frays for racial justice for African-Caribbean and British-Asian communities are not given due credence. I don't know whether that mattered to him. He certainly mattered to me. I felt compelled to write this piece on the morning of his burial. I am eternally grateful for the tenacity of his life's work. Had he, and others, shirked the good fight at a time when confrontation with state institutions were necessary, I, and others of my generation, may have been further exposed to the unadulterated, unjust might of the gavel and the truncheon, the boot and the baton. Very few people possessed the fortitude to demand that a High Court Judge subscribe to the principle of Magna Carta and make provision for an African-Caribbean jury as was his right by law.

He was his own advocate in the UK's highest court and, therefore, he cross-examined and excoriated Crown witnesses. His detractors accused him of being more heat than light. They argued in favor of consolatory utterances to placate the tyrannous, arbitrariness of the voice booming back. Heat *comes* from light. *Power*, as the great American statesmen Frederick Douglass once stated, *concedes nothing without a demand. It never did and it never will. Find out just what any people will quietly submit to and you have found out the exact measure of injustice and wrong which will be imposed upon them, and these will continue till they are resisted with either words or blows, or with both.* **The limits of tyrants are prescribed by the endurance of those whom they oppress.** Mr. Howe devoted his life by speaking his truth into the countenances of wigged judges and cloaked magistrates, bigoted policemen and racist politicians. Oppression from any quarter was not to be tolerated. He fought it as earnestly as he lived. And it is within this context, written on the day of his funeral, that I salute the constancy of Mr. Darcus Howe.

April 20, 2017

JOHN HURT: A MAN FOR ALL SEASONS

B EFORE I EVEN KNEW what John Hurt looked like, or who he was for that matter, I recognized the susurrations of his voice to within a bunny's hair breadth. I first heard him channeled through the shrewd coney Hazel-Rah who, in the 1978 Richard Adams' classic film *Watership Down*, led a fluffle of rabbits from Sandleford Warren across the River Enborne, through the perilous English countryside like a vestigial Moses, into the blessed plot of Watership Down. Hurt loaned his canorous instrument to Aragorn in J.R.R Tolkien's impermeable *Lord of The Rings*, an animated motion picture released also in 1978, possibly the most terrifying of that genre ever made. The brave, beneficent Aragorn of Isildur was Strider to his friends. He was one of the nine companions of *The Fellowship Of The Ring*. He carried the sword *Anduril* in his sheath. Hazel Rah and Aragorn are among the noblest and ablest of characters you could find in fiction. Their companions entrusted them with reverence and respect. This was borne from first embarkation to final destination, shorn from trial and peril, earned across treacherous plain and sanguineous field. Hazel Rah and Aragorn provided forbearance in their haphazard worlds dominated by *savage man, savage beast*. Their bridled stoicism, in the whitest heat of adversity during the blackest of days, are acute life lessons I applied from literature.

They cared that justice was deployed indiscriminately, and not with impermanence. Hurt's willowed euphonics bequeathed gravitas, wisdom and a nobility of spirit into their personages. Hazel Rah and Aragorn are not bettered by the prophets and pietists that the masses revere. Their moral besetting careened into my childhood sentience. It quieted like a fresh breeze through the lone hinterlands of my adolescence, and onto the hostile barrancas of my manhood.

And speaking of animated films with a chilling disposition, Hurt provided the suppurating verbiage for the cadaverous Horned King, the chief villain of the 1985 Disney film, *The Black Cauldron*. His was the levigated timber of Snitter, the hallucinatory canine in *The Plague Dogs*, another Richard Adams offering converted into an animated motion picture. If ever there was an axiomatic, unambiguous inflection that could stoically warn a nation not to die from the ignorance of AIDS, it was his salved and foreboding acoustics. My tender ears heeded his caution whenever the AIDS commercial bearing his stentorian warning appeared on television. My age was not even numbered in double figures when *the big disease with the little name* began troubling the nation's consciousness. *Sign O'The Times*, as Prince adumbrated on a meaty bassline. AIDS was an infectious retrovirus, Hurt warned ominously. Anybody could be afflicted. Man or woman. Irrespective of sexuality and sexual orientation. I believed him without really understanding the message.

The spoken voice is an essential mark of an actor, especially one forged and chiseled by the stage, much less the screen. Welsh actor Richard Burton possessed an exhilarating cadence, especially when embarking upon a monologue of volcanic fury. The same could be said of Paul Robeson, George Sanders, Vincent Price, James Earl Jones, Peter O'Toole, Morgan Freeman, Glenda Jackson, Maggie Smith, Jay Robinson, Peter Ustinov, Alan Badel, Ralph Richardson, Richard Harris, Laurence Olivier, Michael Hordern, Judi Dench, Cate Blanchett... I could name these cats forever. I was able to memorize verbatim their words in some of their performances, much thanks to their mesmerizing heldentenor that knew when to pause momentarily to catch breath and unleash again. Hurt's timber is the perfect reading modulator for the mind when one reads silently to oneself. Of course, the sum of his parts was never limited to narration and voice acting. His irrepressible attributes as an actor of stage and screen were innumerable and versatile: his virtuosity in the expression of *echt* sentiment, his nous in penetrating the curlicues of his characters and projecting them so vividly and affectingly. He stripped bare the nakedness of the noumenon. What is often left is what is least loved. And this was why, as a character actor and as a man, Hurt was most loved. He projected that piecemeal humanity with voracious deliberation. Transgressive filmmaker David Lynch described him as *the best actor in the world*, and for good reason.

He could play diametrically opposing roles. So, in a much later adaption of *Watership Down*, his voice metabolized into that of General Woundwort, the tyrannical chieftain of the Efrafan Warren, the mortal enemy of the Watership Down rabbits. As he was the oppressed serf Winston Smith in the film *Nineteen Eighty-Four*, subject to Big Brother, Groupthink and Room 101, he transmogrified into the repressed, maniacal dictator Adam Sutler in *V For Vendetta*, who experimented and exterminated so-called undesirables in laboratories and concentration camps. He may have been the woebegone, shy, sentimental aberration John Merrick in *The Elephant Man*, but he appeared as the sparkling raconteur Quentin Crisp in *The Naked Civil Servant*. He played an older Crisp in *An Englishman In New York* three decades later from his younger incarnation. He was the barely sentient, wan heroin addict Max in *Midnight Express*. He played the vigorous socialite and fixer Stephen Ward in *Scandal*. He was Bob Champion in *Champions* who, having been stricken with cancer, triumphed at the 1981 Grand National and became a national hero. Yet he was also the roguish opportune Alan Clark, of the BBC mini-series *The Alan Clark Diaries*, who sidled immodestly around the Cabinet Table as a member of Prime Minister Margaret Thatcher's perpetually scheming government.

David Lynch's film *The Elephant Man* is a time-honored classic. Hurt's John Merrick is an intelligent but sensitive young man, trapped in a hideously, grotesque body. He suffers barbarous treatment because of his physical deformities. He endures froward indignities at having to exhibit those deformities at a freak circus. There are plenty plaintive scenes in the movie. In particular, he is provoked by urchins at London's Liverpool Street Station who repeatedly mock him as to why his head was so big. Whilst attempting to escape this vile mockery, he accidently knocks over a young girl. This arouses and excites a crowd. They remove his head covering. They are aghast at what they see. They pursue him until he is trapped. He is left to howl in anguish: *I am not an animal... I am not an animal... I am a human being... A man...* He was more of a human being than his pursuers, I assure you. One cannot credibly call themselves humane if they reject or revile the humanity that accompanies difference. One may not realize how their own heart becomes disfigured and gnaws with rancor and discord when one deprives another of simple and common courtesies that would otherwise have cost them nothing. *The merciful man doeth good to his own soul; but he that is cruel troubleth his own flesh.* (Proverbs 11:17).

That mob scene marked an indelible impression upon me, aged thirteen. For it was from that moment, I held an aversion of crowds. Crowds oft produce madness and thoughtlessness. It enables the coward among the herd to fulfil what would otherwise have been a gratuitous thought. I witnessed rabble behavior at school and college: boys and girls emboldened to say and do things that they would not have dared, had they been alone. I was on the receiving end of such an experience once before. In May 1994, I made hay to a rehearsal in Clerkenwell, central London. That day coincided with the England national team playing football at Wembley Stadium against Norway. At London's Kings Cross Station, I encountered a pack of uncivilized barbarians on route to the game. An impetuous hobgoblin among them took exception to me. I was wearing a West African hat decorated in embroidered golden stars, which may have offended his sensibilities. He walked to less than an inch of my face. I paused. We eyeballed. He bared his splintered teeth. I didn't flinch. If it were just him and I, I'd have decked him with a preemptive strike. His pot-bellied, foul-mouthed minotaur pals called me *a wanker*, extenuating the *errrr*. They made braying, snarling noises. They exhorted him to *punch the black cunt*. Most hobgoblins in his position would have felt temerarious in exacting violence. He had an infantry to support him should things go wrong. But this particular lad seemed overwhelmed by his own cowardice to assail a lone teenager. We weren't getting anywhere. And I wasn't going to hit him first. I decided against standing my ground lest an inconspicuous knife be plunged into my side. Stephen Lawrence's brutal murder occurred barely a year before. It was still fresh in the memory. I chanced by walking away. I made for the escalator. The chants of *In-ger-land, In-ger-land, In-ger-land* bellowed in my ears. I didn't look back. But I was extremely upset by the incident. I told nobody. In the subsequent months and years, I couldn't bring myself to cheer the same England team those reprobates supported. The zeitgeist of Euro 96 dissipated the anger somewhat but not the experience. I spontaneously celebrated Paul Gascoigne's goal against Scotland *with them*. Our England. Their England, not mine. My England, not theirs. Our England. Diabolical! The Liverpool Street Station scene from *The Elephant Man* had planted an orchid seed that germinated further after that Kings Cross Station incident. I retain a disdain for packs, herds, hordes and flocks. I avoid crowds, droves and throngs for their propensity to turn legion. Individual thinkers, among mobs, ought to be mindful of the vicissitudes of their company, and the careworn trauma it could entail. One day, you may be part of a hurricane unleashed upon an individual. *No single raindrop thinks it caused the flood*, mumbled a timeworn proverb. When the individual is pelted by many rocks, no single perpetrator deems herself responsible for the resulting anguish. On another day, it may well be *you* enduring an unremitting headwind. You had simply deferred to being *you* and the right to act and think freely.

As the great socialist martyr Rosa Luxembourg eloquently put it: *Freedom. . . only for members of a party -- however numerous they may be -- is no freedom at all. Freedom is always the freedom of the one who thinks differently.* Mobs have a nose for the most minimal of heterodoxies. Heretics are hurriedly winnowed into the wilderness, with tumbleweed for company. I harbored a hatred for the mocking of so-called outcasts, oddballs and freaks, and the suppressors of contrarian thought and iconoclast intellection.

The latent heroism earmarked by John Hurt's depiction of Quentin Crisp is worthy of reflection. Crisp was a captivating humorist and an arresting raconteur. He was very much in the mold of a Kenneth Williams, a Dorothy Parker and a Fran Lebowitz; ostensive and subversive in equal measure, Lorelei's of unbridled vigor. *However low a man sinks, he never reaches the level of the police,* Crisp once quipped. I know many who'd applaud that! *Fashion is what you adopt when you don't know who you are* is another Crispian philosophical viewpoint one can ruminate on. And consider this preponderant observation: *the war between the sexes is the only one in which both sides regularly sleep with the enemy.* In the film *The Naked Civil Servant,* based on his memoir of the same name, Crisp is initially rejected by almost everyone who meets him. Though he is openly homosexual, he is shunned by the reticent gay community. He is beaten in the streets because he dons wigs and makeup. His natural-born magnetism does, however, succeed in courting friends. When he is tried for soliciting, many of them appear in court as character witnesses. The judge is moved to dismiss the charge. Incidentally, the success of *The Naked Civil Servant* rendered fame to both Crisp and Hurt. Hurt had the manifest good fortune of playing this idiosyncratic wit twice on screen, thirty-three years apart. Incidentally, Crisp described Hurt as *my representative here on Earth.*

In *An Englishman In New York,* Hurt's Crisp has become a minor celebrity. The sequel takes its name from UK musician Sting's 1988 Branford Marsalis' saxophone-laden hit single written in his honor. *Be yourself. No matter what they say.* Hurt's Crisp has migrated from old England to New York. He instantaneously makes his acquaintances in the Big Apple. He partakes in a minor celebrity diet of one-man stage shows and the TV talk circuit. He is a regular guest on *The David Letterman Show*. His agent finds him work reviewing films for a reputable magazine. He even plays the envied part of Lady Bracknell in the Oscar Wilde play *The Importance Of Being Earnest* at the Mercer Street Theater. He, however, discovers that he is not in synthesis with the attitudes of much of New York's gay communities. *I don't believe that anyone has 'rights,'* he remarks dismissively when the tenor of conversation is on gay activism. His careless remark about AIDS *being a fad, nothing more* was unfortunate. He palpably was not cognitive to the disproportionate afflictions visited upon gay communities by AIDS. Thereafter, his publicity was forcibly curbed. He refused to row back on his words. *It is my policy never to lie, never to defend. To recant would be to imply that I don't mean what I say. And I do.* He offered to explain his *fad* quip. His agent replied that the media *doesn't print explanations. They print retractions.* Crisp, described as *being so queer that he wasn't even gay,* and who, of himself said that *he didn't come out because he was never in,* was on better form when making wry observations. Throughout his life, he never deterred from cutting close to the bone.

Ask yourself, he once demurred, *if there was to be no blame, and if there was to be no praise, who would I be then?* A rational question in this age of solipsism. In the final scene of *An Englishman In New York*, Hurt's Crisp addresses his audience. He offers apt and judicious advice: *Persistence is your greatest weapon. It is in the nature of barriers that they fall. Do not seek to become like your opponents. You have the burden and the great joy of being outsiders. Every day you live as a kind of triumph. This you should cling onto. You should make no effort to try and join society. Stay right where you are. Give your name and serial number and wait for society to form itself around you. Because it most certainly will. Neither look forward where there is doubt, nor backward where there is regret. Look inward and ask not if there is anything outside that you want, but whether there is anything inside that you have not yet unpacked.* That advice was duly marked by the hermit who barely left his lodge. Those remarks are pinned on my workstation. An absorbing rebuke against conformity, compromise and acquiescence. *Be yourself. No matter what they say.*

In the 1966 film adaption of Robert Bolt's play *A Man For All Seasons*, John Hurt's character, the raccoon-eyed Richard Rich, is party to a witch hunt against Paul Scofield's Sir Thomas More. This was not Hurt's first film but it propelled him to prominence. The cast included Titans of the Hollywood screen: Orson Welles, Robert Shaw, Nigel Davenport, Vanessa Redgrave, her brother Corin Redgrave, Wendy Hiller and Susannah York. And of course, Scofield, one of the magnificent thespians of the last century. Hurt's Rich was a wily weasel and dangerously ambitious. He appeals to More's Scofield for position among his company. He is twice declined. His inclination towards corruptibility is palpable to the wise More who advises that he would be better served as a teacher. But Rich consorts among More's enemies. He manufactures evidence against the Lord High Chancellor of England in return for the title of Attorney General of Wales. More, in response to Rich's fabrications at his trial, replies: *Why Richard? It profits a man nothing to give his soul for the whole world... but for Wales?* Perhaps Richard Rich had some foresight into the English poet Christopher Logue's clerihew some four hundred and fifty years later when he wrote: *When all else fails, try Wales!* My readings of the Richard Rich of the 15th century construed that he was a malevolent wildebeest, more Machiavellian than Machiavelli's *The Prince*. In Hurt's Rich, we see a tetchy, malevolent nimrod driven by a pathological desire for prestige and position. He would ally himself to anyone. He would do anything. From my readings, the real Richard Rich sounded worse but we must pause to remember that Hurt played him at the beginning of his nefarious career.

Alien is an iconic motion picture for a host of reasons. Hurt finds himself in the role of the luckless Kane. He and two companions are on a reconnaissance mission having picked up a distress signal from an unidentified moon in deepest, darkest space. A phalange-type organism, known as *face hugger*, latches onto his face, impregnates him with an alien embryo, and renders him unconscious. When he recovers consciousness, he and his companions enjoy their *Last Supper*. In the midst of this, he chokes violently. An infant alien rips through his chest, having been incubated within his body. Kane is killed instantly. This scene is widely recognized as one of the most gruesome deaths in cinematic history. We know nothing of Kane, save that he is part of a crew on an exploration of space. We do remember him on the account of his death since it generated a whole chain of bloodcurdling events and sequels. Hurt, rather comically, reprises the role of Kane in the spoof film *Spaceballs*. *Oh no, not again*, he bemoans as the alien being rumbles through his torso and towards his chest cavity.

In the film *Nineteen Eighty-Four*, Hurt conveyed the abjection of Winston Smith from the pages of George Orwell, living and working in totalitarian, feculent London. Having read Orwell's dystopian novel many times, Hurt was how I imagined Winston. The profanation of basic human freedoms, the cruel careworn existence, the round-the-clock invigilation by the state upon the subject, the morose futility and repetitiveness is coagulated upon his granite face. The essential concepts of Truth are subverted. Winston works for a government department named *The Ministry Of Truth*. His job is to *rewrite* history. *Nineteen Eighty-Four* happened to be Richard Burton's last film. I found myself most moved by his stellar performance as the dudgeon O'Brien. The grim scene where he tortures Hurt's Winston with his worst fears and phobias, breaking his spirit and forcing him to betray his love Julia, exhibits his stock breaking point. He is *unpersoned*. Like those subjugated to tyrannous ignobility, he is conditioned with the principles of *doublethink*, or as W.E.B Du Bois would put it, *double consciousness*. He repudiates impulses and thoughts rendered abominable by his shadowy overlords. He publicly repents his sins. He is purged of his *wickedness*. Both film and book purged me of the facets imputed with totalitarianism. *Nineteen Eighty-Four*, as well as other literature and acquirements, reinforced my contempt for dogmas of every description. It reemphasized my will not to subject myself to censors, save for my own feeling, conscious and eternal witness. It reinforced the need to challenge authority and not simply comply with its edicts. It resuscitated my resolve to be mindful of institutions that wield powers that intrude both the private and personal. *Every non-conformist knows, in the depths of his soul, that the place his vanity rejects is the exact same place his nature has assigned him,* wrote Nicolás Gómez Dávila. Respectfully, to the man known as Don Colacho, I don't have any scruples for the club or the crowd.

If you've got nothing to hide, then you've nothing to worry about, remarked a malleable jarhead when we disseminated these matters. *Indeed,* I replied bitterly. *The kahunas are inordinately grateful for compliant serfs like you.* We had just watched a ghastly but pertinent film, *Compliance,* released in 2012. It was, in effect, based on a true story. A depraved pervert had phoned into a fast-food restaurant pretending to be a police officer. He falsely accused an employee of theft. He instructed manager and colleagues to detain the accused. He directed that her phone and handbag be confiscated. He proceeded to request that they search and then strip-search her. Her tribulation is drawn for hours. At the fake officer's prompting, an employee is coerced into sexually violating her. It was only when another employee probed the fake cop's obscene manner, **by asking questions**, did the young woman's ordeal finally end. In the final scene, the manager was interviewed on a talk show. Though she conceded that the episode had been traumatic for the accused, she would not take responsibility. She had simply followed orders! She surmised, therefore, that no blame could be attributed to her. Ten of millions of people in the past century have had their lives extinguished forever by Little Eichmann's who simply *followed orders.* Orderlies, who possess moral cowardice, enable elite gatekeepers. Their abject preponderance for ignorance makes them particularly dangerous. For them, the earth is filled with pollution. To breathe freely, therefore, is a vice in itself. They strive to sanitize the air till one finds it impossible to breathe. Those endowed with earthly power are fallible, flawed and foil for corruption, though they'd admit that in the darkness, *when the demons come.* Yet they are adept at the masquerade.

We see gatekeepers of a similar disposition in another Hurt film called *Scandal*. Conservatives, practically by day and in Parliament, liberals incidentally by night and in boudoirs. Hurt delivered a masterful performance as the osteopath, Stephen Ward, who found himself trapped in the Profumo whirlwind of 1962. Ward is manifestly cosmopolitan and extremely well-connected. His associates are a lethal concoction of satyric Tory ministers, fetching impressionable girls and finagling Soviet agents. When the comely Christine Keeler (Joanne Whalley) is discovered by the intelligence community to be sleeping with John Profumo (British Minister For War), and Eugene Ivanov (a Soviet James Bond without the gadgets) at the height of the Cold War, an infamous scandal ensures. The gangrenous establishment prop Hurt's Ward as the fall guy. He is rendered guilty by his association with the leading players in the scandal. Keeler simply lived in his home, yet he stands accused of being her pimp. His friends pirouette away from him. The Court arbitrates he is guilty, a day after he commits suicide. A habitual sadness lingers through Hurt's Ward throughout the film, whether he be in robust company or lonesome with a quiet drink by night. His eyes are dulled, even whilst he is at his most gregarious. But you see him reach breaking point during his interrogation with the police when he inadvertently snaps an arm of his glasses.

In the BBC mini-series titled *The Diaries of Alan Clark*, Hurt is the lascivious and malapropos Tory MP Alan Clark. He provides some Technicolor among the monochrome gray benches of Westminster, save the notable exception of the lady panjandrum Margaret Thatcher herself. You can see, from this portrayal, how the virtues of gentlemen mask the contours of the rogue. His incessant habit of tripping over his tongue denies him the higher offices of state. He slags off the European Economic Community in the midst of a ministerial engagement. He refers to Africa as *Bongo Bongo Land* during a departmental meeting. He appeared drunk at the

Parliamentary Despatch Box whilst scuttling through a preprepared script. As Minister For Trade, he became embroiled with the Matrix-Churchill scandal. He beds the wife of a South African judge and both her daughters too. Hurt seemed to relish this role, and for good reason. Alan Clark may have relished playing Alan Clark too till his last breath.

In *V For Vendetta*, Hurt is High Chancellor Adam Sutler, leader of Norsefire, ruler of Britain. He is a puritanical fascist, borne from the Hades of 1930s *Mitteleuropaisch*. As Defense Secretary, he plunged the country into a *Götterdämmerung*. His concentration camps are filled with homosexuals, ethnic minorities, Muslims, Jews and atheists. Such *undesirables* are imprisoned for human experimentation. Under his auspices, the St. Mary's virus was created in laboratories. Thereafter, the plague was unleashed upon the population. 100,000 Britons die. Terrorists are conveniently made scapegoats. A purge commences. Amidst the raging chaos, Sutler rises to power. Hurt's Sutler addresses his Council from a large projection screen, bellowing at them as if they were schoolchildren. He earns the hatred and contempt of Creedy, head of Britain's Secret Police. The anonymous *V*, the hero of this picture, cuts a deal with Creedy: Sutler in return for his surrender. And on Sutler's face before his gruesome execution, one countenances the fear of tyrants rendered into lambs when told they had an unscheduled appointment to keep with Azrael, Angel Of Death. I thought of the final moments of Benito Mussolini, Anwar Sadat, Samuel Doe, Nicolae Ceauşescu and Muammar Gaddafi. They had, in turn, arranged ceaseless meetings for Azrael with so many of their countryfolk.

John Hurt's final roles are monopolized by bereavement and mortality. In *Jackie*, an affecting portrayal of Jackie Kennedy (Natalie Portman) in the aftermath of the assassination of her husband President John F. Kennedy, he is a consoling priest. It is a small part. He is the voice of condolence and reserve. *The darkness may never go away*, he advises the young widow. *But it will not always be this heavy.* He compares her plight with that of Celidonius, the blind beggar of St. John's Gospel, whose sight Jesus restored by the Pool of Siloam. *Right now, you are blind,* he tells her. *Not because you have sinned but because you have been chosen so that the works of God could be revealed in you.* In *That Good Night*, his final film, he plays Ralph, a famous screenwriter estranged from his grown son. He is curmudgeonly, elderly and terminally ill. His devoted wife is many years his junior. He worries both about burdening her with his care and then leaving her after his death. He is visited by a mysterious guest, played by Charles Dance. He is offered a painless exit from the world. Perhaps quite predictably at the end, he recites Dylan Thomas' *Do Not Go Gentle Into That Good Night* as the film fades to black.

When I heard John Hurt had died, I was in the company of friends. I excused myself for a moment. Very few people have that residual effect whereby you'd never met them, yet you grieve their death like a friend or relative. The sad news of his demise, at the age of seventy-seven, led my mind to the final scene of the 1978 film version of *Watership Down*. An elderly Hazel Rah is visited by the Black Rabbit of Inlé. The hour of his death had approached. There is a place reserved for him in Osla Heaven. After he slips away by way of sleep, the Black Rabbit leads Hazel Rah's spirit through the grassy meadow and the arcadian heath, and into the presence of Lord Frith himself, creator of the Leporidae world. If there is a heaven solely for thespians, John Hurt will surely be communing with the very best of them.

January 9, 2021.

THE BALLAST OF
THOMAS PAINE

THE BALLAST OF THOMAS PAINE is not taught in British schools, but not for no good reason. We remain tragically remiss of the rancors concerning history and provenance. The emphasis instead is on soothing affectations and shards of truth, which is why this apposite Promethean, who played such a purposeful role in both the American and French Revolutions, has been relegated to a Thetford footnote. He remains an almost unknown in the country of his birth. Churchill, Shakespeare, Cromwell (Oliver, and not his near relation Thomas) and that uxoricidal, teeming, tyrannosaur Henry Tudor junior are the historical lifeblood of a plaintive National Curriculum. Their names are sung in rococo chorus. Their accomplishments eddy invariably as the River Thames. In Thomas Paine, who in the words of the luckless Anglo-American General Charles Lee *burst forth upon the world like Jove with thunderbolts*, we have an incandescent Englishman for all seasons and for all times, a more conscientious man than any of the aforementioned. But alas! He is cast into historical purgatory.

I had stumbled upon Paine after reading extensively on the American Revolution of my own accord, during a dyspeptic summer holiday. I had just finished secondary school and was half-looking forward to college. Throughout that July-August-September period, I can recall reading and ruminating over Paine's pamphlets. I then wondered why no classroom teacher had mentioned him, even in passing, over the previous eleven years. Before embarking on this piece, I asked several among my mottled circle on whether they had heard of, or read on, old Tom Paine. All but one had not heard of him. But then again Brandy Nicholle, of Cleveland, Ohio, is not a product of the British educational system.

Paine was arguably the leading outlier and seditionist of the eighteenth century. From an inimical inkpot, he generated more pungency than the pneumatic, tweeting politicians of our dissipated era. I would readily make the precarious argument that his enlightened precepts, though heretical but atemporal in its *Common Sense*, would make better citizens of Britons and constitute better government. Those ballasts and precepts negate the stoic values congealed around Crown, Church and Country, long before the belated Union Jack drapings of *Britishness*, or whatever schmeared quaintness that it is supposed to represent. Since I am in the spirit of the precarious argument, I will permit myself the indulgence of saying that I had long exempted myself from cornfed mamelukes who can readily accept a fellow primate that claims a dubious lineage to the House of David as their Sovereign Majesty, and then maintain that they and their offspring have a divine right to rule over me and my descendants forever, not minding the polymorphic perversions this entails.

There still exists, from within me, a quaint romanticist regard of a Sir Galahad or a Sir Percival pledging fealty to a King Arthur. The bestiaries of the *faris'* of ancient Arabia and the *equites* of ancient Rome still thrill the cockles, as they did in my youth. Watching moribund motions of knights in bespoke tailored suits on bended knee being anointed by a grandiose sword is a contemporaneous farce, worthy of a horselaugh. Observing further the unbridled joy of our Ri Chun Hee newsbots at the nuptials of the dashing Harry and the sparkling Meghan, it is quite easy to foresee the future of the House of Windsor being immersed in the culture of confected celebrity. *However*, wrote Thomas Paine. *It is needless to spend much time in exposing the folly of hereditary right. If there are any so weak as to believe it, let them promiscuously worship the ass and lion, and welcome. I shall neither copy their humility, nor disturb their devotion.*

His Quaker upbringing hardwired his disdain for authority, and his affection for mankind. His writing explicated the nature of oppression. He understood how to incisively remove oneself from its confining yolk. He did not possess the schizophrenic cast of mind of many radicals and revolutionaries, who after dying the death of a thousand razors, sought to befriend that same tyranny in a mutually exclusive commonwealth. Luminary figures like George Washington, Benjamin Franklin and Thomas Jefferson initially held no conspicuous intent of severing America from her British king. Their quarrel was with the British Parliament over representation and taxes. Their then king, George III, was perceived as a possible honest broker, an arbiter in these matters. Paine recognized him for what he really was: an aberrant, unscrupulous monarch who was deaf, dumb and blind to their problem. When George III's tyrannical interdictions was finally conferred to the mob, his equestrian stature in New York came tumbling down. Paine's unambiguous, illuminating pen helped scythe the umbilical cord from the Mother Country, and a new nation was born. He swayed much of the populace towards independence with his pamphlet *American Crisis*, which remains the all-time bestselling book title in American history. He understood the concatenation between the oppressor and the oppressed.

Men of passive tempers look somewhat lightly over the offences of Britain, and, still hoping for the best, are apt to call out, "Come, come, we shall be friends again, for all this." But examine the passions and feelings of mankind. Bring the doctrine of reconciliation to the touchstone of nature, and then tell me, whether you can hereafter love, honour, and faithfully serve the power that hath carried fire and sword into your land? If you cannot do all these, then you are only deceiving yourselves, and by your delay bringing ruin upon posterity. Your future connection with Britain, whom you can neither love nor honour, will be forced and unnatural, and being formed only on the plan of present convenience, will in a little time fall into a relapse more wretched than the first. But if you say, you can still pass the violations over, then I ask, hath your house been burnt? Hath your property been destroyed before your face? Are your wife and children destitute of a bed to lie on, or bread to live on? Have you lost a parent or a child by their hands, and yourself the ruined and wretched survivor? If you have not, then you are not a judge of those who have. But if you have, and still can shake hands with the murderers, then you are unworthy of the name of husband, father, friend, or lover, and whatever may be your rank or title in life, you have the heart of a coward, and the spirit of a sycophant.

Paine urged that generation of those Thirteen Colonies that this conflagration against a foreign superpower was theirs to contend, to alleviate their children from a danger that will persist if it were not extirpated forthwith. And his ire was palpable against those who were contrary to his position. *I once felt all that kind of anger,* he wrote, *which a man ought to feel, against the mean principles that are held by the Tories: a noted one, who kept a tavern at Amboy, was standing at his door, with as pretty a child in his hand, about eight or nine years old, as I ever saw, and after speaking his mind as freely as he thought was prudent, finished with this unfatherly expression, "Well! Give me peace in my day." Not a man lives on the continent but fully believes that a separation must some time or other finally take place, and a generous parent should have said, "If there must be trouble, let it be in my day, that my child may have peace," and this single reflection, well applied, is sufficient to awaken every man to duty.*

What ought to be normative for any generation is to extirpate the threat of their time, lest it metastases or snowballs into an inveterate malady that persecutes their offspring for all time. When this is done, and the battles are won, the bellicose heroics of our forebears are sung through the ages. You will find *the summer soldier* and *sunshine patriot* among the deprecatory of any generation, trying to coerce acquiescence among the masses with their prematurely ejaculated piffle. These melts have been inculcated by the ecclesiastical mindfucking of hereditary discipline. They are habituated into walking tall upon bended knee. They will forever remain among us. Paine, who was childless, recognized this as a father recognizes his son. It would have been a flagrant crime for that generation of Americans if the British problem was permitted to swell. British rule was unjust, and their taxes even more so. In the nascent United States of America, Paine could see the efflorescence of a great nation. Which was why at this time of indecision and uncertainty, his pamphlets were read aloud in taverns and salons, and to soldiers and their commanders before they took to the battlefield on the morrow. The people were moved to make vehement war with tyranny. *If there must be trouble, let it be in my day, that my child may have peace.*

He penned and pronounced the folly of kings. *A hereditary monarch is as absurd a position as a hereditary doctor or mathematician.* He advocated the abolition of slavery during the infancy of the United States. *I despair of seeing an abolition of the infernal traffic in Negroes. We* (meaning he and his friend Benjamin Rush) *must push that matter further on your side of the water* (in America). *I wish that a few well instructed could be sent among their brethren in bondage; for until they are enabled to take their own part, nothing will be done.* He was a close associate of Mary Wollstonecraft and an expounder of the Rights of Women. *Society,* he writes, *instead of alleviating their* (the female) *condition, is to them the source of new miseries. More than one half of the globe is covered with savages; and among all these people women are completely wretched.* To the care of animals, Paine demonstrated an attentive hand. *. . .that everything of persecution and revenge between man and man, and everything of cruelty to animals, is a violation of moral duty.* He wrote presciently on what was a prelude to a modern welfare system. *To create a national fund, out of which there shall be paid to every person, when arrived at the age of twenty-one years, the sum of fifteen pounds sterling, as a compensation in part, for the loss of his or her natural inheritance, by the introduction of the system of landed property.* And a pension for senior citizens: *And also, the sum of ten pounds per annum, during life, to every person now living, of the age of fifty years, and to all others as they shall arrive at that age.*

The humane idea of freeing men and women taken into captivity from Africa was always going to end up on the cutting room floor of the Pennsylvania State House. Most of the Founding Fathers of the United States of America were rapacious men of property and predation. Enslaved men and women constituted property. Free labor was necessitated into making the new Republic an economic powerhouse. And so the Declaration of Independence was composed with an ironic caveat. Self-evident truths about all men being created equal, endowed by their Creator with unalienable rights to life, liberty and the pursuit of happiness was a bullwhip to the manacled and the shackled. And as for the comity of nations, when Saint Domingue's (Haiti's) founding fathers reached out to their counterparts in Washington DC after freeing themselves from merciless French tyranny, they were instantaneously spurned.

After the formation of the American Republic, Paine's star began to wane after coming of worse in a public dispute with American diplomat, Silas Deane. He unwisely exposed France's surreptitious aid to the Thirteen Colonies during the War of Independence against Britain in a Pennsylvanian newspaper, of which Deane was heavily involved in. The dispute led to his resignation as secretary to the Committee of Foreign Affairs. It was palpable that, from that moment on, he had no political future among the new American establishment. He had made many enemies among the hierarchical classes, save for Thomas Jefferson, who took his advice when president, of purchasing the State of Louisiana from the French, thereby doubling the size of an inchoate United States of America.

He returned to England while another revolution was brewing across the English Channel. His one-time friend Edmund Burke, prevenient father of Thatcherism and patriarch of the modern-day Conservative Party, had been an irrepressible supporter of Irish unification and the American Revolution. He could not, however, bring himself to support the French Revolution and wrote a popular screed against it titled: *Reflections on the Revolution in France*. He warned against the internecine upheaval that betide revolution, fearing it may foam in the Channel and be cast ashore in Britain. Mob rule was most detestable to him. He lamented *the loss of generous loyalty to rank and sex, that proud submission, that dignified obedience, that subordination of*

the heart, which kept alive, even in servitude itself, the spirit of an exalted freedom.
He wrote eloquently in defense of the French Catholic Church (the so-called *eldest daughter of the Church*), which was under an existential threat from Robespierre and the rest. His dewy-eyed reverence of Marie Antoinette, France's Queen, was a distillation of marvel and esteem. Paine's unyielding defense of the French Revolution arrived in the form of *Rights of Man*, where he vied the monarchy and the ruling elite. He was forced to flee England after the authorities incurred a warrant for his arrest. He was absent from the courts when he was convicted of seditious libel. Had he stood trial, he would have swung from the gallows.

When he arrived in Paris, King Louis XVI of France sat aloof in a French dungeon. *Rights of Man* had become an instant bestseller in France (as it was in England) and Paine, in spite of not speaking French, was elected to the National Convention and made an honorary French citizen. However, he made an enemy of the firebrand Jean-Paul Marat by speaking out against the execution of the king. Louis XVI had been America's ally in the war against Britain. He had emptied his nation's coffers in pursuit of American Independence. Marat and his allies voted for regicide, and the king's head was soon separated from his body by a guillotine. Paine was tipped from his seat on the National Convention and into a cooler in Luxembourg Prison, where he was marked for execution. By a stroke of luck, he was fortuitously spared when the white chalk marking him for death was scratched on the wrong side of his cell door. He was freed from the prison after the intervention of James Monroe, then American ambassador to France and later, fifth President of the United States, on the basis that Paine *was* an American citizen.

The publishing of *The Age Of Reason*, which he composed whilst incarcerated, caused Paine's name to fall further into ill-repute. For in it, he excoriated organized religion and the Testaments. *Whenever we read the obscene stories, the voluptuous debaucheries, the cruel and torturous executions, the unrelenting vindictiveness, with which more than half the Bible is filled, it would be more consistent that we called it the word of a demon, than the word of God. It is a history of wickedness, that has served to corrupt and brutalize mankind; and, for my part, I sincerely detest it, as I detest everything that is cruel.* Religion and church were beyond reproach by society in those days. Enlightened folk were inclined to keep their deism to themselves. He, in turn, was excoriated for this work and cast out among the populace. He had also fallen out publicly with America's beloved first president George Washington for not coming to his aid after he was imprisoned in Luxembourg Prison. For these reasons, he was denied the vote because he was deemed a foreigner and an upstart. He was cursed and spat upon in the streets.

After publishing The Age of Reason as an old man, Paine was beaten and turned out of his house and away from his town by his fellow citizens to punish him for blasphemy. I had, even then, a little glimmer of how dangerous it actually is for an American to behave like an American. We've never believed a word we've said from the Bill of Rights onward. What conceivable right do we have to feel smug about the fatwa imposed on Salman Rushdie by fanatical foreigners? We don't do badly with fatwas ourselves. (Bill Holm: The Heart Can Be Filled Anywhere On Earth).

Paine spent the last years of his life under the care of his friend, Marguerite Brazier. When he died on June 8, 1809, his brethren, the Quakers, refused him permanent sanctuary in their cemetery. Six people attended his funeral. Two were African Americans who had traveled twenty-five miles on foot. A third and fourth were a woman and her son *who lived on the bounty of the dead.* But his bones have no resting place. For when his remains were dug up from whence he was buried on his farm, an English radical journalist named William Cobbett transported him back to England, so he could be buried a hero. But Cobbett appeared to be caught up in his own insurgent activism upon his return, ducking the authorities and fleeing from town to village. When he died twenty-five years later, Paine's cadaver was lost forever among his possessions.

Would Thomas Paine have found peace designing iron bridges, as was his pastime, rather than aiding the sword of Washington in a war for independence? Would his name not fall into ignominy had he stayed in Thetford, Norfolk, and earned a quiet shilling from making stay ropes? I have since visited the statue that pays him small tribute on a main road in the town of his birth. The old grammar school that he attended when he was a boy still stands. But alas! *A prophet is not without honor, but in his own country, and among his own kin, and in his own house.* (Mark 6:4).

December 5, 2017.

LOOKING BACK IN ANGER: THE RAGE OF THE WORKING CLASS WRITER

S OME 2,300 YEARS AGO, the Greek polymath Aristotle wrote that both poetry and theater lead to catharsis. For the working-class scribes and lower middle-class dramatists that emerged in the 1950's, a tranquilizing of their inner daemons led rise to a new genre of literature known as *kitchen-sink realism*. These dissentient men were often university-educated bohemians, dispossessed of the opportunities reserved solely for the aristocrat and the highbrow. Their hardy pens, plaintive and brash, were repositories of the drab, cheerless existence partaken of their young lives and soon enough, cinema and stage made capital of their rancor. They were a bedeviling herd of cats with a worm's eye view of the fraught and ossified nature of the grinding poverty and abjection among the working classes. Their works were marinated with identical themes of fury and malcontent against a socio-political structure that sought to suppress them or, at the very least, keep them in their place.

John Osborne was arguably the most important playwright of these times, and certainly the most famous of these *Angry Young Men*, a catchphrase inspired by *Angry Young Man*, the autobiographical book title of Anglo-Irish author Leslie Paul. Up to that point, Noel Coward of *Mad Dogs And Englishmen*, Laurence Olivier of

Richard III and Terence Rattigan of *The Winslow Boy* were refulgent
follow spots of the carefully crafted British stage, gourmandizing
on stuffy period dramas that thrilled the Upper Crust and little
else. Shows like *Relative Values* (a three-act Coward production), *The
Sleeping Prince* (written by Rattigan and starring Olivier and his then
wife Vivien Leigh in its first production) raked the gravel over the
cloistered tracks of elitist England.

I stumbled across Osborne's *Look Back In Anger* (and the word
pusillanimous) from watching a 1989 film production shown on
TV, directed by no other than Judi Dench and starring Kenneth
Branagh and Emma Thompson. It was *risus et bellum* at its finest.
Jimmy Porter (played by Branagh) was a cantankerous young man,
almost unhinged by his ire at the conceptual forces that kept him
downtrodden. His long-suffering wife Alison (played by Thompson)
was a nonchalant representative of class privilege. Her small act of
rebellion against that privilege was to become Mrs. Porter. She bore
the brunt of his unchivalrous rages while she mechanically ironed
the week's washing. Their co-lodger Cliff (played by Gerard Horan)
is an affable peacemaker, everybody's best mate. Alison's conceited
friend Helena (Siobhan Redmond) comes over to stay and, after
some initial hectoring from Mr. Porter, is seduced into his bed by
his boorish charm. Alison flees to her parents after discovering she
is pregnant. Helena absconds after Alison returns, her conscience
having kicked in. Meanwhile, Cliff decamps after deciding to venture
out on his own. In the final scene, Mr. and Mrs. Porter seemingly
call a truce on their connubial class war in a mawkish game of
bears and squirrels.

Thirty years earlier, in the year Nineteen Hundred and Fifty-
nine, *Look Back In Anger* had already been made into a motion picture,
directed by Tony Richardson and starring the legendary Richard
Burton (who played the irascible Porter), Mary Ure, Gary Raymond
and Claire Bloom. A lesser-known film version starring Malcolm
McDowell was produced in 1980. It was on the stage, however, that
Look Back In Anger first appeared before the public. It was not received

well by its initial critics. The irreducible content was deemed caustic and vulgar. However, a lionized review by one of the foremost critics of the day, Kenneth Tynan, (allegedly one of the first people to say the word *fuck* on British television) gave the play leverage. Tynan described *Look Back In Anger* as *the best young play of its decade.* The play almost instantaneously became a success. Osborne was propelled almost overnight as the leading playwright in Britain.

His next work *The Entertainer* (the name borrowed from Scott Joplin's arresting ragtime piece) went on to star Laurence Olivier, and Olivier's future wife Joan Plowright on celluloid. And though Osborne did not ever catapult the heights of *Look Back In Anger*, his place in UK theater is palpably assured. He was an intriguing, controversial fellow, prone towards the crude invective, with which he would so readily spew on subjects ranging from the Suez Crisis to his ex-spouses. He excoriated his countrymen with a letter filled with vile after Britain had the temerity to join that exclusive club of nations that vied with each other over the nuclear bomb. *This is a letter of hate*, he began writing from the sun-kissed beaches of Valbonne, France, where he was holidaying with his mistress, as his pregnant wife Mary Ure was giving birth to a child fathered by another man (actor Robert Shaw). *It is for you, my countrymen. I mean those men of my country who have defiled it. The men with manic fingers leading the sightless, feeble, betrayed body of my country to its death...* I would recommend the magical authorized biography of John Osborne for a comprehensive reading on this anomalous character, written by John Heilpern and titled: *John Osborne: The Many Lives Of The Angry Young Man*. This is a masterful, meticulous and mesmerizing work; a captivating page turner about an incorrigible but charismatic playwright.

A convergence of similar penmanship followed Osborne's path. Writer Alan Sillitoe, of working-class stock, produced two seminal works in quick succession. *Saturday Night And Sunday Morning* told of the scabrous exploits of young Arthur Seaton who sought drink and dames as refuge from the automation of daily life and the drudgery of factory work. The novel was made into a film starring the statuesque Albert Finney in the lead role. *The Loneliness Of The Long Distance Runner* is about a petty thief named Smith. In spite of an offer of a lighter workload at the Borstal were he to win a cross-country race against a prestigious public school, he reaches the finishing line but doesn't cross it. He allows his competitors to beat him, defiant to the bitter end that no reward would make him bend to the dictates of the Borstal's proud governors. *This Sporting Life*, written by the recently departed David Storey, is a morose northern tale about a young man's unyielding desire to become a professional rugby player. His churlish behavior of the pitch proves to be his undoing. *This Sporting Life* was adapted into a film which brought acting great Richard Harris to hell-raising prominence. Meanwhile, Storey, the son of a Yorkshire miner, enjoyed a lengthy career as an author and playwright with works such as *Home* and *Saville* until his death at the age of eighty-three last month.

The original *angry young woman* was a generation or two ahead of her time. Shelagh Delaney wrote *A Taste Of Honey* in ten days, and before her twentieth birthday. *A Taste Of Honey* was a redoubtable script set in Salford about a working-class teenager named Jo, who is impregnated by Jimmy, a sailor of African descent. She rows with her mother and her mother's boyfriend Peter and then moves in with her gay friend Geoffrey. For a teenage playwright in the year Nineteen Hundred And Fifty-eight to write so stridently about lone parenthood, interracial relationships and homosexuality is a pellucid indicator of her irreverent and irreversible courage. Delaney wrote *A Taste Of Honey* in response to Rattigan's play *Variations On A Theme*, which she felt was disparaging to homosexuals (though Rattigan was a closet homosexual himself). Tony Richardson would bring this play of hers to the cinematic screen. The film starred Rita Tushingham, Dora Bryan, Robert Stephens and Paul Danquah. Delaney's second play *The Lion In Love* was a surly depiction of a northern family that consisted of a liquor-loving mother, a spiritless father and a son longing for antipodean shores. Her pen was on the quotidian pulse of her country folk. Her errant plays would go on to inspire playwrights like Andrea Dunbar, creator of *Rita, Sue And Bob Too* and *The Arbor*.

Keith Waterhouse's novel *Billy Liar* was rooted in provincial Yorkshire. Billy, a fantasist and philanderer, lies almost every time he opens his mouth. He harbors dreams of working as a comedy writer in London. But his daily life consists of a dead-end job at an undertaker's office and being engaged to two of his three girlfriends. As with the aforementioned plays and novels, this was made into a successful film. *Billy Liar* starred a young Tom Courtenay. Incidentally, Courtenay also played Smith in the film version of *The Loneliness Of The Long Distance Runner*.

I should hasten to add that several New Wave writers and dramatists were dismissive of this *angry* tag. It never was a convener, as far as they were concerned. The word *anger* is contingent with negative connotations. It is understandable as to why one would flee from any kind of notional stereotype. In Osborne's case, the tag was the brainchild of George Fearon, Press Officer at the Royal Court Theater, and it was bestowed upon him rather disparagingly. Osborne himself later considered it an albatross around his neck. For a while, this indignant wave of disillusion and contempt brought about a much-needed catharsis to literature, stage, screen and the country at large, that breathed oxygen into the plaintive lungs of later writers. Writers belonging to that same period such as John Braine, Arnold Wesker, Stan Barstow, Alan Clarke, Harold Pinter and Joe Orton were to produce pugnacious work in spite of the Colorvision and decadence of the impending sixties. However, there was no propensity towards revolution. Rebellion seldom strayed beyond their pages, but perhaps for good reason. They were soon-to-be embraced by the Establishment.

Alienation descends in structural degrees. The greater the alienation, the deeper the wound. The great African American civil rights leader Malcolm X is oft quoted as saying: *Usually when people are sad, they don't do anything. They just cry over their condition. But when they get angry, they bring about change.* His wounds were borne from the unkindest cut of all. Perhaps some of these writers were not angry enough. Or as it would seem, not at all, as some did indeed testify. In my novel, *The Nepenthe Park Chronicles*, where there is considerable misplaced anger, I put these words into the mouth of the main protagonist Lollipop: *Anger's good, cuz. When peeps see anger... real anger, they step out of your way coz no one wants to get hurt. Anger gives you tha edge. You gotta use dat anger ...or dat anger will use you.*

I would argue that anger channeled intelligently is the ultimate catharsis.

April 14, 2018

MY BROTHER, SERVING
HUMANITY

F ACEBOOK PAGES ARE OFTEN mired with minutiae, drollery and conceit. Most of the fulminations I have seen on Facebook Video fill me with horror. I tend to look away. Or not to look at all. My brother's Facebook page, however, is worth anatomizing and revisiting. Not because he *is* my brother, though that in itself would be a good enough reason, but more so because his page has little to do with his social activity and everything to do with his humanitarianism. Alhaji Ousman Kinteh is the director-general of *Mission Aid Gambia*, a charity that primarily grants sustenance to widows, orphans and senior citizens in The Gambia, West Africa. Scroll down his page. Amidst his daily citations on religious forethought and introspection, you will find his vlogs. In these recordings, he is featured traveling to small hamlets in lackluster districts, where the bare necessities of life are indigent. Thanks to the generous donations of patrons, he brings rice and raiments in abundance to these people. Medicines are procured for regional clinics. Widows and senior citizens are enabled with provisions to help provide for themselves and their offspring. He rebuilds homes that are crumbling. He organizes the repairs of dilapidated roofs so that babes can be spared from the raindrops that exude their homes while they sleep at night. Sponsorship is provided for these same children to attend school so that they may be afforded greater prospects when they become women and men. In these videos, children gently propound their industrious ambitions. I hope serendipity is kind to them.

Alhaji works in conjunction with *Abdullah Aid*, a Muslim charity founded in London by a husband and wife in memory of their infant son, Abdullah. Their charity operates in the most tenuous of regions: In Myanmar, where the Rohingya people are being uprooted and immolated by homicidal barbarians from the Myanmarese army, they provide a haven for the persecuted. In the detritus of Syria, they succor the desolate ones caught between the teeming suffering and slaughter. On the island of Lesvos, Greece, where migrants have survived the Mediterranean, they provide comfort and clean water. And in The Gambia, they aid the poverty-stricken. My brother orchestrates that aid.

The Gambia is a bewitching country of metallic beaches and warm winters. It is a young nation, with a large younger population, pregnant with endeavor and hope made particular by the demise of a tyrant regime who reigned capriciously for twenty-two years. The politics of that pungent rule still lingers. While this land is commonly known in tourist brochures as the *Smiling Coast of Africa*, a discerning visitor would be rendered unsmiling if she were to remove her sightseeing spectacles and pondered thoughtfully beyond the tourist soundbites and gracious hospitality that seems ubiquitous among Gambians. There still exists a dearth of infrastructure. Power cuts are commonplace. Allusions to poverty are palpable. Healthcare and education costs are grossly inordinate to the average wage. A more appropriate sobriquet would be to call this strip of land the *Grimacing Coast of Africa*.

Many daughters and sons of The Gambia, having fled repression into the bosom of the diaspora, are returning home to inject innovation and ingenuity into the nation's lifeblood. They are considerably qualified and better enlightened than their predecessors. Morally autonomous folks like Toure Robinson and Sourra Sosseh have flown from their homes in recent months, having raised money of their own intuitive, to support *Mission Aid Gambia*. This is the land of their fathers no less. They are model benefactors for a new generation.

Businesspersons from India and St. Elsewhere, with greenbacks to invest, do see the potential and promise of The Gambia. They partake in the expansion of industries and the gradual augmentation of infrastructure. They purchase demesne in the fleshpots, for ownership of prime land is everything. Other aspirational Gambians, with zero investment in terms of finance, see greater potential and promise overseas. An unknown number rove the benighted desert and the banal sea, the Sahara and the Mediterranean, to seek the potential and promise of Europe. They surmised that they would rather risk death than to remain at home with nothing.

Alhaji Kinteh had been a businessman in The Gambia since the tender age of sixteen. It was a leavening, life-affirming experience. He managed our father's import and export business for a year. He purchased white goods, tires and household appliances from auctions and wholesalers in London. Then he arranged their transfer by sea to the Port of Banjul, navigating the port authority officials who wanted their beaks wetted with frogskins, to supplement their atrocious pay. Even at that age, he was a wily, unencumbered tradesman. Later that year, I flew out to see him whilst he was in the throes of his work. I'd watch him barter with men three times his age. His haggling reverberated from Wollof to English and then back again. The haughtiest of customers were often confounded during negotiations. And when they finally walked away seemly contented with price and product, he had elicited no quarter. Those that knew him then could readily testify that Alhaji had a hardnosed business head, decorated by charm and chutzpah, and that his aptitude and application would take him places.

After he returned to England, he created a plethora of businesses that made bucket loads of money. He sold mobile phones and vehicles to the public. He established a chain of estate agents and carwash lots across London's East End. In 2006, he created

Ruthless Records and worked with industry stalwarts like DJ Limelight, Morrison, Giggs, Young Spray, Maxwell D and Mike GLC. In only a few years, that independent grime/hip-hop distribution company became the largest of its kind in Britain. But he gradually became disillusioned with the pretentious overtones of the moxie music business, its underlays of soulless tedium and besetting narcissism. Sycophants and the futility of flaunting riches made him sick. He returned to The Gambia in 2010 with an acute need for catharsis and contemplation. Having arrived at the airport, he left behind the urban centers of Banjul, Birkama and Serekunda. He fell into the habitats of some of the poorest people on earth. It proved to be a lucid eyeopener. He arrived at a village, where the inhabitants were too poor to trade in the local currency, the dalasi. Their means of exchange were simple household goods and tools required for everyday living. He was aghast at how some people, who had been endowed with wealth, would turn their noses up at those with so little. The neglect in the provincial villages was apparent. Homes were in a perpetual state of disrepair. Roofs were decrepit from the torrential downpours of the rainy season. Medicines were in short supply. The price of staple foods like rice and cornflower was immoderate. He would never forget an elderly gentleman, Abdou Kanyi, who was in dire need of assistance but held him in high esteem. My brother was unable to aid him, for he was, at that point, experiencing hard times. When they parted, Kanyi gave him a pumpkin which so moved my brother. It was the only thing of value he possessed. He died a short time afterwards.

Our father, Karamo Kinteh, was from a village that is no different to the ones that my brother tarried. He was born in Jassong, some 130 miles from the then-capital, Bathurst. He was orphaned by the age of eleven. He left home for unharnessed horizons when he was no more than a teenager. Kismet delivered him to Dakar, Senegal. He worked on Dakar's dockside while the world was at war for a second time. He would not have been too far from the Thiaroye massacre that took place in the twilight of 1944. Senegalese soldiers and conscripts demanded their salary arrears, unjustly withheld from them, be paid in full. When their demand was rejected, they mutinied. The French were not prepared to arbitrate their grievances. They pointed their impugnable rifles at the Senegalese, who fought to liberate France from the Nazis earlier that year. They shot dead up to seventy-five of their number. From this incident, one can patently envisage the precarious nature of colonial rule, where men were more unequal than they are today, though they be brother-in-arms.

With the great kindling that had affected the world now ending (but its aftershocks ricocheting in the decades to come), our father, having spurned an opportunity to go to America, soon embarked on a ship to Britain from Dakar. He arrived in Cardiff, Wales, sometime in September 1947, after a three-week voyage. In those days, the United Kingdom had a king, a declining empire, and a population living on rations. He lived in London for fifty-five years. He kept his Gambian passport, never trading it for a British one. He married twice and had eight children.

Seventy years on, the third of his five sons resides in The Gambia with his wife and five children, trafficking in charity and hope among the provincial community. *Mission Aid Gambia* is concentrated on the sole principle of the betterment of its recipients. Alhaji treats people with dignity, not pity. His ebullient acumen was honed from years of hustle. He has hired a stern contingent of masons and diggers, laborers and distributors. You need only watch his vlogs on Facebook to watch their work. They rebuild dismembered homes; mend falling roofs and dig new wells for fresh water. Recently, they traveled to a small collective in Ndemban Jola, which squats close to the Senegalese border. Local residents were beneficiaries of *The Gambia Rice Distribution program*. They are supplemented with bags of onions, rice, tomatoes, oil, milk powder and maize. This drop-off was replicated on the fords of Pirang, where village elders came out to welcome him and his helpers. Wells are being constructed in the small town of Jambanjelly. For the health center in Kuntaya, *Mission Aid Gambia* purchased 125,000 dalasis (£2,000) of medical stock.

In Chamsen Sosseh, an octogenarian resides in a woeful habitat, totally unfit for a man of his bearing and age. Fortunately, he falls into Alhaji's *Build A Home Project*. His old house was torn down and rebuilt in weeks to a durable, safe standard. Foundlings have the *Orphan Sponsorship Payout* delivered monthly, to ensure their school fees are readily paid and their welfare needs are taken care of.

And in Jassong, where our father now rests in the village graveyard, Alhaji Ousman Kinteh recently paid homage to our relatives, bringing with him bare necessities in abundance, and consecrating family bonds for our father's sake. His work induces an intrinsic joy he has never known. He does not miss the tics of the rat race, nor London for that matter, though he does return but for a few weeks in a calendar year. And though we live and work on separate continents, he remains my foremost inspiration, and my oldest friend.

October 29, 2017.

WHY LONDON IS
NOT THE GREATEST
CITY IN THE WORLD

W HEN PEOPLE ARE INDISCREET in the art of public conversation, they inexplicably give license for strangers to eavesdrop.
Being privy to such imprudence in London is not uncommon. People
lack etiquette when shouting into their mobile phones on buses and
trains. Young females cachinnate uncontrollably. A pimply man with a
beanie hat shares his music with the entire carriage, as if he's our DJ
and we, his disco. Passengers putting their dirty shoes on commuter
seats epitomizes the vulgarization of the commuter's experience.
The Greek polymath Aristotle wrote that a city is *a unity of unlikes*.
Indeed. Some of the things I've witnessed on public transport is
unlike anything I've seen. Upon the London Embankment where I
am scribbling this piece, one can observe the synchronicity of this
city in the tides of people wafting their way onward, forward and
backward. All roads, judged strictly on appearances, lead to this Gog
and Magog citadel Upon-The-Thames. Etched on every aspect are a
million tales that an Aristophanes, Dickens, Scheherazade or Homer
could convey. Each distrait eyebrow's a bard; each ambled eyeball a
griot. Each furrowed brow a kathakudu. In this spree of wild ap-
proximation, I cannot help but be inspired. Being discreet, in this
inglorious age of barb and rancor, is almost a virtue. Forbearance
is not. But to live in the London of today, you need lashings of it.

I have endured the strain of London to near breaking point. The economic encumbrances are unrelenting, the psychological compressions even more so. Some ten days ago, I watched Mayor Sadiq Khan at Trafalgar Square describe London as *the world's greatest city*. I have heard him repeat this fatuity several times before. It did me no good to hear him say it again. London is withering, not flowering under his watch. Many of his parishioners toil with poverty. Their public and social services are too frequently inadequate. They are not of the greatest or greater standard as befitting the greatest city, but that could never temper his vainglorious self-centeredness before the flashbulbs of the international media. London is the greatest city in the world because he happens to be her mayor. London is the greatest city in the world because he happens to be a Londoner. London is the greatest city in the world because he projects her miscellaneous virtues upon his civic mask. The social decline of London is not the sole fault of the current mayor. This *lackluster* city has been receding because of discrepant politics, local and national, before the turn of the century.

Only days later, I overheard a searing debate between city workers on London's supremacy over all cities, or her lack of. Their conversation inspired this piece. These thirty-somethings were in the vicinity of the Glass Testicle, otherwise known as City Hall, the HQ of Mayor Khan. I was drinking black coffee and sending WhatsApp messages from my iPhone at a table nearby. Their recriminations about the woes and winsomeness of London rumbled noisily. Both sides of the argument were intriguing. I stopped messaging. I sipped my coffee slowly. I eavesdropped.

An alabaster-skinned chap in a smart black suit arched a brogue ungallantly into London's gonads. His accent indexed his Skagerrak roots. Though I could be wrong. London was a urinal, he choked, vitiated by the burg air. The pavements were paved with dog poo. Too many of her citizens were uncouth. They pissed, spat, shat and barfed on the sidewalks. They tipped domestic rubbish on public streets. Rent prices were exorbitant and devoured a considerable amount of the tenants' earnings. The cost of living was extortionate, beyond reason. Night train services were abysmal. The weather was woeful, save for a few chance weeks per year. Oligarchs and Baron Greenbacks, saturated in the perfumes of Arabia, Rublyovka and Tunbridge Wells, enjoy the champagne supernova heights overlooking Hyde Park and the Thames while the majority of Londoners toil for a stipend.

His companions felt his generalizations were out of line. Their cliched objections were akin to a bleating crescendo. It was flagrantly unpleasant to the ear. London, they argued, was inarguably the world's greatest city. They had collectively visited Tokyo, Mexico City, New York, Accra, Singapore and Berlin (among other places) and yet London's pluralism remained unrivalled in comparison to her sister cities. She was the intersection of the earth's communities. People worshipped at temples and taverns, mosques and raves, churches and theaters, synagogues and football stadiums. Her historical landmarks bore witness to her timeless stridency. Contemporary cultural hubs like Brixton and Brick Lane were regentrified hives of diversity. The Southbank and Shaftesbury Avenue were barns of performative expression, where the foremost names in theater and the arts electrified audiences. Was it not testament to London's quirkiness and peculiarity that most of her police force patrolled the streets unarmed? The terrorist attack of last week demonstrated her innate cordiality. Citizens aided their kinsmen bleeding on Westminster Bridge after a deleterious scumbag waged a diabolical crusade of death with a Hyundai Tucson for a weapon. Londoners exhibited their unity with a candlelight vigil at Trafalgar Square and other notable landmarks.

The man in the black suit was not buying the *I'd like to teach the world to sing* Coca Cola commercial affectations by Nelson's Column. His once pallid cheeks were now an incarnadine hue. The stout and Pepsi Max»s still flowed but his shish kebab looked as cold as the salad. Displays of solidarity and selflessness in the wake of a terrorist attack were not unique to London, he said. It was insulting to suggest otherwise. He'd witnessed adamantine resilience in Tel Aviv in the wake of similar slaughter. Hearts hardened against terrorism wherever it was waged. As for London, expect it to fall further and the economy to falter, thanks to Brexit, as the heart of the nation seeks to reimagine the monophonic days of yesteryear...

The debate concluded without me. I had to make haste to a scheduled appointment and so the All Seeing Sobek only knows if their argument was ever settled. What is patently obvious is that London is different things to different people. However, I weigh heavily on the side of the alabaster chap.

So many people migrate to this polis and partake in the building of skyscrapers not seen since the Biblical Tower of Babel. The God of the Old Testament confounded the uniformity of language, brought forth new languages and scattered Man to wander throughout the Earth, thereby dispersing the monoculturalism that once existed. Contemporary London, by that reckoning, is very much a subversion of the ancient land of Shinar. Three hundred languages are spoken in this city-state. Man hath wandered from afar into this perforating cathedral, primarily on the strength of Sterling and learning, but also to substantiate better futures for themselves, their families and their kinsfolk in their countries of origin. Many natives to London have fled to the outskirts of the M25 and beyond, commuting to London for work purposes, leaving behind old neighborhoods they no longer recognize. Nostalgia reminds them of the good old days of milk floats and the rag-and-bone man. The cost of London has emaciated returns. One need only appraise the demarcation lines beneath the carapaces of cities and towns to know of the resentment and loathing sizzling and popping beneath the panoramic purlieus like a lava river. No wonder Jihadi jumpstarts and racist rogues are breeding furiously among us.

I have been native to this town my entire life. It has not been dear to me. My affection for London has gone unrequited for decades. I will ask what my city can do for me. It need not ask what I would do for her. I would do plenty without her having to ask. But I will not permit myself to subscribe to any form of chauvinism, lest of all proclaim the city of my birth to be greater than the thousands of cities that exist elsewhere. Why should I extrapolate mythic proportions about London? I see no greatness. I see mass iniquity. I see a numbing conformity. I see Londoners being shortchanged in terms of utility and welfare. I see emanating divisions. I see a gross outbreak of pococurantism. Many people are readily inclined to use their phones to film an extremity for the benefit of Facebook than to intervene or call the emergency services. I hear spasms of gratuitous violence and mindless slaughter. The schizophrenic disposition of *the Great Wen* is debilitating. Her avaricious appetites are such that my pockets are near empty. The dearth of social housing renders no security. Pinguid landlords profit from this crisis. Food banks are a prerequisite for putting food on kitchen tables. Wages alone are insufficient. The working poor are but a paycheck from poverty. Air and water quality is dire which inextricably breeds maladies for the body and mind. Scalping eyesores and searing skyscrapers form a fatigued collage that are a mishmash smudge along the London skyline. Beneath these buildings sit some of the poorest boroughs in Britain, where beleaguered families struggle to make ends meet. They wrestle in continuum among themselves about the bare necessities of life. Notwithstanding these diminishing returns, London inordinately qualifies as a great city. But the greatest city in the world? Fuck off!

April 2, 2017.

WHAT I LEARNT FROM THAT DAY IN SEPTEMBER

T HE YEAR 2021 MARKED the twentieth commemoration of the September 11 attacks in America. Our imponderable attitude to time compels us to gape in awe at the temporal passing of years. *Has it really been twenty years?* Has precisely two decades slipped so inconspicuously since I stood aground in my former boss' office, among a kindle of co-workers on a Tuesday afternoon, staring aghast at the cyclopean screen hanging sturdily from a pallid wall? The most consequential news of the century thus far ruptured its quadraphonic speakers. Both World Trade Center buildings in New York teemed with macabre smoke. Two airbuses had slammed into its flanks apiece. We bristled with shock-horror. The boss shooshed the room. Speculation as to the cause was abound and bruited. Whose was the Black Hand that *directed this storm?* Thousands of forlorn and frightened souls were reportedly trapped in those towers, eighty storeys high. The fiery incalescence, intensified by billowy flames from those airbus jet engines, had unafforded them an incogitable choice between Scylla and Charybdis - an infernal death by smoke and incineration or a thirteen-hundred-foot leap to certain destruction below. Some phoned their dearest to say goodbye. This egregious imposition was unpalatable as it were sudden. Would they *go gentle into that good night?* Why must they, their futures fading abruptly into deepest, cruelest, unfathomable black? Some flung themselves from open windows to escape the pernicious smoke. Those that could not exit the furnace, their remains would surely be lost forever in the impending subsidence. I imagined the overwrought pandemonium in both towers. The motion picture *The Towering Inferno*, of Steve McQueen and Paul Newman fame, came to mind, twenty times multiplied by the power of twenty. I had watched the film barely a week from September 11 for the first time. But that was only a film, mind you.

Civilian aircraft, without exception, were ordered from the skies of the United States. Terse instructions were issued to all aviation transport to land at their nearest airport. They risked being shot down by the United States Airforce otherwise. International flights were diverted to Canada and Mexico. Major tunnels and bridges in Manhattan were closed. More breaking news conveying reports that the Pentagon, on the banks of the Potomac River in Arlington County, Virginia, had been hit by a Boeing 757 sounded absurd to the absorbable ear. The White House and Capitol Hill were rumored targets to yet another supposedly missing airplane. The tenants to these seats of American power were hastily evacuated. U.S fighter jets scrambled to the heavens and patrolled virulently from on high. A Middle Eastern news channel, via Sky News, reported that the Democratic Front For The Liberation Of Palestine claimed responsibility *post facto*. They recanted their statement almost instantaneously once they realized the scope of this heinous act of terrorism was far beyond their meager reach. Especially after the American government was already calling this quaternary of hijackings *an act of war*.

The full-throated media speculated the whereabouts of President George W. Bush. He was last seen in Sarasota, Florida, reading to a classroom of schoolchildren. Vice-President Dick Cheney was said to be hiding somewhere in Washington DC in the care of the Secret Service. I countenanced him in a serpentine labyrinth-city under the nation's capital, with a lektor-like metal suitcase on his lap, containing the nuclear codes that could herald Megiddo and a thousand plagues as a retaliatory response to whomsoever was responsible. A colleague suggested we, too, evacuate our offices on Whitfield Street, W1T. The Saatchi and Saatchi building stood in the shadow of the hideous BT Tower. Her assertion was that a plane could be hijacked on route from Heathrow Airport and be made to crash into that landmark. The boss reminded her that we were 3,500 miles from New York and, therefore, out of the tentacle reaches of their barbarism. Simultaneous attacks in different places by homicidal terrorists was the new rage, said she. See Tokyo Subway Train attack by Aum Shinrikyo, 1995. See Tanzania and Kenya embassy bombings by Al-Qaeda, 1998. She segued news channels, BBC to CNN, Sky News to Fox News. Newsbots were perforating the biggest story of their journalistic careers, interviewing Security, Defense and Terrorism experts who claimed to know a thing or two about the *modus operandi* of terrorists. The Canary Wharf Tower and The London Stock Exchange was emptied of its employees. Mass evacuations were conducted in Manhattan and Washington. The news ticker scrolled the bottom of the cyclopean screen, awash with the miscellaneous temblors reverberating from America on this onerous of days. Finally, one after the other, the twin towers crumbled to the ground. Harrowed co-workers felt we'd be safer under the clouds. We made for the exit. We were grateful for the draughty September air.

I was melancholic by the time I returned home that evening. It felt as if it was the end of the world. I spoke to my mother and brother by phone. After watching an extended showing of BBC 2's *Newsnight*, I turned on the radio. The mood was of solace, shock and condolement. Alternative opinions and suppositions from radio moreporks were nuanced and sundry. American foreign policy had long been snarky and duplicitous, some callers argued on a radio phone-in show. The State Department had long interfered clumsily in the business of nations. Their intrigues had sowed strife. They had propped up ghouls and hags the world over. Intertwined in these rational conversations were a gaggle of conspiracy theorists, online and elsewhere. They extolled Black Ops and the *shifty fingers* of the State of Israel for a controlled demolition job well done. I had long known that a good masquerade was incomplete without the inclusion of a complot of contriving Jews, operating the puppet strings of marionette Presidents and kings. The Jews of New York, it was claimed, were given forewarning of the twin towers attack. They had been advised to stay clear from Downtown Manhattan. This rumor was wantonly repeated, though hundreds of Jewish bodies lay crushed beneath the Twin Tower rubble. My *Liebchen* was made bitterly upset by the prescriptivist and insurmountable prejudice that lay dormant in the simmering breasts of conspiratards. She was not political. Neither was she partisan. She was Jewish. Anti-Semitism, she said, would never recrudesce. Its endurance was made possible by the meathead. It was the first refuge of the highbinder. A few midnights later, the BBC World Service reported that five Israeli nationals had been arrested by the FBI on September 11. They were seen filming the aftermath of the subsided towers. Their jubilation at the scene aroused suspicion. Two of the five men were identified as Mossad agents spying on Arabs in New York. I relayed this news story to *Liebchen*. She felt there was enough here for conspiratards to spin calumnious fables. A few days later, she sat waiting for a train at Goodge Street Tube Station. She witnessed a colony of tattooed troglodytes on the platform, braying at a parliament of hijabi's with their babes in prams. *What you gotta say bout all those innocent people killed in America?* bellowed one of the frothing oafs. Liebchen said she was ashamed that nobody came to their aid. She felt greater shame at herself for doing nothing. She had been paralyzed by fear. The plumes that rose from the pyrolysis of the World Trade Center threatened to sully our basic humanity towards others. Many took refuge in their tribal warrens.

Notwithstanding what was inarguably the greatest upheaval in terms of world events in my life thus far, I still hoped our forays in Britannia would not be tinkered too much. I was a ne'er do well precariat. My coevals and I were in our early twenties. We were waist-deep in our unfair share of domesticated problems. Most of us were on losing streaks. We were of a larval disposition. Our mizzenmasts threatened to snap in the intrusive winds headed our way. The light at the end of the tunnel was naught but a runaway steam train. Any legislation designed to curb what civil liberties we had was an inimical sword clad in an ominous sheath. Several political and social commentators predicted that an unprecedented political and social volte-face was imminent. Many of them possessed a Hobbesian view, irrespective of their ideology, religion or political leanings. They were prepared to pile Pelion upon Ossa to belabor their point. The nabob politician oft proclaimed from the Parliament Dispatch Box that terrorists will not sour our democracy. In the same breath, he advertently votes for sour injunctions because of those same-said terrorists. He cordons (and curbs) the civil liberties once enjoined by the quotidian man and woman. He opts for the sanctuary of a securitocracy. Air travel to domestic and foreign destinations were specifically commutated into preventing a recurrence of aviation barbarism. These commutations remain today. The British police desired some of the naked powers of a *Mukhabarat*. Injunctions granted the government the privilege to retain telephone and Internet records of any UK subject it deemed a threat. Subject that is, not citizens. We are *subjects* of Elizabeth Saxe-Coburg Gotha and her heirs. Laws permitted a foreign national in Britain to be interned indefinitely without trial. Expedient legislation were passed in the name of national security. Control Orders were forged into tablets of stone applicable to sixty million people, but duly applied to perhaps some six thousand. If that. Rather our lawmakers give the devil the benefit of the law, they duly became a Parliament of Ropers. They cut through a great road of civil freedoms in pursuit of him. If only Robert Bolt's Sir Thomas More from his acclaimed play *A Man For All Seasons* was able to address the House Of Commons thus: ... *And when the Last Law was down, and the Devil turned round on you, where would you hide, the laws being flat? The country's planted thick with laws from coast to coast — man's laws, not God's — and if you cut them down, and ye are just* **the Parliament** *to do it, d'you really think you could stand upright in the winds that would blow them? Yes! I'd give the Devil the benefit of the Law,* **for my own safety's sake.** Indeed. Those who support laws that infringe the civil rights of others should be mindful that those same unwarrantable laws be turned mercilessly against them. Maximilien Robespierre, the incorruptible soldier of the French Revolution, sent many enemies to the guillotine. His surviving foes would return the favor. *Like Saturn, the Revolution devours its children,* observed Jacques Mallet du Pan who witnessed what *The Great Terror* wrought. *At the Sierra Maestra, we executed many people by firing squad without knowing if they were fully guilty,* wrote Che Guevara of the Cuban Revolution. *At the times, the Revolution cannot stop to conduct much investigation. It has the obligation to triumph.* Like the practitioners of a marauding social media who gobble heretics over their heterodoxies. One of the herd could sedately become an inversed fatted calf, spit-roasted by a thousand tweets, if her mind ventures too far afield. *A patriot is he who defends his country against its government* wrote Edward Abbey, a favored American author of mine. Many MPs of that Parliament behaved as if patriotism meant hanging steadfastly onto the coattails of Prime Minister Tony Blair.

Societal schisms deepened between segments of the Muslim community and sectors of wider society. This simmering feud were not birthed by 9/11. They had sprung from the paucity of integration and gulf of prejudice borne from the decades prior. September 11 merely poked a red-hot pole into an already suppurating wound. There was genuine fear that boors, clodhoppers and steers, emboldened by their warped hatred of anything remotely beyond their limited understanding, may resort to violence. On September 15, 2001, a Sikh-American gentleman named Balbir Singh Sodhi was shot dead by an ignoramus gun nut who mistook him for a Muslim simply because he wore a heavy beard. Two days later, President Bush visited a mosque in Washington. He appealed for tolerance. *Islam is peace,* he said. *Terrorists don't represent peace. They represent evil and war.* Tony Blair claimed a copy of the Koran accompanied him wherever he went. So-called Muslim community leaders, who volunteered themselves as spokespersons of their faith on UK soil, were gathered before him. They were asked to put their names to a statement condemning the attacks orchestrated in the name of their faith, notwithstanding the fact that Muslim lives had also been lost and mourned in that same tragedy. Muslims were expected by the media to answer for Muslims, as if they were a monolith. Defending a personal belief system is one thing. It *is* personal. By definition. Having to postulate soluble answers for the actions of Muslims whom you never met, to soothe the suspicions of Bob Taylor from Billericay, that British Muslims were not a Fifth Column, was an absurdity. Placating the belfry choler of a Benedict Carmichael-Bridge from Tunbridge Wells had the delicate tinges of an inferiority complex. Muslims were as diverse and denominational as Christians. Individual Muslims were free to practice some of the fundamentals of Islam and discard others. Some drank beer, fornicated in cheap hotels and watched pornography as if Allaah wasn't watching. But there was a seeming never-ending supply of Muslim commentators on TV and radio who were all too willing to walk into booby traps and manholes and speak on behalf of *all* Muslims. I understand. These were unprecedented times. They felt themselves under siege. So they did what they did. They signed Tony Blair's memorandum. And whenever one of their number walked into a TV studio or a radio booth, they ritually declared Islam *a religion of peace.* (It isn't. No major world religion could credibly accede to that shibboleth). They proceeded to condemn terrorism. (Who wouldn't? Even Bin Laden didn't think himself a terrorist). I already realized these mouthpieces were midgets in the grand scheme of things. They held little sway in Muslim Britain, never mind the Muslim world.

A younger generation of British Muslims, whose religious and political awakenings were precipitated by the Bosnian war of 1992-95, judged them as stooges and sell-outs. They scanned the Muslim world with an indignant lens. They deduced a common denominator.

Whether it be Bosnia or Bangladesh, Kashmir or Kosovo, Pakistan or Palestine, Muslims were habitually oppressed by a polar axis of evil: America, Britain and Israel. They concluded that the Muslim world was ruled by manikins and marionettes, prepped by The White House, Downing Street and Beit Aghion. Ten years removed from 9/11, I watched a video in a college common room, where the atrocities orchestrated by the heinous Serbian army upon Bosnian Muslims were such that many wept and were moved to anger. And this bloodshed occurred less than a thousand miles from where we stood at Sir George Monoux Sixth Form College. Hanif Kureishi's 1997 film *My Son, The Fanatic* articulated the generational divide - the disconnect between an immigrant Muslim father, having adopted many British customs, and his British-born son, despising the debauchery of Britain and clinging steadfast to zealotry and dogma for the preservation of his soil. It is a depressive story. Pertinently, however, it makes its point. In the immediate aftermath of 9/11, I can recall logging onto *Hizb-ut-Tahrir's Khilafah* website. I had attended college with some of their then prominent members. Their reports focused on one of their figureheads in Egypt, Maajid Nawaz. They lauded him as if he were the Elephant King in Barbar. He was on a recruiting gig in Cairo. The Egyptian authorities arrested him soon enough. He spent four years in their dungeons. After his release from jail, he was *not about that life!* Blair's Muslim community leaders were better integrated and suitably agreeable. Many were members of his Labour Party. Their mumblings were inevitably co-opted by the fanaticism that titillated intrigue and ignorance. Images of American flags being burnt by small herds of Muslims in Pakistan, Palestine, and elsewhere in the Middle East charged the *monstrum horrendum* community. A fringe group headquartered in Britain named *Al-Muhajiroun* praised the September 11 terrorists as *The Magnificent 19*. The media sought out the meathead, not the so-called moderate. They gave them several hours in the sun. The meathead always had the initiative. Not the so-called moderate. He always played catchup.

Islam's cardinal texts prohibit its adherents from committing suicide and partaking in indiscriminate suicide murders. The Koranic inferences are cognoscible on the subject. ...*And make not your own hands contribute to destruction but do good. For Allaah loveth those who do good.* (Chapter 2: Verse 195). ...*And do not kill (or destroy) yourselves. For verily, Allaah hath been to you most merciful.* (Chapter 4: Verse 29). *Do not take life, which Allaah hath made sacred, except by justice and law (i.e., capital punishment): thus does he command you, that ye may learn wisdom.* (Chapter 6: Verse 151). The *sahih* Hadiths unequivocally affirm that suicides will reside in *Jahannam* on Judgement Day, a place of torment and burning. Western nations fear the inevitability of the next suicide bombing within their cities. Terrorist hordes plot their next martyrdom operation, wherever the heretic or infidel be found wanting. Foundational Islamic texts esteem the martyr who gives his life for *Jihad* on the battlefield. They are venerated in the afterlife. The suicide faces damnation in hell. The question, therefore, of what constitutes martyr and suicide becomes as contentious as determining freedom fighter from terrorist. It need not be if we come to an understanding from a logical inference. These terror ghouls strike retributively inside the *Darul Harb* (Abode of War). They advocate that the enemies of Islam unconscionably wage *fitnah* in *Darul Islam* (House of Islam). America, *the Great Satan*, snuggly falls in the former domain. So too does Britain, the *Little Satan*. Incidentally, Muslims, of approximate sub-denominative beliefs, are the main victims of these bloodstained cruels. The terrorists plant car bombs in souks. They strap explosives to their bodies whilst mingling with worshippers at Friday prayers. They lie in wait of children outside schools whilst their combustibles tick. I don't want to propound forever the latent arbitrariness of either suicide or martyr. They are not comparative. They are, admittedly, interchangeable in the minds of many. Adam Lankford's 2013 book *The Myth Of Martyrdom: What Really Drives Suicide Bombers, Rampage Shooters And Other Self-Destructive Killers* expounds on the mindset of the tendentious martyr. The author provided analytical insight into the psychological disposition of Mohamed Atta, hijacker-in-chief of the 9/11 terrorists, save for the pathological component that energized the psychosis of religious fundamentalism. The fanatical, doctrinal ingredient should not be diminished from any deconstruction. It is a primary constituent of his being. You need only read the various attestations attributed to Atta. This world is merely a prison for such men. Of course, the feelings of abjection, isolation and anxiety leaves cicatrix mental scars. But he believed he'd be purged of temporal earthly sin and suffering. His afterlife ascension to a celestial, eternal Elysium indemnifies this belief. Though he might be disheartened or angered by Ibn Warraq, author of the screed, *Why I'm Not A Muslim*, who wrote an article in early 2002 for The Guardian newspaper titled *Virgins? What Virgins?* Based on a book by Christoph Luxenburg titled *Die Syro-Aramaische Lesart des Koran*, he contested the sedulous conviction that seventy-two untouched houris awaited Atta and co in Paradise. Owing to a Syriac translation of the Koran, *white raisins* would be their recompense instead.

The narrative of the nineteen dolts from the Wahabi offshoot terror group Al-Qaeda was submitted through the media by US government agencies. Fifteen were from Saudi Arabia. Two were from the United Arab Emirates. One, Mohamed Atta, was Egyptian. The other, Lebanese. Their hollowed martyrdom, never mind hallowed, flung themselves headlong (to borrow a quote from my literary handiwork *The Nepenthe Park Chronicles*) into *an ineffable Erebus that went on eternal until the timeless endless end.* The loss, on 9/11, in human terms were grievous and substantive. Thousands were reportedly killed. Many thousands more were purportedly missing and injured. A UK government spin doctor flagrantly deemed it a *good day to bury bad news.* The world's attention would not be clogged to the usual skulduggery frothing in Westminster. I listened to Talk Radio after midnight. Hosts debated nothing but the devastation of Tuesday. Their tones of voice were unanimously in accord of a military fight against Al-Qaeda. Caller contributions ranged from the cerebral to the fatuous. I discussed this subject with a friend of mine. He quoted Machiavelli: *There is no avoiding war. It can only be postponed to the advantage of others.* At first glance, a war, fought in all its known orthodoxies, seemed complex. America was not attacked by a nation-state. Al-Qaeda were a band of outlaws thinly spread across borders, including that of European nations. Their leadership were *guests* of the Taliban in Afghanistan. In Greater Khorasan, it had been *Yalda* since the seventies. One wondered whether the sun would rise there in the foreseeable future. The Taliban preyed upon the stricken, impoverished, benighted Afghan population. Women, in many instances, were treated no better than livestock. Their wretched helplessness was expected to forbear the pestilence of indiscriminate Cruise and Tomahawk missiles falling upon their houses. The Afghans had suffered strafing from empires before. Two centuries previous, British troops stormed their territory in two attritional wars to safeguard Her Majesty's interests in the Indian subcontinent from the Russian Empire. The British called this marshalling of this passage to India *The Great Game.* A generation ago, on Christmas Eve 1979, the U.S.S.R, heirs of the Russian Empire, invaded Afghanistan. They had long held the Kabul government in a chokehold. Soviet forces used chemical weapons, as well as rape and slaughter upon the civilian population, never mind egregious inflictions upon the Mujahideen. The Mujahideen melded together to resist the invasion. They considered the defense of their homeland an obligatory religious decree. This was *Jihad* in its purest, physical form. For in The Koran, Chapter 2 verses 190-193, you will find this injunction: *Fight in the cause of Allaah against those who fight you, but do not transgress limits. For Allaah loveth not transgressors. And slay them wherever ye catch them, and turn them out from where they have turned you out, for tumult and oppression are worse than slaughter... And fight them on until there is no tumult and oppression, and there prevail justice and faith in Allaah; but if they cease, let there be no hostility except to those who practice oppression.* In the same scripture, Chapter 8 verse 65: *O Prophet! Rouse the Believers to the fight. If there are twenty among you, patient and preserving, they will vanquish two hundred.*

If a hundred, they will vanquish a thousand of the unbelievers. And finally in Chapter 9 verse 5: *Fight and slay the pagans wherever ye find them, and seize them, beleaguer them and lie in wait for them in every stratagem (of war)* . . .

Transnational Jihadists like Osama Bin Laden, Abdullah Yusuf Azzam, Ayman al-Zawahiri and Ahmed Said Khadr flocked to the Afghan Badlands. They bolstered their Muslim *Ummah* with their trust funds. They stung the Red Goliath repeatedly with their stratagems and stupendous courage. They were skilled in sabotage and assassination. An assortment of nations, which poetically included the Islamic Republic of Pakistan, the People's Republic of China, the Kingdom of Saudi Arabia. the United Kingdom of Great Britain and Northern Ireland and the United States of America, lassoed ordnance and finance for the cause of *Jihad*.

The C.I.A was also involved in covert activity in Afghanistan from 1979 to support the *Mujahideen*, father of the Taliban. *Operation Cyclone*, as it were known, was their most expensive expedition to date. It lasted well into the nineties. A policy of plausible deniability meant their footprints were untracked by the higher echelons of their own government, much less the average American. The Soviet Union withdrew in 1989, weakened by political constraints in Moscow, worn by Mujahideen's Russian bear traps. Tens of thousands of their young men had been killed and maimed. Fast forward to 2001. The Americans were coming! The British were coming back. The sons of the Mujahideen, the Taliban, awaited them. President Bush demanded the extradition of Osama Bin Laden, architect of 9/11. The Taliban insisted evidence of his involvement. Though they were bound by Pashtun Laws of Hospitality, they intimated that he could stand trial in Afghanistan. The American government rejected their proposals. Congress, minus the sole vote of House of Representative member Barbara Lee, plumped for military action. Figureheads in Washington were content with the wisdom of this maladaptive, sanguinary response. They named the enterprise *Operation Enduring Freedom*. Furthermore, an entire executive branch of government was created, the Department of Homeland

Security, to precipitate their War on Terror. Currently, it is the third costliest division of government, incorporating the dominion of immigration, antiterrorism and federal emergency management. When President Bush announced Tom Ridge would spearhead this bureaucratic behemoth, I doubted he paid heed to the caution of a conservative predecessor, Ronald Reagan, who warned that *government does not solve problems, it subsidies them.* Whoso truly believed that this cumbersome department would solve the problem of terrorism? Who could have foreseen two decades later that, after employing more than 200,000 people and spending more than $50 billion per annum, America still trembles at the whiff of terrorism? Who could argue for the certitude of American taxpayers subsidizing the IRA on the British mainland, Contra rebels in Nicaragua and the overthrow of democratic-elected governments the world over?

The American hubris, *prima facie*, intrinsically reckoned herself a benign superpower and an exceptional force for good; that *Pax Americana* is an exporter of human freedom and emancipatory will. America had been the chief guarantor of the *New World Order*, first prescribed by men like Woodrow Wilson and Winston Churchill and, in our own times, by George Herbert Walker Bush. Wilson of a century ago, when much of *the* earth were under the sway of the imperial powers, addressed the US Congress thus: *Peoples are not to be handed about from one sovereignty to another by an international conference or an understanding between rivals and antagonists. National aspirations must be respected; peoples may now be dominated and governed only by their own consent.* **Self-determination** *is not a mere phrase. It is an imperative principle of actions which statesmen will henceforth ignore at their peril. We cannot have general peace for the asking, or by the mere arrangements of a peace conference. It cannot be pieced together out of individual understandings between powerful states.* America was indubitably the *arsenal of democracy*, as prescribed by Franklin D. Roosevelt, at the wrathful clanging of world war in Europe. She was an adamantine foe of totalitarianism, Nazism and

Communism. Her sons were to lay buried overseas having liberated mainland Europe in the two world wars against bankrupt ideologies. America had supplanted the world's worst tyrannies, wherever they terrorized and tormented. She rebuilt *less happier lands* out of the smog of destitution and despair. She devised and bankrolled the Marshall Plan, which aided the rebuilding of Western Europe after World War II. She was the lynchpin of NATO, which first buttressed and then broke the Soviet Union. She reconstructed Japan from a psychopathic imperial power into a modern industrial nation. She molded Saudi Arabia from a desert kingdom into a guzzling plutocracy. She safeguarded the newborn State of Israel against *saif*-wielding theocrats in her neighborhood. She benefacted the Irish Republic, once scourged by imperialism and vicious sectarianism. She is still called upon as an arbiter between nations. She is damned for interfering conspicuously in the internal affairs of Somalia in 1992. She is damned for not intervening overtly in the internal affairs of Rwanda in 1994. Interventionists desire that she be bilateral. Isolationists prefer an apathetic foreign policy. Those who blame her for the world's woes rather that she hadn't begun *destroying monsters* in the first place.

Her soft power made Americans of us all. We consume her culture. We gorge her food. We look out to her from the 51st State. Wheresoever she steers herself politically, economically and culturally, we seemingly cannot be rendered unaffected. Successive UK governments, of whatever political stripe, claim a *special relationship* with America. Whilst this is palpably true in the realms of our respective intelligence services, UK-US relations appear lopsided everywhere else. This probably explains why UK bureaucrats and functionaries are so touchy-feely about the perception of Britain, irrespective of the politics of the ogre that occupies the White House. Sir Christopher Meyer, UK ambassador to the United States at the time of 9/11, wrote a meaty memoir titled *DC Confidential.* It was there, I read, that he was instructed by a senior mandarin in Downing Street to *get up the arse of the White House and stay there.* Former

UK Prime Minister Harold MacMillan famously advised that the British ought to be the ancient Greeks guiding the American Rome. I doubt old MacMillan envisaged this being orchestrated from the fundament of a former colony, tolerating the flatulence and feces that fuels international politics these days.

I have visited America twice before 2001. I've yet to return. Such was the ubiquity of her culture in my formative years, she was the country I most identified with outside of my own. I had read about her extensively and belatedly in novels. I had watched her irrepressibly on TV. Books by Cormac McCarthy, Bret Easton Ellis, Hubert Selby Jr, Ernest Hemingway, Toni Morrison, Jack Kerouac, Chuck Palahniuk, Phillip Roth, Alice Walker, Mark Twain, Saul Bellow, Hunter S. Thompson and John Steinbeck hadn't endeared me to their fraught depictions of America. These writers spew the excess, the scalping, the transcendence, the self-loathing, the psychosis, the hubris, the pestilential, the unpalatable violence that forged their county into the molten edacity it had become. If it were for the procured jaws of the great American Novel, composed by some of the great hands of world literature, I may not have visited. America's image on TV and film, however, was comely and inviting. Baywatch and Beverly Hills 90210 were great billboards for stylized Californian tourism. America was the home of *Knight Rider, NYPD Blue, Friends, Doogie Howser M.D, Quantum Leap, Highway To Heaven* and countless other shows. Like the devil, she had the best tunes. She was the birthplace of Michael Jackson, Prince, Madonna, Whitney Houston and Mariah Carey.

I took a cruise controlled, rollercoaster ride from Los Angeles along Highway 101 to San Francisco with my old school buddy, Imran. We drove seven hours in a hired Ford Taurus. We stopped overnight in Carmel, where Clint Eastwood once reigned as mayor. We woke to the ethereal waves of the Pacific Ocean eddying to the morning breeze. Our fledging eyes beheld the Christmas tree lights of Las Vegas. We avoided the cat houses and the casinos. We were good boys. Gentlemen, in fact. We clubbed in Los Angeles at a place called *The Palace*. I danced with a girl named *Houdini*. After I bought her a drink, she disappeared forever from sight. I often think of the pure beaches of Santa Monica and Venice, where I met an array of eccentric characters, the like I've not met since. I've yet to see, however, the Big Apple in all its bravura and commingled wonder. Mazhar, my *compadre* since the playgrounds of Leytonstone School, visited Ground Zero a year from the attack. A dear pal of mine, Helen is a regular guest of New York. She once harbored a dream to live there. I'd like to have flown to Washington DC, Chicago, and America's many sprawling metropolises. I still harbor aspirations of broadening my iterations from sea to shining sea. I often wished I possessed the arrant wanderlust of my friend Kishmeister. Whilst I remained in *The Hermit's Lodge*, he vacated in the wondrously byzantine. He reconnoitered the Land of the Rising Sun. He sipped Saki with the Japanese. He surveyed the Fragrant Harbor. He segued into Dubai and the Burj Khalifa. He is my Uncle Traveling Matt from *Fraggle Rock*, who sends me attestations and texts whilst he travels. I wish I were as hotfooted as the Lilliputian Italian *scrittore*, Oriana Fallaci. She forensically examined the heterogeneous good, bad and ugly of the latter twentieth century with a roving mind and a cutlass pen. I will return to her and her métier in due course. What of the lionized British journalist James Cameron who, according to a polemicist of almost immeasurable repute Christopher Hitchens, *had swum in all five oceans and fucked on all five continents* as a result of his globetrotting endeavors? And what of Hitchens himself, who visited the so-called *axis of evil* triumvirate of North Korea, Iran and Iraq? The Americans I met in California and Arizona were essentially a people wrought with industry, felicity, frankness and charm. America seemed a place of the parvenu. A realm that rewarded resourcefulness and rigor. Breakfast buffets were epic affairs. And so were the steaks and milkshakes. There were obvious variances with their putative use of the English language, but the Californian dehiscence and spirit was particularly infectious and regaling. Even the self-proclaimed war president George W. was known for his folksy good manners.

We are rabid consumers of America's lusty innovations. Our lives have been exponentially transmogrified by the Internet, Amazon, Apple, Facebook, Twitter, Microsoft, Netflix. We rely on these as if their equivalence were air, water, earth, fire. Portable devices are like appendages of the body. Rather than trawl through an encyclopedia, we ask *Alexa*, never mind Wikipedia. America's supranational and seductive culture have cattle prod our emotions into reacting to mere trifles. American values provide perennial problems for immiserated belief systems that boast incessantly of their exclusivity and divinity but wither and whimper when subjected to challenge and provocation. Her decadence habitually tempts and mesmerizes but coagulates revulsion and contempt. This is a perception not limited to foreign feeling. Conservative doctrinaires seemingly weep for the uncurbed vices that prompts the buckle of the Bible Belt to loosen. America has long threatened extirpation of ideologies and doctrines that preceded her independence. I have partaken in quarrels over the caprice of American foreign policy, especially in relation to Israel, and rightly so. She is entitled to be judged by the standards she set. It is paradoxical, however, to observe state actors and officials operate in the calibrated manner of their disparagers. The rest of the world is perverse with wanting America on their own terms. Or demanding American leadership. Or, at the very least, keeping faith her side of the bargain. America has innumerable, conflicting agendas on a single policy issue. She is a polycephaly. The interest groups that drive her are self-serving. Their motivations can be found in coffers and chads, clad in the Stars and Stripes. Whenever she acts upon her national appetites, even her so-called allies feel a sense of betrayal. Her admirers fall for her countenance of earthy honest broker. Her idealism gleams like her cities. America, like her neo-imperial brethren Britain, Russia, China, France or quite frankly any Sir Olifaunt of any time, have avaricious self-interests. Every great nation and civilization have been forged by Mars' spear and Thor's hammer. America is no exception, roaming the earth like Leviathan, searching for monsters to destroy in the name of liberty and whatever else. Old John Adams would have shaken his head at the mere notion. The foreign policy of any great power is duplicitous by definition. They change face and tact on a whim. They possess recurring powers of reinvention. Any expectation that they behave nobly when they enter nations and discover treasure beneath the soil of that nation must be met with credulity. Since man sprung from the earth, his base initiations have caused him to conquer his brother. America casts dreams that cannot be replicated by any nation. Her comeliness is seductive. Many had chosen her, by migrating from *less happier lands*. Some are resourceful enough to perpetuate their version of the so-called American Dream. Valhalla or Jannah. Eden or Elysium. Asphodel Meadows or Paradiso. Whether that dream be illusion or illumination depends on the fortitude, fortune and focus of the individual.

It was George W. indeed who *rode the whirlwind and directed this storm* after the terrorists struck on that day in September. *Americans are asking, why do they hate us?* he remarked during his somber address to the Joint Session of Congress, nine days removed from 9/11. *They hate what they see here: a democratically elected chamber… They hate our freedoms: our freedom of religion, our freedom of speech, our freedom to vote and assemble and disagree with each other.* George W's rationale were painfully erroneous. These agents of Terror were not envious of the proceedings of the House of Representatives and the Senate as he supposed. They were finetuned to the principle of *shura*, ordained by Allaah in the Holy Koran. After His *Shariah* was established in the land, a *shura* council would debate policies among themselves and advise their Caliph. That, in their eyes, was far superior to Congress and the House of Horrors (i.e. Houses of Parliament) whose diabolical objective were *to spread mischief and corruption through the earth*. Freedom of religion meant nothing to them. Allaah's religion indomitably counted. They were vehemently hateful of secular, permissive, Sodom and Gomorrah societies that wrought decadent rights for women, gays and atheists. Gays and atheists would be slaughtered like cattle in their dream world if they didn't renounce their wickedest ways. Women would be largely confined to purdah. If they wished to travel, they required a *mahram* for company. American foreign policy, meanwhile, bore primal resentments. They enabled larcenous cutthroat rulers in the Arab and Muslim world. America's core objective waged oppressive and suppressive war against Muslims the world over. Like Satan himself, *The Great Satan* had *assaulted them from before them and behind them. From their right and their left...* (The Koran, Chapter 7: Verse 17). The United States, Britain and France were godparents to their existential enemy Israel, usurpers of Palestinian land and prison wardens of the Palestinian people. The 9/11 attacks struck at the heart of this evil empire. And over the next twenty years, their affiliates had sown death at its various outposts: London, Paris, Istanbul, Madrid, Mumbai, Bali, Dar es Salam and Nairobi.

Some religious meatheads within American society itself provided an answer to the 9/11 question that was palpably not of this world. The dissonance spewed from the hoary mouths of bull-horned ecclesiastical racketeers and their ancillaries was that the triune godhead had determined that America was debauched. 9/11 was punishment from heaven, they said. Televangelist Baptist preacher Jerry Falwell blamed *pagans, abortionists, feminists, the gays and the lesbians, the ACLU and People For The American Way.* Brother pastor Pat Robertson and fellow demagogues propounded similar theories from their pulpits. The media industrial complex rumbled unfavorably. Falwell and his fellow fomenters then said sorry. I wondered what God thought of this backtracking from these vicegerents who claimed to be ventriloquizing his will on earth. I Imagined Nathan or Samuel of the Old Testament providing an inquest as to why fire and brimstone had rained inexplicably upon the obelisks and temples of the people of old. The Lord, their God, loathed their hellraising and sodomizing in the streets, they explained. The peasants and proletariats cried foul. They were triggered by such offensive language. So Nathan and Samuel contortioned their statements to mollify their anger, though their original explanations was supposedly God's unalterable position. One pondered whether Nathan and Samuel had consulted the Lord over their hasty retraction. One further wondered as to who had the greater right to offense, God himself or the hysterical pride of worms who behaved like gods but were godless themselves? Could Nathan and Samuel, thereafter, be deemed credible again? As supposed men of the Book, it would have been better for the likes of Falwell and Robertson that they kept the following injunction: *Whoever keeps his mouth and his tongue, keeps himself out of trouble.* (Proverbs 21:23).

Some weeks after September 11, 2001, I watched an unflinching Prime Minister Tony Blair give a speech televised by Sky News. He offered the British people's condolences to their American counterparts. *We were with you at the first,* he wept. *We will stay with you to the last.* To his credit, he did not deliver a platitudinous warble about *thoughts and prayers,* and all that jazz. He appeared sincere but you can never tell with this master thespian. His solemn address fastened the Union Jack indivisibly to the Stars and Stripes. He had already forged a hail-fellow-well-meet bond with President Bush. *America has no truer friend than Great Britain,* remarked the American President before the Joint Session of Congress, nine days removed from 9/11. *Once again, we are joined together in a great cause. So honored that the British Prime Minister has crossed an ocean to show his unity of purpose with America...* Blair had been in attendance to hear those panegyrics that evening. He was graciously applauded. Now he was in Britain adjuring the case for war. British boots, he pledged, would go wherever American troops feared not to tread. Critics, in media outliers, questioned the consequential price tag of Blair's unanimity. It was often overlooked that the Bush Administration began life primarily focused on domestic policy. Their early months were marked by an ambitious tax cuts program and rising unemployment. The viscous neoconservative candle burnt so patiently until the explosion of September 11. Thereafter, Bush, Cheney, Rumsfeld, Wolfowitz and Co. fast became a stentorian, Motorcycle Hells Angels crew riding through Asia, armed with Derringer pistols, waging enervating wars in Afghanistan and Mesopotamia. Bin Laden was sought as if he were Billy The Kid. *Wanted dead or alive*, Bush brazenly told a pack of journalists. His administration were reportedly prepared to invade as many as seventy countries. *Our grief has turned to anger*, he told America. *And our anger to resolution. Whether we bring our enemies to justice or justice to our enemies, justice will be done.* Bush starkly informed Congress, the American people and the world that *every nation, in every region, has a decision to make. Either you are with us or you are with the terrorists.* He would not stomach neutrals. I was a little miffed by this declaration. I certainly wasn't with the neocon camp. Lesser still was I with the terrorists. I'd rather sit this out while these *two tribes go to war.*

Blair had long envisaged moments like these. Whilst Bush governed in Texas, he delivered a keynote speech at the Chicago Economic Club in April 1999. He advocated that the good guys (Great Britain, United States, France, NATO), their capes flapping in the breeze, ought to intervene or invade (depending on your viewpoint) the bad guys (Slobodan Milosevic and Saddam Hussein) when they were up-to-no good in their own backyards. Blair had taken a leading role in stopping the bloodshed in Kosovo. He deployed British forces to partake in a peacekeeping operation in East Timor against Indonesia. He sent British troops into Sierra Leone to quell an internecine conflict that had overseen the barbarous amputation of civilians. He reportedly contemplated invading Zimbabwe after the government of Robert Mugabe began the systematic confiscation of farms that were the supposed reserve of *white settlers.* Some tyrannies were exempt from the Blair Doctrine, of course. Especially if they were neo-imperialist, possessed nuclear weapons, had germane and economic ties with the U.K and the U.S or were too costly to invade in terms of troops and treasure. Who could tell how the North Koreans would respond to a preemptive strike, especially with South Korea and Japan in range of their warheads? How many American and British lives would be sacrificed to invade and occupy Iran? How about World War III

with Russia over its caniformian encroachments in the Baltic and
Black seas? Or a fracas with the Chinese over Hong Kong by way
of HMS Illustrious?

So Blair toured the Middle East with the aptitude of a U.S
Secretary of State. 9/11 turbocharged his enthusiasm for the
reinvigoration of the Blair Doctrine. He found bedfellows who
pioneered the *Project For The New American Century*. He squeezed palms
with autocrats in Syria, Egypt and Saudi Arabia, peradventure
pickings themselves for regime change should an exigent American
military work up a ravenous appetite for game. Syria sent an estimated
20,000 troops to fight on the side of the U.S, U.K and France against
Iraq in the Gulf War of 1990. In 2002, Syria voted in support of
National Security Resolution 1441 on the side of the U.S, U.K and
France, forcing the Iraqi regime to comply with weapons inspections
and disarmament, and threatening *serious consequences* if they did not.
The *serious consequences* phrasing became a rod of contention. The U.S
and the U.K vied for war. France, allied with Russia and China did
not. Nobody cared that Syria's despots could also stand accused of
identical crimes ladened against Iraq's monocrat. Saddam Hussein
was belatedly condemned for the massacre of the Kurds of Halabja
in 1988. Syria's Saddam, Hafez Assad, oversaw the slaughter of tens
of thousands of his own citizens at the Hama Massacre in 1982.
While Hussein was made a pariah for his excursions into Kuwait and
Saudi Arabia, Assad's sanguineous sashays into Israel and Lebanon
did not disqualify his country's participation at the United Nation's
top table. Shame, then, that Syrian government did not follow the
bouncing ball! For when the so-called Arab Spring seasoned, and
Bashar Assad moved to quell the uprising in the manner of his
departed father, the U.S, U.K and France turned their fighter jets and
aircraft carriers against him. And had it not been for the swinging
dicks of Russian forces in his country, Assad Junior may well have
been swinging from a scaffold a la Saddam. Or sodomized with a
bayonet a la Gaddafi. Incidentally, Blair did not visit *axis of evil* state
Iran. He sent his Foreign Secretary Jack Straw instead.

My late father portended a time when Islamist terrorists would build foxholes in Europe, and that they'd operate more zealously than the IRA. He was a devout Muslim. He'd lived fifty-five years in England until his death in October 2002. He'd migrated from The Gambia in September 1947. He held court in his spacious lounge at No. 1 Boscombe Avenue, Leyton E10 on Sundays to an impressive set of gregarious intellectuals. Among them was Amon Saba Saakana, author and owner of publishing imprint Karnak House. He wrote several books that included *Colonialism And The Destruction Of The Mind* and *Blues Dance*. Muhammad Kabsoun, ranging an approximate six foot five in height, was from The Sudan. He'd be tragically killed in a plane crash several years later, having gone to serve as an attaché of sorts with the then Sudanese government. There was Muhammad Ismail, a Black Hebrew Israelite, I believe. Even as a child, he spoke to me with such deliberate courtesy and unaffected tenderness. I could never forget his kindness. There was Muhammad Faisal, of the Nation of Islam. I knew not of his association with the Black Muslims until his final visit to our Leyton home when I was nineteen. He and his family have since migrated to America. There was the historian/ anthropologist Danjuma Bihari, an accrued well of knowledge, whose education and travels took him across the Americas, Africa, Europe, the Middle East and Asia. Whenever I phoned him for advice I'd have a pen and a notepad ready to draw water from his upswirling fountain. These men examined the contemporaneity of the African Caribbean diaspora within the context of the wider UK society. They discussed topical news subjects and religious matters. I can vividly recall them debating whether they thought it wise for Patrice Lumumba, who happened to share a birthday with my father, to so robustly respond to King Baudouin II's maddening speech on Congolese Independence Day, when his position in government was far from secure, with an impromptu speech of his own. I found their doughty but civil interrogations of each other's viewpoint riveting. I was not permitted to speak among adult company. I often ached to. I'd sit silently in the corner like a dormouse and study the genial discourse of men. In one session, they detoured onto an event that occurred in old West Berlin, old West Germany in 1986. Several American soldiers had been wounded and killed after a bomb exploded at the *La Belle* nightclub. The American government, without tangible evidence, blamed Colonel Gaddafi's Libya. They vowed retribution. American bombers flew from their military bases in Britain. They rained bombs upon Tripoli and Benghazi. My father told his guests that he'd not be surprised if a generation of young men sprung from the sands of Cyrenaica, the ruins of Beirut or the camps of Gaza and planted bombs in Britain, mainland Europe and America. They'd be more callous than the IRA, he said. They'd give no telephone warnings nor show any mercy. Their zealotry would be unbounded. They would not permit their countries be meddled and struck with impunity. These were the days when westerners like Terry Waite, John McCarthy and Brian Keenan were swept from the streets of Beirut, Lebanon and blindfolded in basements by Islamic Jihad. These were the times when Salman Rushdie's *The Satanic Verses* provoked the ire of many Muslims. The Ayatollah Khomeini of Iran issued a *fatwa* calling for his murder. The grievously offended burnt effigies of the author. They drenched copies of the bestseller with petrol and set alight its pages. I can recall sitting in Lea Bridge Road Mosque during a Friday sermon as the Imam raged with unbridled indignation at the author's perceived blasphemy. His bare-knuckled fulminations in Urdu were punctuated fiercely with the name *Salman, Salman*. I was a boy of ten or eleven. I sat among the middle rows. The congregation yelped and spat in response to the heretic's name. They broke into vituperative-rhyming chorus at impromptu intervals as if they invoked a curse. Many years later, whilst reading Sir Thomas More's final piece *A Dialogue Of Comfort Against Tribulation*, a passage brought my mind back to the mood in the mosque on that day sometime in 1989: ... *Another sort there are, who will seek for no comfort, nor yet receive none, but in their tribulation (be it loss or sickness) are so testy, so fuming, and so far out of all patience that it profiteth no man to speak to them. And these are as furious with impatience as though they were in half a frenzy. And, from a custom of such behavior, they may fall into one full and whole. And this kind of heaviness in tribulation is even as dangerous as the high branch of the mortal sin of ire.*

A year or two removed from this incident, I was in another quasi-religious, ghastly setting. The zealots present behaved like prepossessed zombies, babbling vehement, vociferous invocations with breakneck, repetitive speed. I was the only kid in the room. To this day, I cannot recall how I ended up through that Looking Glass, but there I was. It was late at night. I'd have been better served asleep in bed. My family had played host to a supposed hierophant from Senegal. They were not party to his mysticism or his sect. However, he had been permitted to invite his disciples to partake in this hysterical, unharnessed, squawking exhibition of delirious chanting and inaudible wailing. But I saw to it, from that moment onwards, that I would never subject myself to another bleating incantation again. When I think back to that experience, I am inclined to repeat Colonel Kurtz's last words in the 1979 film *Apocalypse Now: . . . The horror. . . the horror...* As for Salman Rushdie's *The Satanic Verses*, the notion that an author should be killed because of his craft, no matter how profane, was aporetic. Nobody could ever tell me what I could or couldn't read. Whenever I was told a book was banned or censored, I sought it out even more. When the British government sought to ban Peter Wright's *Spycatcher*, I craved to beg or borrow a copy to ascertain the fuss. I was filled with glee when I beheld the book with my own hands. I finally did read *The Satanic Verses* whilst at college. I concluded the furore a jig in a jeroboam. But with American planes pummeling the Libyan desert, followed by orchestrated book burnings of *The Satanic Verses* in ebbing cities like Bradford, West Yorkshire, my father spoke of a premonitory time when such spawned anger would kindle such an explosion in the seats of American and British power *that the world would be turned upside down.* He outlived 9/11 by thirteen months.

But he was not the only one, from that distance, who saw this clash between anarchical fundamentalism and Western neo-imperialism coming. Author Robin B. Wright had written and spoken for decades, with imperturbable relish, about the symbiosis of C.I.A rogue policy and the pitiless terrorist menace from its Middle Eastern seabed in Egypt, Iran and Lebanon. Her books *Sacred Rage: The Crusade of Modern Islam* and *In The Name Of God: The Khomeini Decade* calibrated the ideological vectors and grievances that metastasized into kidnappings, assassinations and wholesale bombings of civilians. In a 1988 ITV documentary titled *The Sword of Islam*, she predicted, with sibylline precision, the further rise of militant Islam well into the 21st century. She advocated a policy of rapprochement, which enjoyed degrees of success against ideological foes such as Red China and the Soviet Union. Here was a scholar of experiential and prescient ability. Andrew J.R Mack's 1975 essay *Why Big Nations Lose Small Wars: The Politics of Asymmetrical Warfare* interrogates *a pre-theoretical perspective* when faced with a problem like Afghanistan. An enemy like the Taliban need not win militarily. If the political will for the fight dissipated in Washington, and public opinion became debilitated by the longevity of war and an expanding roll call of dead soldiers, then the conflict would be practically lost. He contrasted insurgencies in Morocco, Algeria, Tunisia, Cyprus, Aden, Indochina and Indonesia, where mighty hosts were smitten and forced to withdraw their soldiers and ordnance. He quoted former U.S Secretary Henry Kissinger's 1969 observance of The Vietnam War: *We fought a military war; Our opponents fought a physical attrition; Our opponents aimed for our psychological exhaustion. In the process, we lost sight of one of the cardinal maxims of guerrilla warfare: the guerrilla wins if he does not lose. The conventional army loses if it does not win.* Afghanistan, like Vietnam, would be waged on two quicksilver fronts: the battlefield and the social polity of the United States. I'd have thought the Bush Administration would have charted minds like Ms. Wright and Mr. Mack before luring themselves to the so-called *graveyard of empires*. When I surveyed modern history and pondered the statecraft of tactical theorists like Talleyrand, Von Clausewitz and Bismarck, who sought the best bad alternative in response to the crises of their times, I am, in my mind, certain that men like Tenet, Wolfowitz and Baron Goldsmith pursued options of impermanence. Their conclusions propelled their governments into pyrrhic entanglements that killed millions and cost billions. Our world was devoid of statesmen of the caliber of Cicero and Hammarskjöld at government level. Practical men who sought alternatives than the blood rush to war like France's Dominique De Villepin and the UN's Kofi Annan were spurned. The harlequins of Halliburton and the stooges of Sandline International waved their batons to the tune of the military-industrial complex. Profit and procurement have long been granted preeminence over peace and concord.

I felt intrigued into knowing what America, on the anvil of 9/11, thought of herself. Her armed forces stood poised to invade Afghanistan. Swathes of the media regurgitated whatever their government said. There seemed scant appetite for inquiry, scrutiny and perusal. I was peculiarly enthralled as to the variegated thoughts of American intellectuals and writers on the point of 9/11. I looked for women and men with repute. How were they interpreting this seismic event? Was introspection part of the national discourse? Was American open to a third way, other than the belligerent talk and the bombing lark? Since fifteen of the nineteen homicidal fanatics were Saudi nationals, and stains of impudent Wahabism was on mission creep through the streets of Western Europe, when would the president announce Allied preparations for the invasion of Bin Saud's Arabia? Where was the Jimmy Beslin of our age? I was for the radical journalism of Hopewell Chin'ono, Roger Cook, Jeremy Scahill, John Pilger, Laura Poitras, Glenn Greenwald. Ersatz journalism had laid siege to the orthodoxy, echoing the cry for Vulcan and Mars. I sought interpretative reading, not ideological reporting.

I staggered upon the Roman-American patrician Gore Vidal. He was an insatiable writer with an irreverent mind. He had wittily described the U.K in an interview with the London Independent, as *an American aircraft carrier.* Britain had behaved as much since Prime Minister Margaret Thatcher permitted the Americans to fly their planes from the USS Britannica for the 1986 bombing of Libya. *America, full time power,* he famously remarked. *On the march, looking for enemies.* He was a stern critic of the Bush Administration, and administrations preceding it. He doubted the official 9/11 version of events. Nonetheless, I was thrilled to have discovered him. *Burr, Myra Breckinridge, The City And The Pillar* and *Live From Golgotha* were wolfed down enthusiastically, one after the other. One couldn't underestimate the avoirdupois of his polemic fiction. I was also enamored with an Anglo-American journalist named Christopher Hitchens, whom Gore referred to as his *dauphin.* They would later suffer a separation of paths. Hitchens was an eloquent cheerleader of the War on Terror. He was a cuckoo in the nest of the so-called political Left. He'd become best known for his heresies against God and organized religion in a compelling book titled, *God Is Not Great: How Religion Poisons Everything.* I enjoyed his rumbunctious style of debating on *C-Span,* which appeared on the *BBC Parliament* channel on weekends. *C-Span* was unlike the banausic effusions of the *BBC, CNN* and *Sky News.* Their debate shows were regularly spearheaded by the channel's founder, Brian Lamb. Divergent opines were offered from across the political and media aisle. Listeners were invited to phone in and offer their piece. Hitchens was one of the few public intellectuals brazen enough to connect 9/11 with Iraq's Saddam Hussein. Abu Musab Zarqawi of Al-Qaeda had sought refuge and convalescence in Iraq, he argued. Nobody of that stature could possibly enter and leave Iraq without Saddam Hussein's express permission. Hussein had a track record of supporting international gangsterism. He provided succor to the hijackers of the Mediterranean cruise ship, *Achille Lauro.* He compensated kinsmen of suicide bombers in Palestine. He dispatched chemical weapons during the Anfal Campaign, killing tens of thousands of Kurds. American and British Intelligence claimed he was on the verge of acquiring nuclear missiles. Israel and Iran felt threatened. Saddam's Iraq was their existential enemy. The American government made the 9/11/Saddam Hussein link only tepidly. Hitchens mired them repeatedly. I was glad, however, to have met his acquaintance through his maître literature. He was an insuperable debater and a funny man. I read *Love, Poverty And War: Journey And Essays* with a serendipitous breath. *Letters To A Young Contrarian* was one I wished I waded long before I read it.

Revered essayist and author Susan Sontag was reprehended, by much of the media, for three paragraphs she wrote for *The New Yorker*. She offered some self-scrutiny of America which was discarded at first glance. She scythed through the trite watchwords being served about 9/11. *The voices licensed to follow the event seem to have joined together in a campaign to infantilize the public,* she wrote. *Where is the acknowledgment that this was not a 'cowardly' attack on 'civilization' or 'liberty' or 'humanity' or 'the free world' but an attack on the world's self-proclaimed superpower, undertaken as a consequence of specific American alliances and actions? How many citizens are aware of the ongoing American bombing of Iraq? And if the word 'cowardly' is to be used, it might be more aptly applied to those who kill from beyond the range of retaliation, high in the sky, than to those willing to die themselves in order to kill others. In the matter of courage (a morally neutral virtue): whatever may be said of the perpetrators of Tuesday's slaughter, they were not cowards.* What she wrote seemed fair and fitting. Her piece was neither spiffy nor self-flagellating. Few, however, thought it convenient to forensically explore the hatred that bore this attack in its immediate aftermath. Especially when many remained uncertain as to whether their loved ones were alive or dead. Her piece provoked a maelstrom. But I felt a dose of matured reality required shooting into the nation's antecubital vein.

After World War II, America practically franchised several foreign policy initiatives to the Central Intelligence Agency. The C.I.A became kingmakers. They installed Cat Paw's as heads of state by nefarious design. They helped unseat the democratically elected Mosaddegh of Persia in 1953, thanks to *Operation Ajax*. The also-democratically-elected Arbenz of Guatemala was ousted by Black Ops methods a year later. The attempted overthrow of Sukarno of Indonesia was a failure, but thousands of lives were lost in the culminating bloodbath. America destabilized the nascent democratic nation of Congo by surreptitiously removing its President Lumumba and planting the despot Mobutu, propping him with dollar bills and machine guns. He became one of the richest men in the world in the 1970s, joining the ranks of the Shah of Iran, another C.I.A myrmidon. America's inordinate interference in Indochina, replacing French imperialism, metamorphosed into what became commonly known as The Vietnam War. An estimated half-a-million Vietnamese civilians were slaughtered in their homeland because of a superpower's psychosis over Communism. The C.I.A abetted I.D.E.A stooges in Greece and presided over the sequels of catastrophes during the Korean War. They trained insurgents to stage coups in Syria and Cuba. They administered an agglomeration of disorder in Chad (Habré) and Lebanon (Gemayel). America removed tyrants in the Dominican Republic (Trujillo), Brazil (Goulart) and Chile (Allende), yet solidified them in Greece (Papadopoulos), Philippines (Marcos), Grenada (Blaize) and Chile (Pinochet). The C.I.A funded Nicaraguan Contras against the Sandinista, trained death squads in El Salvador, not to mention peremptory operations in Cambodia, Laos and Bolivia. In the proxy wars against the *evil* Soviet Empire, nothing was left to chance. *There are no innocent civilians*, remarked Curtis LeMay in a dissonant interview with Michael Sherry, author of *The Rise of American Air Power: The Creation of Armageddon*. I wondered whether LeMay would have applied that same fallacy had he witnessed the terror of American civilians in New York and Washington. He was the architect of the strategic bombing of Japanese cities in World War II. Had his advice been heeded, Cuba and North Vietnam would have been flattened too. *There are no innocent civilians*, croaked the old frog. *It is their government, and you are fighting a people. You are not trying to fight an armed force anymore. So it doesn't bother me so much to be killing the so-called innocent bystanders.* One can hazard a guess as to whether Osama Bin Laden would have approved such philistinism.

A day after 9/11, Ward Churchill, a professor of Ethnic Studies at the University of Colorado Boulder, published an essay titled *Some People Push Back: On The Justice Of Roosting Chickens.* The pepper-grey piece elicited little attention at the time it was written. Churchill connected the attacks on the World Trade Center and the Pentagon with the American bombings and economic sanctions on Iraq. *On the morning of September 11, 2001,* he wrote, *a few more chickens — along with some half-million dead Iraqi children — came home to roost in a very big way at the twin towers of New York's World Trade Center. Well, actually, a few of them seem to have nestled in the Pentagon as well.* The *chicken coming home to roost* phrasing was borrowed from Malcolm X's comments in the immediate aftermath of President John F. Kennedy's assassination in Dallas, Texas, 1963. American duplicity in foreign lands had wrought it so, Churchill wrote. He challenged the pervading notion that the World Trade Center casualties were blameless victims. *As for those in the World Trade Center... Well, really. Let's get a grip, shall we? True enough, they were civilians of a sort. But innocent? Gimme a break. They formed a technocratic corps at the very heart of America's global financial empire — the "mighty engine of profit" to which the military dimension of US policy has always been enslaved — and they did so willingly and knowingly. Recourse to "ignorance" — derivative, after all, of the word "ignore" — counts as less than an excuse among this relatively well-educated elite. To the extent that any of them were unaware of the costs and consequences to others of what they were involved in — and in many cases excelling at — it was because of their absolute refusal to see. Most likely, it was because they were too busy braying, incessantly and self-importantly, into their cell phones, arranging power lunches and stock transactions, each of which translated, conveniently out of sight, mind and smelling distance, into the starved and rotting flesh of infants. If there was a better, more effective, or in fact any other way of visiting some penalty befitting their participation upon the little Eichmanns inhabiting the sterile sanctuary of the twin towers, I'd really be interested in hearing about it.*

The *Little Eichmann* concept provoked a thought experiment in my mind: the notion of everyday people ploughing mechanically into a system. Their anodyne output produced destructive results elsewhere. Alas, they were so detached and anesthetized they didn't notice! German-American author and theorist Hannah Arendt had postulated such a supposition in arguably her most celebrated work, *Eichmann In Jerusalem: A Report On The Banality Of Evil*. Adolf Eichmann had overseen the worst genocide in human history. He'd been tasked with supervising *The Final Solution*. Arendt argued that Eichmann was both unremarkable and unimaginative. He could not think independently. He was not bright academically. He followed orders without inquiry. He acted as he was bidden. He demonstrated no pathological or ideological hatred towards Jews. He broke no law. And he was in the employ of a democratically elected German government. So what was his wrong?

Churchill asked the same hardboiled question of our societies. I discussed his essay with others. Many felt ruffled by the assertion. They were more Winston than Ward with their response. America was not the equivalent of Nazi Germany, most said. Neither was Britain. We may say so, I replied, but that question would be better served if we asked it of the Chagossian. Or the Taíno, the Kalinago, the Pequot, the Narragansett, the Beothuk. Or the Cheyenne, the Arapaho, the Yuki and the Aboriginal Tasmanians. Moreover, the Nazis, to the Nazis, were not *Nazis*, if one could follow this pattern of thought. They never referred to themselves as *Nazis*. The National Socialists, as they presented themselves, were admittedly a cultured people among their kind. Their Hanseatic mythology diffused the presumption of superiority. They were patriots who revered the Fatherland. They were loving fathers and mothers to their children. They enjoyed the music of Handel, Beethoven and Mozart on their phonographs. They watched Weber, Wagner and Strauss in opera houses. They were directly inspired by America's institutional racist laws. They didn't consider the mass slaughter of Poles, Jews, Gypsies and Slavs barbarous. They considered the murder of sub-human folk necessary to preserve the *Third Reich*. I should hasten to add that Adolf Hitler himself was an admirer of the British Empire, and how that Empire, whom the sun would never set on, ruled half a billion Indians with a few thousand bureaucrats from Whitehall. The British Royal Family had inextricable ancestral links to Bavaria. The House of Hanover, whose reign included that of Queen Victoria, had ruled the British Isles for two centuries. Had Hitler sought territories on another continent, the British establishment may not have minded as much. One would do well to recall that in 1884, the Germans, under Otto von Bismarck, invited the Belgians, the British, the Americans, the French and a host of European others to decide who would own what of Africa. Hitler's fatal error was to construct his *Lebensraum* in the heart of Europe a ala, Austria, Saarland, Sudetenland, Czechoslovakia and Poland. The British and French Empires could not, and would not, accept any brigandry on their doorsteps. It was this that led to World War II.

Thus was Churchill's rebarbative critique, co-ordinated to give heads a shake! In the comfort of their homes, Middle America tuned into Walter Cronkite and Dan Rather, who reported on the extenuation of American foreign policy. They listened, mostly with indifference, to these mild-mannered, avuncular men. Off-camera, American warplanes extirpated people and property. And after CBS and ABC news had finished their evening transmission, *The Falcon Crest, Friends* and *I Dream Of Jeannie* followed, to the mirth and amusement of many homes. The next day, Middle America climbed into their vehicles or caught the subway to work. After collecting a thermos of coffee from Starbucks, a run-of-the mill bureaucrat powered the remunerative wheel with little punctuation. The passive administrator processed his work like an automaton. In effect, they powered industries, institutions and economies that were by-products for carnage and corruption elsewhere. If *for the want of a nail, a kingdom was lost*, then a push of a button could render a million dead.

* * *

Around the Ides of March 2003, I tuned into the *BBC Parliament* channel to watch the British House of Commons vote for a *fait accompli* long resolved in Washington. Iraq was the next phase of the *War on Terror*. Britain had some forty-six thousand troops, two hundred aircraft and thirty-three ships poised for battle, at a cost assemblage of billions. The Americans were numbered in the hundreds of thousands. They bought their best warplanes and their largest aircraft carriers. The other participants of the so-called *Coalition of The Willing* lugged a few boots, tinny armored cars and rangy artillery pieces. I was aghast at the puckishness of that day in Parliament. It was as if these men and women had gathered in the chamber before a round of foxhunting. I had envisaged lawmakers made solemn by the bloodred dread of armed conflict. I expected emollient speeches like that of Robin Cook, former Leader of The House, who resigned from government the day before. He could not, in good conscience, support an Iraqi invasion. I wasn't expecting wholesome resignations. But I had supposed a funereal tone, of reflection, and contemplation on innumerable civilian souls and military deaths in the foreboding hours. I recalled conjuring a story that might well read true: Of a man named Asim. He lived in downtown Baghdad, founded by Caliph Al-Mansur in 762 A.D as *Madinat as Salaam* (City of Peace). He was apolitical, with a young family. He cared for his elderly parents. He prayed five times daily. He toiled the earnest hours. The cost of living was skewered by maddening inflation, thanks to international economic sanctions and the regressive failures of the Iraqi autocratic machine. Nevertheless, he and his entire family would soon be killed by a stray bomb from an RAF jet. And that sortie was flown at the will of a facetious Parliament, who voted in the favor of this action. I imagined the House of Commons adjoined to the 1920s ballroom featured in the 1980 horror picture, *The Shining*. Ciphers drifted from the muggy, sententious drivel in the Commons, into the Overlook Hotel to vote and swig drinks, and then back again to hear more drivel. Labour MP Oona King seesawed a speech that eventually swung yay for war. Tory MP Alan Duncan behaved like a two-bob Partyman baddie from Michael Keaton's *Batman*. Folks like Tony Benn, Jeremy Corbyn, Diane Abbott, Tam Dalyell, George Galloway, Kate Hoey, Dennis Skinner and Angus Robertson voted no. The media industrial complex accused them of being tyrannophiles. I paused to think whether Parliament was this exuberant during the fogs of war in 1914, 1939, 1956 and 1982? Perhaps it was that dreamy Twin Peaks state that rendered many MPs with amnesia about the whole thing since. Having set fire to the Middle East, they belatedly discovered Iraq was already free of weapons of mass destruction. I have heard many plead since that, had they known better, they'd have voted no too. That left me in no doubt as to the chicanery of politics. Having set ablaze North Africa in 2011, when Britain and NATO toppled Colonel Gaddafi after intervening in Libya's civil war, the British Parliament demonstrated that they were prepared to boil their cabbages twice.

I took refuge in more books. Bob Woodward's *Bush At War* shone a flattering torchlight over the countenance of the White House following the first hundred days after 9/11. Contrary to Bush's media image, the book depicted him a bold, irreproachable president, guided by gut instinct. He may not be displeased by that description. Woodward was granted exclusive access to the Dogs of War. I got the impression he reciprocated their favor by analyzing nice. This was an inevitable consequence when journalists sail too close to politicians. Their integrity is inevitably compromised. Their optics become tidal-locked. Woodward was a legendary reporter in his own right. He came into prominence after probing the Watergate Scandal, which culminated with the spectacular resignation of the woebegone President Nixon. Bush's counterterrorism chief Richard A. Clarke also wrote a book titled *Against All Enemies: Inside America's War on Terror*. He alleged that Rumsfeld wanted war with Iraq from the get-go. Deputy Defense Secretary Paul Wolfowitz doubted whether Bin Laden could have pulled a terror scheme of that magnitude without state sponsorship. There was a conceited attempt to establish a link with the Iraqi Government from the outset, in spite of the intelligence community disproving their involvement. They eventually settled for the fibrillating *weapons of mass destruction* theory. I read Patrick Cockburn's *Dangerous Liaison: The Inside Story of The US-Israeli Covert Relationship, Out Of The Ashes: The Resurrection Of Saddam Hussein* and *Saddam Hussein: An American Obsession*, which he cowrote with his brother Patrick, also an author and journalist. While the fires still smoldered under the twin towers rubble, meatheads in the American government targeted Saddam Hussein in their crosshairs. They bitterly rued having not finished him off in the Gulf War of 1991. The Baathist butcher, having lost Kuwait after illegally occupying it, had slain Kurds and Shias for rising against him. The problem of Saddam marinated throughout the 1990s and early 2000s. Why not the tribunes like Wright and Mack, rather than the hawk Cheney and falcon Rumsfeld, I again wondered? Perhaps Wright and Mack had opined, like the Roman philosopher, Seneca the Younger, that the sage ought to let the Republic destroy itself. Controversial polemicist Ann Coulter, herself an acquired taste, wrote of destruction of a sort. She championed a medieval crusade, probably on the scale of Jerusalem 1099AD. *We should invade their countries, kill their leaders and convert them to Christianity*, she wrote incorrigibly in the *National Review*. They subsequently fired her. I wondered how much slaying this would-be Boudica was prepared to do her herself and how she'd fare in the missionary business in grand old Mesopotamia.

Chris Hedges' book *War Is A Force That Gives Us Meaning* was a brisance to my mind. As a foreign correspondent for the *New York Times*, he'd tread many battlefields. He'd overseen the excavation of mass graves. *We demonize the enemy so that our opponent is no longer human*, he wrote. *We view ourselves, our people, as the embodiment of absolute goodness. Our enemies invert our view of the world to justify their own cruelty... Each side reduces the other to objects — eventually in the form of corpses.* Hedges examined how war affected nations that waged them. If war was like a drug, America had overdosed. It wasn't just Lieutenant Colonel Kilgore, of the film *Apocalypse Now*, who *loved the smell of napalm in the morning*. Foreign and war correspondents did too. As the bombs pounded Afghanistan and, later, Iraq, I sensed the adrenalin rush in their reporting. The *shock and awe* campaign made frigorific television. I saw bombs fall but not people. I heard the sirens ring but not the wails of human beings. Nevertheless, the war was a ratings success. David Rieff and Roy Gutman's *Crimes Of War: What The Public Should Know* included essays from CNN journalist Christiane Amanpour on Bosnia, BBC correspondent Jeremy Bowen on Chechnya and Sydney Schanberg, an American journalist, who reported on Cambodia. His chilling accounts inspired the 1984 war film *The Killing Fields*. Herein this filial book lies the contradictory and hypocritical nature of war as crystalized in its content. What constitutes a war crime, terrorism and conventional warfare aren't universally defined. The bombings of Dresden, Hiroshima, Nagasaki, Vietnam are open to conjecture. I supposed it depended on *who* orchestrates the slaughter and, more importantly, *who* wins the war. For it was always the losers who stood trial for war crimes. In former Pakistani President Pervez Musharraf's memoir *In The Line Of Fire*, the United States Deputy Secretary of State Richard Armitage, it was said, had threatened to bomb Pakistan *into the Stone Age* if his country refused to cooperate against the Taliban. Not another war crime then?

I was, for a moment in time, in love with Asra Nomani, who spoke in the softest voice about the barbaric murder of her journalist friend Daniel Pearl in Pakistan. His crime was that he was Jewish American. He was decapitated and his body cut into ten pieces by terrorists of the worst kind. Italian *scrittore* Oriana Fallaci was another name that fell into my lap. She had stoked the Muslims of mainland Europe into a frenzy not seen since *The Satanic Verses*. *The Rage And The Pride* and *The Force Of Reason* were two Badalisc screeds she wrote from the grotesque mist of September. 9/11 appeared to obscure her cognizance into curating Muslims as a race of people. *Those who drink orange juice* was a queer euphemism she assayed regularly in *The Force Of Reason*. She was an atheist. However, her perceived threat of politically propelled Islam in Italy forced her into the bosom of the Holy Father in Rome. She had enjoyed a distinguished career as a journalist. Rolling Stone magazine described her as *the greatest political interviewer of modern times*. She interviewed many luminaries that powered the latter half of the 20th century. She sat with the Shah of Iran and the Ayatollah Khomeini. Not at the same time of course. (*The Ballad Of The Imam And The Shah* by English poet James Fenton was a delectation about the two foes, and the insane catastrophes they wrought upon the great Iranian people). With Khomeini, Fallaci was impertinent. *How do you swim in a chador?* she asked without a tincture of irony. She was requested to wear one during the interview. *Our customs are none of your business*, replied the Imam. *If you don't like the Islamic dress, you are not obliged to wear it.* To which, she answered: *That's very kind of you, Imam. And since you said so, I'm going to take off this stupid, medieval rag right now...* She initiated dialogue with Nguyen Van Thieu of South Vietnam and Vo Nguyen Giap of the North. *How corrupt are you?* She asked the former tersely. She interviewed Israel's Golda Meir and India's Indira Gandhi. Of Gandhi, she got her to publicly defend her *dreadful methods* on birth control, which included the forced sterilization of men. Meir was deemed praiseworthy. *In my opinion even if one is not all in government with her*, she gushed, *with her politics, her ideology, one cannot help but respect her, admire her, even love her. I almost loved her.* Her examinations were compiled into a book titled: *Interviews With History And Conversations With Power*. I found her interview style fascinating. I had once harbored ambitions in journalism. That aspiration had long dissipated. Had the intent lingered, I'd have gladly been a Fallaci! She was unpretentious and aggressively so. *If they're afraid of me, that's too bad!* She never pretended to be objective. *When I take the subway in New York and see ads for newspapers that claim 'facts, not opinions,' I laugh so hard the whole subway car shakes. What does that mean? I'm the one interpreting the facts. I always write in the first person. And what am I? I'm a human being!* She was not in awe of official titles or offices. *Whether it comes from a despotic sovereign or an elected president, from a murderous general or a beloved leader, I see power as an inhuman and hateful phenomenon... I have always looked on disobedience toward the oppressive as the only way to use the miracle of having been born.* These words are framed above my workstation. I'd recommend Cristina de Stefano's book: *Oriana Fallaci: The Journalist, the Agitator, the Legend* for a comprehensive read into the life of this remarkable human being. As a young girl, she'd been a partisan against fascism. Islamofascism, as she saw it, had taken afoot in Italy in her old age. She was committed to fighting by use of the pen. A self-proclaimed Muslim leader Adel Smith attempted to sue Fallaci but found himself on the wrong side of the law having been sentenced to prison for forging checks. Perhaps an adverse parable of sinners casting the first stone is befitting.

Twenty years on, the permeations of 9/11 have irreparably altered civil society. London has since experienced 7/7, Lee Rigby, Westminster Bridge, London Bridge. Manchester saw the bombing of children at an Ariana Grande concert. Paris suffered the slaying of journalists and cartoonists employed by the satirical magazine *Charlie Hebdo.* Cities across Europe and the world have endured similar evils. The perpetrators were predominately homegrown, rendered bitter and warped by a brew of grievance and mythopoeia. America rendered several prisoners during its War on Terror. They were imprisoned in Guantanamo Bay in violation of *habeas corpus.* Minors were also detained. There were innumerable reports of torture including sodomy and sleep deprivation, waterboarding and beatings. *They're living in the tropics. They're well fed. They've got everything they could possibly want,* remarked Vice-President Cheney when interviewed by CNN about the condition of these *enemy combatants.* Some remain in captivity at the time of writing. I've been appalled, however unsurprised, by successive U.K governments. They have committed political and social seppuku in slow motion. They have traded civil liberties for fear. They snuggled up further to powerful sections of the cloying, duplicitous media. Their *de haut en bas* lecturing, whether it be on the European Union, Brexit and Covid 19, are insidious and patronizing. The pearl-clutching and polarization of vast spheres of British public life, over the two decades, has driven me into semi-isolation. We remain trapped by the eidolon foghorned from America. The political perversity of President Trump, the General Woundwort of American Presidents, culminated into the infamy of Capitol Hill on January 6, 2021. Contrast that, if you will, to the evening of 9/11. Senators and House members, Democrats and Republicans, stood on the steps of that same Capitol building, singing an impromptu, stirring rendition of *God Bless America*. That show of unity was admirable but incomparable to the images of horned vagabonds attempting to replicate a 21st century Monty Python storming of the Winter Palace on January 6, 2021, in Washington DC. On 9/11, New York's mayor Rudolph Giuliani was dubbed *America's Mayor*. He was a standard bearer of American resolve. His visibility as the leading elected official on the New York frontline, coordinating with the emergency services, inspired his country. On 01/06, he metamorphosed into Trump's ventriloquist, regurgitating the verisimilitudes of a stolen General Election. As I write this, the American military are conducting a fraught exit from Afghanistan as if it were Saigon: The Sequel. I concede that it is much less disastrous than the original. Afghans, employed by the U.S and U.K militaries and contractors, are naturally concerned for their fate. Some have secured visas to leave the country. Others have not. Those who have left may never return to their homeland. Those who remain are *remaindered* to the merciless Taliban. *You have the clocks. We have the time* was a refrain repeatedly intensified with the passage of time. The Taliban, who allegedly made reference to this phrasing, were right. American troops could not hold Bagram Air Base forever. Afghanistan was no more than a satrapy under their protection. Inevitably, it'd sink into becoming a medieval theocracy. I've heard western journalists on television crow over the plight of women and gays in Afghanistan, as if the initial purpose of the 2001 invasion was to impose feminist and LGBTQ+I principles in that Cocytus wilderness. Gore Vidal had famously dubbed his country *the United States of Amnesia*. His rationale is self-evident if we gaze back twenty years, never mind two hundred and forty-five. Many are hard pressed to remember the objectives of the American military in Kabul. Some are perplexed as to their achievements in that woebegone place. Martin Luther King once said that *we have guided missiles and misguided men*. There is a case to be made that every major foreign venture undertaken by the United States since the Second World War was unwarranted. But such is the beastly disposition of every empire in human history. I stare at the TV as Afghans cling to the wheels of American military aircraft. They are determined not to be left to theocratic tyranny. As the plane sailed through the sky, they fell back towards the earth, to certain destruction below. The Taliban, like the North Vietnamese back in 1975, are set to swallow their country whole again. Their Jihad looks complete. Their innumerable martyrs and suicides are promised paradise. They do not number them. America contemplates her 2,420 dead soldiers in Afghanistan. Britain's military have yielded 456 deaths. Both their governments have concluded their deaths were worth it. In terms of blood for treasure, they may well be right.

August 17, 2021.

THE NECESSITY
OF HIP-HOP

*Y*OU CANNOT KICK A *man in the gut and then tell him how he should* *scream!* This was a vehement refrain of a friend of mine, often made to justify the presupposed blowbacks that pursued the footfalls of racism. He has asked not to be named. He lives in Paris, that sclerotic City of Light. He lectures on the history of art. His caboodle of hip-hop records dwarfs my own. His acquisitions serve as an irradiated timeline, from The Sugarhill Gang to J Hus. Vinyl stacked to digitally stored. He remembers his determinative years with pathos. He was born in the Fifth Republic. His antecedents hail from Algeria. His mindfully inoffensive parents lived in Biskra, on the fringe of the Sahara Desert. They fled their country during its bitter war of independence against the Fourth Republic. Hundreds of thousands of people were slaughtered in this understated conflagration. His family settled in the *banlieue*. They cobbled among a synthesis of French speaking peoples from across the globe. They worked cul-de-sac jobs with polite deliberation. They counseled their children to dress in the mantle of forbearance. My friend was taught to practice obsequence before the predation of malevolent police officers. He was instructed to show deference to insidious teachers. If he dared wrestle with chimney sweeps, the authorities may depict him as one. If he appeared remotely threatening, he may only be given employment with impenetrable ceilings. If he were kicked in the gut, he was advised to elicit a temperate sigh and plod on. Whilst some were certain of their manifest destiny, he was bedeviled by a beleaguered inauthenticity. The Fifth Republic was committed to its laïcité principles. Marianne insisted upon *ceteris paribus*. Authority smiled upon the dutiful and the earnest. If he followed the script, he would reap the reward of her intelligible privileges.

He read the works of dead poets and radical thinkers (some French, others not). He surmised that folks like him were prepped into becoming Janissaries. He resented this type of conditioning. It compromised his integrity. He was ostensibly French. He was a citizen and, therefore, nobody's guest. Perhaps it was normal for the convoluted crosswinds of *kulturkampf* to rage civil strife from within himself. He once told me how the clanging of weaponry and the firing of ordnances ricocheted within his skull by night. The internal war oscillated within. The winner takes soul. His world was smothered by smaze and conjecture. His future seemed unpropitious as he was inordinately misunderstood upon every turn. He reproached his parents for their casuistry. He despised authority for its calumny. He was rigidly on the side of, what he would call, the *speculative classes*.

An alternative family were forged in the banality of the *banlieue*. These kindred fellows had variegated roots sprung from Senegal and the Seychelles, Guinea and Guadeloupe, Cape Verde and Cote d'Ivoire. Pernicious troubles were wrought by a society that spied them with visceral suspicion. Even the local baker felt his shop was poised to be robbed when all they desired was bread. Their germane experiences and pastimes cemented their bond. They reclined in each other's bedrooms. They composed their own rap songs, in French, Arabic and English. They dissected each other's cassette recordings of NWA and Naughty By Nature, Ice-T and A Tribe Called Quest, Public Enemy and KRS One. These lyrics tessellated their angst. These incautious rappers performed without trepidation.

Their conscientious ire spared no quarter. *Cop Killer, Fuck Tha Police,* and *Fight The Power* were spawned from temperate fury, adroitly rhyming with reason. Their perorations were understood by dissenting kids, who felt humiliated by Marianne on the streets. Hip-hop tempered their foolhardy disposition. Its syllogisms were something they could subscribe to.

Hip-hop was borne from subversion, contemporaneously supplanted in the Bronx, New York. Its immanent roots lay in Africa, long before the bondage ships shored, bearing yoke and chains. The Soninke, Toucouleur, Fulani, Mandinka, Wolof and others had, among them, bards and griots. They recited verses to the balafon. They declaimed couplets to the accompaniment of a bloodless drum. Occasionally, the tongue required no *obbligato*. Their recitals often referred to the nostalgia of famed ancestors. In the early decades of the 20th century, Paul Laurence Dunbar, The Jubalaires, Luke Jordan, Lonnie Glosson and Blind Willie McTell were among those, whose syncopated cadence to a swift tempo, were early manifestations of what was later called hip-hop. Hip-hop's repackaging and resurgence in the seventies emanated through the world, not unlike the manner of Typhon, son of Tartarus and Gaia, who, according to Hesiod's *Theogony* was *terrible, outrageous and lawless,* and that ... *His hands were strong... The feet of the powerful god were weariless. From his shoulders were a hundred heads of a dreadful serpent dragon, licking with dark tongues. The eyes on the monster's ineffable heads flashed fire beneath their brows. (From all the heads, as he looked, burned fire). Voices were in all his dreadful heads, emitting sounds of all sorts, unutterable by gods. Sometimes they spoke so gods could comprehend. Sometimes they emitted the cry of a bull, unchecked in might, proud of voice. Sometimes the cry of a lion having a shameless spirit. Sometimes sounds like puppies, a wonder to hear. Sometimes he hissed and the lofty mountains rumbled.*

Hip-hop's explosion into Middle America disconcerted the staid senators on Capitol Hill. They worried for the deracination of their offspring's generation. It was as if their own parents never feared the specter of punk and rock n roll. Little Richard and Elvis Pressley, Johnny Rotten and Sid Vicious caused moral panic to the generations that preceded Fab Five Freddy, Africa Bambaataa and Big Kap of The Flip Squad. However, the gods of Olympus, unsettled by the young storm giant, would totally empathize with the likes of Tipper Gore. The overwrought clamor of the hip-hop *homme fatale ... emitting sounds of all sorts, unutterable by gods,* meant their albums were accompanied by parental advisory stickers. Like Typhon, hip-hop was wrung with voluble tones and innumerable tongues: searing, unstanchable, adversarial, cerebral, eccentric, poetic, logical, brazen, Baudelairean. Hip-hop contained contrasting resolutions therein: Abstract, Conscious, Crunk, Dirty South, Gangsta, G-funk, Latin, Underground. *Sometimes they emitted the cry of a bull, unchecked in might, proud of voice; Sometimes the cry of a lion having a shameless spirit. Sometimes sounds like puppies, a wonder to hear. Sometimes he hissed and the lofty mountains rumbled.*

Furshlugginer critics have long disparaged hip-hop with their fastidious judgement. They scathed its fleshy appetites. They scorned its cultural outgrowth of beguilement and nihilism. They condemned it as a promoter and projector of intercommunal violence. They decried the lyrics laden with imprecations and misogyny, murder and Mammon. Gangsta rap videos was a bespoken quarry of opportunist condemnation. I readily recall the British police, aided by parliamentary MPs, harassing and repudiating UK hip-hop collective, So Solid Crew, circa 2000. Street violence was grossly attributed to their songs. Venues were advised against hosting their performances, lest brannigans broke out on the dancefloor. No other music genre accrued more social liability than those who sought to rhyme from a microphone. A society, who spared reaved violence in operas such as *The Rape Of Lucretia, Guillaume Tell* and *The Abduction Of Seraglio,* had an innate problem with Snoop Dogg, Eminem and Dr. Dre videos! One supposed it a matter of taste, I supposed. *You know I spit it but hate to love to admit it,* rapped Method Man of the Wu-Tang Clan on their track *Frozen,* from *The Saga Continues* album. *They're criticizin the lyrics. Guess everybody's a critic.*

I push the limit while rappers is pushing gimmicks. I use to push my pen and then add it to the premise hook. Yeah, still talk about it and I still live it. Underground without a shovel and still digging! Society inexplicably demanded rappers be *role models* and *loco parentis.* Why, I wondered. An artist must be unbound by the Mary Whitehouse moralizers of our times, whose unidimensional endeavors to sanitize the landscape to their bland, boring tastes are an absurdity. Hip-hop attracted a sensationalist level of scrutiny because its marauding catechisms spoke to the angst of youth everywhere, from Turkey to Trinidad and Tobago. But Typhon was a challenge to the gods, and not mortal men. Even when the young Cadmus played the pipes for him whilst he rested, he promised him no harm.

I can recall the aplomb of Ice Cube's unflinching enunciations, the undulated embroidery of the Notorious B.I.G, the rapid pulsations of Bone Thugs-n-Harmony, the phrenic verses of Naughty By Nature's Treach, the rapt baritone of Nate Dogg, the feverish lament of Eminem, the rhythmic precocity of Black Thought, the intellectual thrust of Imhotep Gary Byrd. *We wear the crown!* The cohering polysyndetons of DMX. *Who we be.* The swashbuckling dexterity of these wordsmiths, their mercurial brocade of linguistics, are unlike any composition in the English language in our modern era. I loved the cleverness of their syntax, injected with verve and wisdom. As a budding litterateur, I felt emboldened to experiment with idioms. When I listened to Black Thought, arguably the Coryphaeus of hip-hop lyricists, expounding himself on *Twofifteen* thus: *Who keeps it a hundred when everything's partial? Dignity and sanity is what the game cost you,* he was giving notice of a precarious time when fairmindedness was at sea for both peons and princes. Rakim, in *Let The Rhythm Hit Em,* espoused a verse that spoke to my sapiosexual tendencies. *Before I get that Fifi I met, whisper I wanna reach her intellect. Kiss her 'cause I wanna give her the most respect.* Tupac had abundant lines oft-quoted the world over. *Don't settle for less,* he rhymed from the acclaimed *Me Against The World.* This track gave caution against hymenopterans that served as a fucking nuisance. *Even a genius asks questions. Be grateful for blessings.*

Don't even change. Keep your essence. Inspectah Deck, of the Wu-Tang Clan, no stranger to lexical juggernauts, unleashed a temblor on the track *Triumph: I bomb atomically. Socrates' philosophies and hypotheses can't define how I be droppin these mockeries. Lyrically perform armed robbery. Flee with the lottery. Possibly, they spotted me...* My Parisian friend positioned himself under the political wing of KRS One: *Take a look at the police and how they treat you,* he rhymed from *Pick It Up,* of the album *Maximum Strength. Take a look at these corporations that cheat you. Democrats and Republicans are all see-through. Now we voting for the lesser of two evils. Man, don't let em deceive you. This is an autocracy, not a democracy. But to call this a democracy without mock interest in the laws of society, that's called hypocrisy.* When Nas, of *N.Y State Of Mind,* and then The Game, of *Dreams,* declared *sleep is the cousin of death,* I argued with many that *Death's own brother* (was) *sleep,* according to Virgil's *Aeneid.* Hypnos was the twin brother of Thanatos, not his cousin! My protestations were robustly swatted aside. Nas and The Game held far greater sway.

Hip-hop would, respectfully, be nowhere without its Daughters of Memory. No apotheosized narration of its history could be rendered legitimate without citing Sylvia Robinson, founder and CEO of Sugarhill Records. She quarried The Sugar Hill Gang's *Rapper's Delight* into one of the first hip-hop songs to enjoy commercial success. Music fans were further propitiated when she engineered further achievements with Grandmaster Flash And The Furious Five. Their 1982 hit record *The Message* is lauded among the greatest hip-hop tunes of all time. Robinson also signed an exclusively female hip-hop/funk trio called *The Sequence,* led by the *Black Diamond Of Soul* herself, Angie Stone. Dr. Dre borrowed a chorus interpolation from their most successful hit, *Funk You Up,* for his own 1995 candescent offering, *Keep Their Heads Ringin.*

Pebblee Poo, widely acclaimed as the first female M.C ever, worked closely with DJ Cool Herc, who is principally recognized as the father of the hip-hop genre. She remains a fixture on the scene and in her local community, five decades down. Monie Love was raised in London. Yet she found herself in New York, aged nineteen, recording her debut album, *Down To Earth*. Her most successful single *It's A Shame (My Sister)* was a *deductam carmen*, to borrow a phrasing from the Roman poet Ovid. Her conscientious locus was a pivot to the social politics in America, and further into the events of Rodney King, Latasha Harlins and the L.A Riots of 1992. Before Jazzy Jeff, there was Jazzy Joyce, a sampler turntablist of the highest order. Before King Louie, there was Queen Latifah, exhibiting her virtuosity in the recording booth and in front of a camera screen. She collaborated with Monie Love on a zesty song, *Ladies First*, taken from her 1989 debut album, *All Hail The Queen*. She took prominent roles in hip-hop films like *Juice* (which featured Tupac Shakur) and *Set It Off* (which starred Jada Pinkett Smith). M.C Sha-Rock, of Funky Four Plus One More, is widely considered the first female rapper. She wrote a book titled: *The Story Of The Beginning And End Of The First Hip-hop Female M.C.* The tome served as a deft bildungsroman about her tribulations in the industry. M.C Lyte was the first female solo rapper to release an album stocked with noteworthy hip-hop content titled, *Lyte As A Rock*. During her decades long career, she concerted with artistes as varied as Sinead O'Connor, Moby and Beyonce. Roxanne Shanté, of *The Juice Crew*, was beholden to the notorious *Roxanne Wars* against her arch-rival *The Real Roxanne*. Both artists played out a helter skelter, lyrical back-and-forth that numbered over ninety songs. Even the Tupac vs Biggie Smalls, Jay-Z vs Nas and Eazy-E vs Doctor Dre skirmishes were circumscribed to a handful of volleys. Shanté retired from the music industry, aged just twenty-five. Salt N Pepa were one of the biggest female hip-hop acts of all time. They produced hits like *Push It*, *Let's Talk About Sex* and *None Of Your Business*. My favorite album of these times was Neneh Cherry's *Raw Like Sushi*. Hers was the first album I purchased with my own pocket money. I only began scribbling rhyming verses after reading her interview in *Smash Hits!* where she encouraged fans to compose and perform their own rap songs.

I have an eidetic memory. I can recall the exact date when I first became aware of hip-hop: New Years Day 1986. My family and I watched the film *Breakdance* (also known as *Breakin*) starring Adolfo 'Shabba Doo' Quinones, Michael 'Boogaloo Shrimp' and Ice-T. My younger brother Ousman and I imitated the knee and back spins, the windmill and the robot choreography in our living room. The film, as well as its sequel *Breakdance II (Breakin II)*, featured hip-hop's other elements – turntablism and graffiti. My turntablist friend Kishmeister is a master at synthesizing and scratching. You could not separate his deft cuts with an anorexic rizla paper. Every homophonic beat is amalgamated by an analogous bell. He led me to Leake Street in Lambeth, London, where the tunnel walls are refulgent with graffiti innovation and design. His weekly *Beats Theory* shows on pirate radio keeps me abreast of contemporary hip-hop. I tune in regularly. He is a fervid supporter of the British music scene. He plays hip-hop tracks performed in Japanese, Hindi, Spanish, French, Arabic and Portuguese. He humbly follows the pathways of Grandmaster Flash and Grandmaster Flowers, DJ Cash Money and DJ Cheese, DJ Grand Wizard Theodore and DJ Cool Herc. I should hasten to add that, on August 13, 1973, Herc's older sister Cindy Campbell organized her birthday party at 1520 Sedgwick Avenue in The Bronx, New York. Herc played cuts from his eclectic collection of records through the night. The birthplace and birthday of hip-hop, in its universal and recognizable manifestation, are invariably attributed to that address and date.

My French pal earned a fistful of francs playing records at birthday parties and school raves during the days of *La Haine*. Some years later, after arriving in London to study at the Imperial College London, he and his friends would walk along London Underground's Central Line after midnight with aerosol cans. They'd coruscate TFL trains and property with luminous paint. He was an enormous admirer of Jean Michel Basquiat, the great New York artist and neo-expressionist, whose ingenuity and flair made fans of Andy Warhol and Madonna. He informed me of Taki 183, the Greek-American graffiti artist, who adorned New York's subways and bridges with ruminative expressions for the speculative classes; of Lee Quinones, another artist of that radical ilk, who declared that *Graffiti is art and if art is a crime, please God, forgive me.* And there was Keith Haring, who sprayed socially conscious messages on safe sex and AIDS all over that *Sturm und Drang* city. Complications of that wretched virus eventually killed him, aged thirty-one. My French pal desired to emulate Basquiat, Taki 183, Quinones and Haring, not to mention Kenny Scharf, Patti Astor, Michael Holman, Futura 2000 and the Zeus of hip-hop himself, Herc.

Hip-hop was by no means a nascent genre in the late eighties in Leyton. I was heavily dependent on pirate radio and Ousman for the new offerings of the moment. We had no MTV at home. The top end of the charts was dominated by kitsch pop songs. But we obtained a salubrious diet from Cypress Hill, Scarface, Dead Prez and LL Cool J. We patiently worked our way across the radio airways. Once we'd successfully separated Naughty By Nature's *OPP* or Eric B and Rakim's *Follow The Leader* from the crackling frequency, we were galvanized. *In this journey, you're the journal. I'm the journalist. Am I eternal or the eternalist?* I wrote rap songs with the aid of instrumental tapes. I performed under the *nom de guerre, The Godfather,* a name adopted from an acclaimed Spoonie Gee number. I was quite okay at rapping. Ousman later created Ruthless Records, which became the largest independent grime and hip-hop distribution company in Britain during the noughties. My younger brothers SI and Seaker dabbled in studios and taped their own songs. Their copacetic rhymes were unfailingly better than anything I ever produced in a recording booth.

De La Soul's debut album *3 Feet High and Rising,* its successor *De La Soul Is Dead,* Arrested Development's *3 Years, 5 Months and 2 Days In The Life Of...,* P.M Dawn's *Of The Heart, Of The Soul And Of The Cross,* and A Tribe Called Quest's elaborately titled *People's Instinctive Travels And The Paths Of Rhythm* were albums I owned after securing a substantive increase in pocket money. Ousman brought home substantive albums that were made infamous by their temerity and subversiveness: Dr. Dre's *The Chronic,* Eazy-E's *It's On 187um Killa,*

Nas' *Illmatic*, Mobb Deep's *The Infamous*, The Fugees *The Score*, Jay-Z's *Reasonable Doubt*. He also delivered VHS cassette recordings of films: *Juice*, *House Party*, *Boyz N The Hood* and *Menace 2 Society*. These movies titles are now deemed classics.

The hip-hop movement is an exsanguinated, spiritus force, in spite of aforementioned corollaries and novelty songs that perforated the charts on occasion like Skee-Lo's *I Wish* Camp Lo's *Luchini AKA This Is It*, Vanilla Ice's *Ice Ice, Baby* and Afroman's *Because I Got High*. Hip-hop consolidated my adherence to language. It possessed boundless transgression, anarchic poetry and rhythmic prose. It weaponized a brand of consciousness, a viable third way from society and home. In return, hip-hop was singed with opprobrium from the media industrial complex and gateway politicians. The genre has been repeatedly sought for censorship since the 1980s, whether visual or verbal.

Everybody is for freedom of speech so long it is *their* freedom of speech. Everybody upholds the liberation of opinions so long as it is theirs and their thought tribe. They tolerate ruffles of disquiet but within limitations. Many pertain to advocate Voltaire but aren't prepared to abide by his misattributed quote: *I disapprove of what you say but **I will defend to the death your right to say it**.* (The phrase was incidentally taken from Evelyn Hall's *The Friends Of Voltaire*, published in 1906 under her pseudonym Stephen G. Tallentyre). Those who cannot defend, *to the death*, speech they consider repellent must stop masquerading as free speech advocates. They must halt their pretence that they are heirs to the Enlightenment and classical liberalism. Of Partners In Kryme, the first hip-hop act to top the UK music charts with their hit single, *Turtle Power*, they promulgate these venerable verses: *Since you was born, be willing and able: to defeat the sneak, protect the weak, fight for rights and your freedom to speak.* Of Public Enemy, who amplified universal truths in their epic anthem, *Fight The Power*: ***Our freedom of speech is freedom or death. We've got to fight the powers that be!*** Of Frederick Douglass, who knew more of liberty than any person born free today, he had this to say: ***Liberty is meaningless where the right*** *to utter one's thoughts and opinions has ceased to exist. That, of all rights, is the dread of tyrants. It is the right which they first of all strike down. They know its power. Thrones, dominions, principalities, and powers, founded in injustice and wrong, are sure to tremble, if men are allowed to reason of righteousness, temperance, and of a judgement to come in their presence. Slavery* **cannot tolerate free speech.** *Five years of its exercise would banish the auction block and break every chain in the South.* Of John Milton, in his oft-praised polemic, *Areopagitica*, he wrote thus: *Let her (Truth) and Falsehood grapple. Who ever knew (of) Truth put to the worst in a free and open encounter?* **Her confuting is the best and surest suppressing.** Which is why I am prepared to defend hip-hop as a collective, whether I agree or not with its expressionist and predatory appetites.

Hip-hop exposed the shame and the saga of the inner street and the outer suburb. Brooding rappers, with riled wounds, said hateful things. But they were within their rights to say them. I'd further argue that any limitation of speech should extend only to protecting the sanctity of the individual, not the sanctimony of ideology. The individual should not be slandered because it is the individual, not her ideas, that are sacrosanct. The immutable components that make us human: i.e., gender, race, sexuality should be ringfenced from trolling and abuse, and awarded protection and guarantees from the law. Defamation and incitement to violence have naught to do with free speech. Perpetrators should face crimination. Ideologies require no such protection, no matter its immersion within the human psychosis and sinew. The Kantian and Koranic lens require scrutiny. Tertullian and Turing must forebear critical observation. Any ideology ought to live by the merit of its truth, or retreat into darkness by the infamy of its falsehood. Divine revelation need not require human protection. Detractors are prone to pick apart any body of work, and rightly so. But they ought to afford the same level of scrutiny upon their body of ideals, rather than jealously guarding whatever it is they hold sacred. The memorialist Francoise Bertaut de Motteville wrote of Cardinal Richelieu in her memoirs published 1723, that *according to the methods of the cardinal himself, who, as I have heard his friends tell, was in the habit of saying that with two lines of a man's handwriting, an accusation could be made against the most innocent, because the business can be interpreted in such a way, that one can easily find what one wishes.* Inferences and aspersions could be depicted in any text, according to one's prejudices. Whether the author's proposes creeping normality, throwback contentions or a revolution too far, it would be miserly to approach his texts in the manner of Richelieu. Why seek a few disapproving sentences to compound the author and her entire handiwork? If you are riled by her writings, you can always close the book!

As my French pal, Kishmeister, Ousman, myself and likeminded others would concur, hip-hop gave rise to a recalcitrant thought process that advocated self-determinism and self-awareness, self-empowerment and self-respect. In these desolate times, authenticity and skepticism are encapsulated as virtues. And what position in life are nobler than an authentic, skeptical disposition? *Be real!* was a common refrain in hip-hop culture. The philosophical injunction on *being real* to oneself and to others is a return to First Principles. We were raised on a bed of nails. We were finetuned into appraising the world in its innumerable facades, in our towns and yonder. By Enceladus, it made us men, not mice. It rendered us tall, not cowered. *They talk. We live. Who cares what they say?* (Jay-Z: *What We Talkin About?* – from *The Blueprint 3*). *We* arbitrate events from a distance, like birds of prey. Like a barn owl, who watches the mice scurry at the faintest hint of sound. As a falcon does when he spies, from the sanctuary of a tree, two animals dueling for territory or spoils. And not unlike the condor, who envisages what lies ahead having traveled far, and made wise by what went before. We need not be like pigeons, flapping our touchy wings to every distraction and disturbance, reacting to every caw and cluck. The information sewage, confected by the *pezzonovante* online, titillates *great vengeance and furious anger.* As Montaigne wrote in his essay titled *Of Vanity: What, then, ought prating to produce, since prattling and the first beginning to speak, stuffed the world with such a horrible load of volumes? So many words for words only.*

My middle-aged ears have become inclined towards contemporary homegrown prophets like George The Poet, Mos Def, Lowkey, Common, Akala, Giggs, Kendrick Lamar and J. Cole, whose earthy, judicious throes reverberate across oceans and through time, from those West African bards who first set the whole thing in motion.

June 18, 2018.

ON FATHERHOOD

M Y LIFE CHANGED IRREVOCABLY on the morning of Sunday
May 06, 2012. I had just become a father. My wife Nyima
was on the phone to her parents in Sweden. Our newborn lay
asleep in a hospital crib. I looked out from the sixth-floor ward
window of the Royal London Hospital. Whitechapel had been
sprinkled by either rainfall or morning dew. I could not tell what
from which. I was ensorcelled. My senses were captive to the
occasion. I felt myself swoon into an unbridled state of euphoria.
I had never before or since experienced such feelings as I did that
day, and in the days that followed. *I am a father. I am a dad.* I loved
my son long before I was touched by Mnemosyne. I will love him
for all of perpetuity, long after I've slipped into oblivion. If you
were to offer me all the perfumes of Arabia, it would be scant
consolation to cradling my son after that spellbinding moment,
when he percolated into life before me with a billowy cry. The
wines in the cellars of ancient Babylon, too, would not suffice.
Neither would the rarest oysters, *in the deep bosom of the ocean buried.*
Ownership of the ancient libraries in Timbuctoo, Athens and
Alexandria might cause my head to turn for a slight scintilla of
a moment, but upon second reflection, they would still fall a few
hundred million miles short of the Pleiades.

I nicknamed him *Wriggles* some months earlier, not knowing whether he'd be girl or boy. We had chosen not to know the gender of our child when Nyima underwent her final scan. We thought it would not matter. It did! The curiosity almost killed me. I lay close to his mother when he was twenty-four weeks old. I watched his tiny limbs making swift crosscurrent waves from within her womb. I named him so, for he sure was a wriggler. He kept that momentum relentlessly up and until birth. By the time the midwife placed him in his mother's arms after what was a very straightforward delivery, he was already sound asleep with barely a murmur.

I took a month from work (two weeks paternity leave plus two weeks annual leave) to support Nyima at home with our child. She was the primary parent. I was facilitator-in-chief. I did everything but breastfeed. That permitted Nyima to rest and recreate at will. I was enthralled and enchanted by his basic flicker and copious twitch, his every belch and hearty sighs, his occasional cough and constant dribble. These moments felt surreal to behold. I'd watch him sleep silently in his cot, awakening within me the verses of Sonnet 29 of Dante Gabriel Rossetti's *Inclusiveness*, which includes the line: *What man has bent o'er his son's sleep, to brood. How that face shall watch his when cold it lies.* I beseeched those words to be truth; that my firstborn, who I gape upon now, will look over me after life has drained from my body. For this firstborn of mine will be entrusted with me when I am no more, and will commit my body into the ground, in whatever town Death contrived to take me.

Simply Red's 1992 hit single *For Your Babies* served as part of the soundtrack to his cradlesong. A particular verse in the chorus *I don't believe in many things, but in you I do* was apt because it spoke on my behalf. Other songs were not dissimilar in tone and poignancy. *Baby Mine*, from the Disney animated film *Dumbo* and mesmerizingly sung by Betty Noyes, was the first lullaby that caused Wriggles to garble in accompaniment to the melody. The soundtrack included *They Long To Be (Close To You)* by The Carpenters, Roberta Flack's *The First Time Ever I Saw Your Face*, The Ronettes' *Be My Baby*, Sweet Child

Of Mine by Guns N Roses, *The Look Of Love* by Dusty Springfield
and *You Are Not Alone* by Michael Jackson. These songs and others
were lulled repeatedly whilst he slept and played.

Nyima and I were deluged with old wives' tales and well-
intentioned advice from family and friends. Their information often
conflicted. We were a team with regard to parenthood. We seldom
quibbled. Our near perfect universe fell afoul to the prejudices that
overshadowed the professionalism of some of the clinicians involved.
A healthcare worker at the local GP praised me for handling my child
before proceeding to ask if I was Nyima's friend? I duly informed
her that the boy was mine. Why on earth, I added indignantly, would
she be prone to think that I was simply a friend of the mother
but not the father of the baby? She was patently embarrassed. But
she was the architect of her own embarrassment. Another bizarre
incident occurred some weeks later when we returned to the clinic
for a routine check-up for Wriggles. A young practitioner asked why
was I *hogging the baby to myself*? She'd watched me cradle him while we
waited half-an-hour in the lobby and may have taken offense that
my son was never in the possession of his mother at any one time.
I had, by then, experienced a handle of these febrile types, who
harbored their own predisposed views of men and fathers. I chose
not to dignify the sow with a comment.

As far as I am concerned, fatherhood is an indispensable duty.
It is not a gratifying raiment to cloak when convenient, and then
remove whenever toilsome. I cannot readily wane or negate this
responsibility. Precarious voices may host divergent opinions on
the status of fathers, or whether in fact fathers *are* needed at all.
Each to their own. I speak solely to the fixed necessities of *my* son,
and *my* future children. Wriggles requires a dutiful temperament,
befitting his needs. *The child is the father of the man*, wrote the English
Romantic poet William Wordsworth. And so it is incumbent that
this *sweet child o mine* is steadily equipped with the prerequisite
tools, that his critical faculties and perceptual facilities enable a
prosperous life. His mother and I build a home, wherein he is safe

for cultivation and erudition. If he were to ask about Santa Claus or the Tooth Fairy, the response will be one no less of truth. I am raising a man, and a man of African descent no less. He cannot be lacking in emotional intelligence. He cannot remain in a state of sophomoric slumber. Whether he comes to me *tabula rasa* or in a state of innatism, preparatory learning from a male perspective must abound and flourish. I must wean the boy from the man at the precise phase of his development. Role models won't do, particularly in this most vacuous of ages. Let the musician rock n roll and trash his hotel room. Let the actor hell-raise herself into a stupor. Let the footballer pursue his orgasmic dream on a ten million pound per year contract. Let the reality TV star sell her soul for less. But let me do my work.

For soon, he will be without the shade of my umbrella. He must forge his own path. I will not live vicariously through him. Nor will I want him to sacrifice any part of himself for me. I love him enough to set him free. I have my own objectives to fulfill, which is why I do not feel guilty when I work long hours and I come home to find him already asleep. One day, he will be his own man. Whatever his decisions of the future, I do not want him thinking or believing that I was a hindrance. The Lebanese poet Khalil Gibran, in his most famous work *The Prophet*, lends some thought on this when asked about children: *Your children are not your children. They are the sons and daughters of Life's longing for itself. They come through you but not from you, and though they are with you, they belong not to you. You may give them your love but not your thoughts, for they have their own thoughts. You may house their bodies but not their souls, for their souls dwell in the house of tomorrow, which you cannot visit, not even in your dreams...* For now, my bosom is his pillow, my shoulders his climbing frame, my sleeve his handkerchief. *O dearest, dearest boy! My heart for better lore would seldom yearn, could I but teach the hundredth part of what from thee I learn.* (Anecdote for Fathers by William Wordsworth).

Thus far, I have written eighty letters addressed to Wriggles. Should I not live to see him become a man, he can read my private thoughts. These letters are for his eyes only. In these private notes, I express myself openly. I am both unrefined and eloquent. I offer distilled advice on how to circumnavigate the crucibles in life's amphitheater. I write about introspection and identity, philosophy and feelings, finance and false consciousness, cinema and social media, politics and peradventure, sex and skepticism. I tell incidents I experienced, situations I shared with nobody. I narrate anecdotes from history and mythology, whereby he can draw lessons and strength from. I relate to him his family's history; his mother's genealogy half a millennia to the lands now known as Senegal, Guinea, Nigeria and Mali, and his father's antecedents that go back even further in time to a part of the world now called Mauritania and The Sahel.

As I write these words, he has stopped playing with his toy monkey, Crazy Legs. He has run up to the table that I am sitting by. He has proceeded to climb onto my shoulders. I must cease writing in case he falls.

June 19, 2017.

WHEN SATURDAY CAME...
AND WENT

T HERE WAS A TIME, not too long ago in England, when football
fans were fed a staple diet of pendulous football matches
that kicked off on Saturdays at 3pm. The football calendar was
unfailingly staid and vanilla. Select fixtures, apportioned in small
doses, were broadcast live to the nation on terrestrial television.
These tentative affairs were set aside for Sundays. Midweek contests
were played on Tuesdays and Wednesdays. Football were often
Trumpian fire and fury embroilments, contested in desiccated
stadiums and on muddy pitches. Tackles registering on the Richter
scale were inexorably made by the likes of Stuart Pearce and Julian
Dicks, Thor and Malaga, Neil Ruddock and Bryan Robson, Vinny
Jones and Terry Hurlock. No quarter granted. No mercy requested.
No metatarsal spared. The wounded party would be upright and
jogging again after a wet sponge was applied on the infringed area.
But it was not only the sledgehammers and sickles that caused
the couloirs to quiver and the gods to wince during these frenetic
encounters. Coruscations and craft emanated from the boots of
Gazza and Sheedy, Beardsley and Barnes, Mirandinha and Merson,
Hoddle and Waddle. *Diamond Lights*. This was before the *fin de siècle* era
of the Premier League when racism, hooliganism, and the tragedies
of Bradford, Heysel and Hillsborough scarred the countenance

of English football. I came to know and love football during this metastasized period.

I was swiftly enamored to Everton Football Club, the aristocrats of English football. It was not a deliberate act of contrarianism. My friends were predominately Liverpool and Arsenal, Tottenham Hotspur and West Ham United. Everton and I have a connubial relationship that has lasted thirty years, plus some. *I did not choose. I was chosen.* At the inhibited age of seven. During the 1984 FA Cup semi-final, after Adrian Heath plunged the winner into the Southampton goal during the dying embers of this fixture, I pledged fealty. I hadn't heard of Everton before then. I was in love with them thereafter. Whenever they played their matches henceforth, I checked the latest scores on *Teletext* and *Ceefax* every ten or so minutes, retreating either heartened or distraught but forever hopeful that a muscular header from Graeme Sharp or a saintly strike from Kevin Sheedy's left boot would contrive a winner into the opposing team's net. The Toffeemen were a *gesamtkunstwerk* in those days. Fellow Evertonian and legendary anchor man Elton Welsby endeavored to summarize the afternoon results on ITV during a small teatime *Final Results* window. The BBC used the sturdy vidi-printer. Through a prelapsarian lens, I watched Everton jostle for league supremacy with Mersey neighbors Liverpool. Meanwhile, the likes of Aston Villa, Chelsea and Manchester City floundered through the First Division trapdoor, screaming. Such are the vicissitudes of empires.

When Saturday came, *Saint and Greavsie*, ITV's flagship football fanzine show with its Aztec Gold theme by Silsoe, was mandatory lunchtime viewing. Jimmy Greaves was laden with banter. Ian St. John appeared to enjoy his wit more than I. These were two master marksmen of their profession, previewing games insouciantly. The BBC's football coverage was more earnest. Perhaps so, because the public collectively paid for the service. They produced a formidable line-up of Bob Wilson, Ray Stubbs, Des Lynam, Tony Gubba, Barry Davies, Jimmy Hill, Trevor Brooking and John Motson. Football was discussed in *mot juste* tones, as if they were seated in an agora, contemplating the civic virtues accentuated within a football framework: excellence, sportsmanship, beauty, mindfulness, skill, majesty, guile, courage, endurance, vision. They debated the dark arts - professional fouls, Fergie Time, and the Hand of God himself.

These were the Saturdays that heralded epic sporting smorgasbords like *Grandstand* and *World of Sport*, with Des Lynam and Dickie Davies as their respective helmsmen. On such a day, before the existence of Sky Sports, I rotated the radio dial to 909 MW and procured BBC Radio 5, and the gang of Jimmy Armfield and Stuart Hall, Alan Green and Mike Ingham for an afternoon of comprehensive football reporting and commentary. These were the times when English clubs, barred from European competition as a result of the Heysel tragedy, took part in a puppet cup competition known as the Simod Cup (later called the Zenith Data Systems Cup). The finals were contested at a sparsely attended Wembley Stadium to little hurrah. These were the days when plucky Luton Town, accoutered with the Stein brothers (Brian and Mark), upset *boring, boring* Arsenal (as they were then known, for their comatose 1-0 victories) in the dwindling throes of the Littlewoods Cup Final. The Gunners were already reeling from Luton goalkeeper Andy Dibble having saved a penalty from the usually dependable Nigel Winterburn. Nottingham Forest were regular guests at the old Wembley Stadium of the Twin Towers, playing against Joe Royle's Second Division outfit, Oldham Athletic, who themselves had the likes of West Ham United, Manchester United and Everton sweating from their cup exploits. I recall the Owls of Sheffield Wednesday. They were Polyphemes in the top Division. Their squad included talents like David Hirst and John Sheridan, Nigel Worthington and Nigel Pearson, until their acute demise in the nineties, of which they have yet recovered. These were the years when Wembley Stadium was the reserve of finals only. Semi-finals were played predominately at Villa Park and Maine Road, Hillsborough and Highbury. Coventry City and the Crazy Gang would win the FA Cup in consecutive seasons. Sutton United, Woking and Wrexham A.F.C were packed with the sling and the aplomb of David, son of Jesse. These were the days of *Nessun Dorma*, the Divine Ponytail, Panini sticker albums, Gazza's tears and *Football Italia* on *Channel 4*. In the midst of the nineties, I careened upon Everton Clubcall, an ingenious means of making money from the bonehead fan, who desired briefings on the latest rumblings from the bowels of their football club. The cost of a call was £1 a minute. My first mobile phone bills were £100 plus monthly affairs. T'was the Internet that killed Clubcall.

The Premier League was the rising tide that lifted some boats. TV revenue and billionaire owners propelled exponential financial progress for football clubs. The devils in the vault were no longer curtailed by tradition. The glamor of the FA Cup has long dissipated. The Champions League is the new Holy Grail. Football is no longer confined to the flintlock months of August and May. Transfer speculation and pre-season tours are adumbrated from May until August, and that is without the elongated spectacle of a World Cup or European Championship. Football is an omnipresent leviathan; the national psyche has long asserted that the game lasts considerably longer than the ninety or so minutes prescribed by the referee. Fans spew their emotional incontinence on radio talk shows if they choose. Suppositions concerning managers and players are strung out like some cheap American soap opera. *The Bold and the Beautiful. The Young and the Restless. Days of Our Lives.* The private lives of footballers are under intense scrutiny, policed by a marauding and nosy public. A seemingly offensive tweet could exhibit fines worth thousands of pounds. Even the colorful aspects of certain managers and club owners have fallen prey to greater emphasis. We have already seen the rise and fall of the WAG. We thank the merciful Lord for that.

This season, dithyrambic fans will flock once again to Anfield Road, Old Trafford or unto any other Dancing Floor of Ares. Pewter skies, torrential rain or hell freezing over will not hold back the devout multitude. Their loyalties will be pushed beyond the brink. But still they flock to these amphitheaters, though the ticket prices burn holes in their pockets. They'd readily pay an *obolus* to Charon, to be ferried across the Styx River, so that they could watch their team play beneath whatever sordid sky in Sarmatia. Such is the price of the Europa League. They will purchase new kits with minimal embroidery changes churned out per season. Ticket prices can be tinkered with at will, bearing no reduction to crowd attendances. Fan(atic)s are blindingly loyal. They sit astride upon every shore and nation, adorned in the colors of their heroes. Football clubs know that whatever is drenched by the rain can be dried by the wind, and so they grow fatter and richer still. My friend Kishmeister had declared, at the end of every season, that he has forever washed his hands of his beloved Tottenham Hotspur. He decried the ardor invested in supporting Spurs was exhaustive; a needless affair that spawned eternal despair. But like Michael Corleone, when he thought he was out, *they pulled him back in.*

I surmise that football is a better sport than it was in the so-called good old days, in spite of vergences like the *Sky Six* (formerly known as the *Sky Four*). The construct of an elite mini-league of six clubs chafes me no end. The media, plus the fans, have ineluctably enabled the *Sky Six* a platform to pursue privileges and power at the expense of other clubs in the Premier League. They will rue that day when it brings forth the collapse of the game as we know it. Clubs look beyond their working-class roots towards a global fanbase and corporate sponsorship. The FA are madly confected in their ambition to sanitize football from human error. The terraces are no longer awash with racist catcalls. The riot police are not summoned too often from their sties. And who would really want to swap Maine Road for the Etihad, Roker Park for the Stadium of Light, Ayresome Park for the Riverside Stadium, save for those who place nostalgia above the promise of a better tomorrow? Soon Everton will abandon the hallowed Old Lady for a new home on the Mersey River. Goodison Park, meanwhile, will reap a greater good for the community it serves. Football, once viewed through *Ceefax*, is observable through a plethora of phone and handheld

devices. Society tends to give us more of our wants, less of our
needs. Whatever found wanting in football, you will find lacking in
the society that inhibits it. But the refulgence for an Everton game
burns as bright as ever.

August 9, 2017.

READING LORRAINE HANSBERRY IN THESE NARCOLEPTIC TIMES

O NE OF THE OLDEST books I currently have in my possession was given to me by my temperate mother. *Les Blancs: The Collected Last Plays Of Lorraine Hansberry* was peculiarly selected from the numerous nondescript books at a summer jumble sale hosted at Barclay Junior School in Leyton during the Britpop era. I still don't know how my mother bartered for that small tome or how much she paid for it. Considering from whence it was purchased, she most likely exchanged it for a few pieces of shrapnel. Book enthusiasts will know the exhilaration of obtaining a most wanted or celebrated book written by a maven at bargain price. This rarely happens to me. The jubilance is all the more delicious when it does happen. Books, that I most desire, frequently cost me an outré penny. I have since developed an insatiable habit for scavenging cult classics in quaint bookshops. Besides, I'd rather take home an impenetrable tome than a comely companion. I've had better luck with impenetrable tomes. Tomes, and most notably companions, should not be judged simply on their aesthetics alone.

Les Blancs: The Collected Last Plays Of Lorraine Hansberry lay idle in my closet. We became reacquainted at some speculative hour months later. I was an unfledged *schmerzensmann* lollygagging, for most hours, in a messy bedroom. I was in the midst of yet another coarsened

period of auto-alienation in a morass of teenage misery. I remember
the time vividly. It was the week when Louis Farrakhan, of the
Nation of Islam, led his Million Man March into Washington DC.
It was the week when Everton Titan Duncan Ferguson got locked
away in a hoosegow named Barlinnie for a haywire on a football
pitch. Amidst smeary paperbacks of Hubert Selby's *Last Exit To
Brooklyn*, Angela Carter's *The Passion Of New Eve*, Paul Schrader's
screenplay *Taxi Driver* and other melancholic leanings, I rediscovered
Lorraine and her revelatory permeations. I had been mad to have
rendered her book idle. I found socio-political discernments in her
mélange of fictions. Her troika of igneous plays adumbrated a sober
light upon the chiaroscuros of human pathology and dialysis. Her
acute scripts unfurled into the expansionary realms of present, past
and dystopia. She died before she completed any of these works.
One can only wonder how those last plays would have truly played
out had she vectored them herself. Her ex-husband and literary
executioner Robert J. Nemiroff was able to reconstruct any unhewn
sketches and scenes.

The first of this ternion of plays is itself called *Les Blancs (The
Whites)*. The title was partially inspired by Jean Genet's theater
piece *Les Negres: Clownerie (The Blacks: A Clown Show)*, which was being
shown in Broadway at around the same time Hansberry was penning
her masterpiece. *Les Blancs* is set in downcast Zatembe, a fictional
African state under the thraldom of a Perfidious Albion. The play
centers around a Mission, where the settlers provide health and
human services to the common people. For Dr. Wily DeKoven,
coming to Zatembe had *saved his life*. For Dr. Marta Gotterling,
coming to Zatembe had *brought fufillment*. The overseer of this facility
is Reverend Nielsen, who considers the people *his children*. That *is*
according to Dr. Gotterling. But more on that later. The protagonist
of this theater piece is a ruminative soul. He carries an onerous
burden upon his lorn vertebrae. He is the Hansberrian Hamlet. He
is *Tshembe Matoseh, the Wanderer, who has come home with the white man's tongue.*
What was said to the Shakespearian Hamlet could be addressed to

him also: *Good Hamlet! (Tshembe). Cast thy nighted color off, and let thine eye look like a friend on Denmark (Zatembe). Do not forever, with thy vailed lids, seek for thy noble father in the dust. Thou know'st 'tis common. All that lives must die, passing through nature to eternity.*

Tshembe had settled happily overseas with his European wife and biracial son. He returns to his gurning motherland for his father's funeral. His father, Abioseh Senior, a figurehead in the revolt, had been commander of a revolutionary militia known as the Freedom of the Land Army. With his father deceased, Tshembe is expected to steer its helm. He is told he is stuck in neutral and couldn't gear himself in taking sides. This is a factor in his indecision on whether to partake in the Terror or return to his young family in England. And though he declares that he has *renounced all spears*, he is haunted by an abstract premonition of what is to come: a female warrior would appear before him and dance to the exhortatory bassline of war. Like Hamlet, he is slow to unsheathe his indignant but ambivalent sword. He is limned by caution and doubt. A contrast of his quandary could also be appliqued to Orestes who, having suffered the murder of his father Agamemnon, kneels before his tomb and prays: *Hermes, Lord of the dead. Look down and guard the fathers' power. Be my savior, I beg you. Be my comrade now. I have come home to my own soil, an exile home at last. Here at the mounded grave, I call my father. Hear me — I am crying out to you . . .*

Tshembe's Romish older brother Abioseh Jr. has assimilated with both European thought (physical) and European religion (metaphysical). He has been anointed as Father Paul Augustus. He is poised to be ordained in the turbulent mantle of Catholic priest. He scorns the *Kwi* robes of his forefathers. He is in chorus with the orisons of his despoilers. He propitiates their good will. He adumbrates their ill-intent. He claims to be committed to God, civilization and Africa. He chides Tshembe for believing in nothing, acting on nothing. *You neither serve God nor man.* He is vehemently opposed to any uprising. He is the Hansberrian Laertes, the insidious, miseducated, misinformed kind that is a benediction to a shrewd devil. He believes the Government of Zatembe will eventually summon the likes of him to be part of the new reigning order because they *cannot go back to the old ways*. Forthwith, they will exist a mutual respect between the likes of him, the new guard, and the old colonial order. There is an interesting scene when the brothers confront each other at their father's funeral: Tshembe is cloaked in the *mystical robes of ancient and contemporary Africa*; Abioseh Jr. is draped in the *mystical robes of medieval and contemporary Europe*. They argue their cultural positions till their back-and-forth becomes a dithyrambic crescendo of *Kwi* incantations and a liturgical Latin cantata, with neither abating. When Tshembe pleads with Ntali (otherwise known as Peter), an insurgency leader, to halt his attacks against the occupiers so that Amos Kumalo, a Jomo Kenyatta replica, can seek a peaceful solution with the colonizers, Abioseh becomes Judas Iscariot and betrays Ntali to Major Rice, the taint chief commander of the colonial troops. Kumalo, having arrived from Great Britain, is arrested. Ntali is shot. This awakens the masses and exacerbates the burgeoning conflagration.

Tshembe's youngest brother Ngedi (otherwise known as Eric) is the spawn of Major Rice, who raped Aquah, the mother of Abioseh and Tshembe. Old Abioseh may have been a gallant knight in the eyes of his countryfolk but he could not succor protection or vengeance for his wife. Aquah dies whilst in the throes of giving birth to Ngedi. Or rather, she was left to die by the Reverend Nielsen who deemed it deserving of her fate for having been raped in the first place. Ngedi would have died also had it not been for the intervention of the Reverend's wife, Madame Nielsen, whom everyone had sanctified like some Lady of Loreto on the account of her Western graces. The young man had grown up, immutably troubled by his origins for which he is blameless. He overcompensates by throwing his entire lot on the side of rebellion. He brooks the coarse admonitions of his brothers. They harbor hauteur aspirations for him. Abioseh wants him schooled at St. Cyprian in the priesthood. Tshembe wants to take him home to

Britain. When he is espouses ambition to fight the colonizers, Tshembe scolds him: *You are half European. Which part of yourself will you drive into the sea?* This, he says, without a tincture of irony and perhaps without a forethought that this corollary could be brought against his own son in later years. Tshembe had named his son Abioseh after his own father and John after his wife's father in recognition of the boy's dual heritage. His lad was conceived in love. Ngedi is a similitude of Zatembe. He is the produce of pillage, conquest and colonialism. Like his country, his gloaming contours appeal to lonesome men from faraway places. Dr. DeKoven ornaments his intimate appetites by plying him with liquor, cigarettes and facial cosmetics. Tshembe sneers at these powders: *If you cannot quite be a white man, you have decided to become a white woman.* He says this, though he lacks Ngedi's bravura and aplomb when it comes to dealing with a common enemy. Ngedi replies: *He* (Dr. DeKoven) *is kind. No one else is kind...* Through his acute worldliness, and his partial detachment from his fellow settlers, Dr. DeKoven is well-sighted enough to see the grotesque political thunderstorm permeating the landscape. *I have saved hundreds of lives,* he says. *All of us here have. I have arrested gangrene, removed tumors, pulled forth babies - and, in so doing, if you please try to understand, I have helped provide the rationale for genocide.* He can, at the very least, appreciate the futility of his activism. *This Mission has been here forty years. It takes perhaps twenty-five years to educate a generation. If you look around, you will not find one African doctor. Until they govern themselves, it will be no different.* The Good Doctor's rationale for this is stark: *The struggle here has not been to push Africa into the Twentieth Century -- but at all costs to keep him away from it!*

The strange case of the piteous gofer known as Peter is worth dwelling on. He is acutely ailing from the double consciousness that Ralph Waldo Emerson, W. E. B. Du Bois, Franz Fanon and others had expounded in their literature. In the presence of the settlers, he genuflects into coughing *Bwana*, master. He is abject and servile. Whether this is some method of survival, servitude or pretense, it must pain his soul to live it. Among his own people, he stands upright. He projects himself with eloquence and purpose. In Tshembe's father's house, he boldly declares that he is not Peter, but *Ntali, the name our people gave me*. He is a spokesman for the People's Council, a democratic body charged with freeing their nation. He chides Tshembe for comparing their plight to Hamlet, a European fable. He relates the tale of Modingo, an African apologue, that bears more relevance to their quandary. Modingo, a hyena, was selected to arbitrate the conflict between the hyenas, who were the native settlers, and the elephants, who subscribed to *Lebensraum* because of their size. Modingo, meaning *One Who Thinks Carefully Before He Acts*, also *sees too much to take sides*. He requests time to contemplate both positions. Whilst he deliberates and procrastinates, the elephants drive out the hyenas and seize the lands for themselves. For this reason, and from that day thereafter, hyenas can always be seen chuckling bitterly to themselves. They were outfought by irrationality while they *reasoned* with their problem. Ntali counseled Tshembe with received wisdom before metamorphosing back into a crouching serf whenever an Englishman or American pranced back into the picture. When Major Rice addresses him as *Ntali* as opposed to *Peter*, he knows his cover is blown. He is cut down in cold blood whilst he flees.

Among the primary characters of *Les Blancs* is American journalist Charlie Morris. He permeates his Western infrared lens onto the African ultraviolet landscape. The shibboleth exchanges between himself and Tshembe ricochet through the pages. Morris cautions in favor of nonviolence and peaceful protest. These propositions were neither options for Hamlet nor Orestes, both of whom share the problem of Tshembe. The problem of Hamlet was *to be, or not to be: That is the question. Whether 'tis nobler in the mind to suffer the slings and arrows of outrageous fortune, or to take arms against a sea of troubles, and by opposing end them. To die: to sleep;* The problem of Orestes was immutably stark: *Neither the life of anarchy nor the life enslaved by tyrants, no, worship neither. Strike the balance all in all and God will give you power.* Morris' own antecedents, presuming they were American at the birth of his own nation-state, did not protest or reason non-violently when wrenching themselves from the manacles of that same Perfidious Albion: ... *And the rocket's red glare, the bombs bursting through air, gave proof through the night that our flag was still there...* Tshembe, having to equate the Zatembe Warrior Woman with Joan of Arc, Queen Esther from the Old Testament and Dolores *La Passionara* Ibárruri, for an American journalist to arrive at an understanding of a people's inalienable right to self-rule, by way of violence, raised a sardonic chuckle from me. As an educated man, Morris would have been schooled in his own country's war against a foreign tyranny; of the Virginian Patrick Henry who made the blunt declaration of *give me liberty or give me death* when calling for the separation of the Thirteen Colonies from the Kingdom of Great Britain; And of Thomas Paine whose robust promulgation was that *when all other rights are taken away, the right of rebellion is made perfect.* And of that great abolitionist and American John Brown who, upon hearing the word *caution* said *I am eternally tired of hearing that word caution. It is nothing but the word of a cowardice.* Hansberry herself had exhorted the *white liberal* to stop being a liberal and become an American radical embodied by the likes of William Lloyd Garrison, Cassius Marcellus Clay, John Brown, Harriet Beecher Stowe, George Thompson and Lysander Spooner. She believed that African Americans should grant no quarter in the pursuit of their natural rights. *Blacks,* she declared, *must concern themselves with every means of struggle: legal, illegal, passive, active, violent and non-violent. They must harass, debate, petition, give money to court struggles, sit-in, lie-down, strike, boycott, sing hymns, pray on steps — and shoot from their windows when the racists come cruising through their communities.*

Initially, Morris was determined to discover Tshembe's political alignments during their discourse - marking, classifying, branding in order to know him. Was he a communist? Had he studied Marx? What did he think of Russia? Did he hate all white men? Tshembe's answer is intimated and thoughtful. *I do not hate all white men - but I desperately wish that I had. But I am afraid that, among other things, I have seen the slums of Liverpool and Dublin and the caves above Naples. I have seen*

Dachau and Anne Frank's attic in Amsterdam. I have seen too many raw-knuckled Frenchmen coming out of the Metro at dawn and too many hungry Italian children to believe that those who raided Africa for three centuries ever loved the white race either. I would like to be simpleminded for you, but - I cannot. I have - seen. By the same token, Tshembe is able to compartmentalize his latent *adorare* for the *white man's daughter* i.e. his European wife, Dr. Marta Gotterling, Madame Nielsen. He speaks of them with refulgence whenever they are mentioned and to almost every character who gives him leave to do so. Morris, to his credit, evolved from his short time in Zatembe. However, he is not quite the radical that Hansberry had envisaged for the likes of him. As he is preparing to leave the country, Tshembe berates his Western infrared lens will permeate the African ultraviolet landscape when he scribbles his bias about Zatembe in America. Morris fires back: ... *Get off my back, you hypocrite! What makes you so holy? A week ago, you gave me a song and dance about the white intellectual 'plumbing' your depths. Well, stop presuming on mine! Stop writing my book. Stop telling me which side to come out on because it's so much easier to fill your eyes with me than to look at yourself ...Tshembe, we do what we can. We're on the same side ...I'm me - Charlie Morris - not the white man.* He is not Reverend Nielsen. He is not Major Rice.

Reverend Neilson and Major Rice masquerade themselves as gods amongst men. These retrenched, paternalistic ogres act without encumbrance or conscience. Their spoliations may have elicited some protest from Morris but they commanded the authority to override any velleity. Major Rice caterwauls about curfews as an effective mechanism for marshalling order. He has a mechanized army to enforce his will. Reverend Neilson has the Lord and Jesus Christ. Which means they are either excused or elided for their actions. Old Abioseh was afflicted by their perverse métiers. He was among those who beseeched the Reverend over the pressing issue of independence. After reading their petition, the Reverend, according to Dr. Wily Dekoven, dispersed the crowd with the queasy words: *Children, children, my dear children. Go home to your huts before you make me angry. Independence indeed!* Thus, the protest ended. Old Abioseh was instinctively aware of his limitations. He could do nothing more but seethe with anger. He did even less when his wife is raped by Major Rice. These instances manifest his powerlessness. Incidentally, Major Rice's own wife had borne him two daughters. They lived happily, presumably in a nice part of Zatembe, a place they call home. Merciful heaven help the man who puts a dirty paw on the hairlock of his womenfolk! All three are in purdah. They are mentioned only in passing. They remain nameless. Notably, the Reverend himself doesn't make an appearance in the play but we do hear of his grisly death. Upon his demise, the younger Abioseh pays a disfigured tribute to the widow of the man who left his mother to die. *Madame, your husband was an extraordinary human being, above race, above all sense of self.* But Abioseh was a man of bathos and intense self-delusion, to state so empathetically that the man responsible for his mother's death was an *extraordinary human being*. This served as a reminder that Man, for the most part, immerses himself in meager slights but cannot avenge grotesque offenses. I recall reading Niccolò Machiavelli's *The Prince* which first alluded me to this type of human extremity. He wrote: *However, one has to remark that men ought either to be well treated or crushed because they can revenge themselves of lighter injuries, but of more serious ones they cannot. Therefore, the injury that is to be done to someone ought to be of such a kind that one does not stand in fear of revenge.* I would expect men like Dr. Rice and Reverend Nielsen to have read this treatise, since it was for such men these words were written.

The donnybrook conversations between the characters in *Les Blancs* resonate to this day, sixty years after Hansberry had committed them ceaselessly to an epidermis exposition for all time. She was never chanced to visit Africa. She was birthed with an Afrocentric cognizance. This metaphysical discernment would not recoil from her writings as an adult. As a child, she recalled looking at the map of Africa. She sought to locate herself therein. Unable to do so, she embraced the entire continent. She recalled watching newsreel footage of Italy's Fascist troops invading Ethiopia. Her mother, Nannie Perry Hansberry, who outlived her by a year, explained that those Fascist Jackboots from Rome had been blessed by Pope Pius XI. Having received a holy invocation from the vicar of Christ on Earth to do God's Will, they proceeded to drop bombs from planes and fire bullets from rifles on a benign people who had neither wronged nor threatened them. Perhaps it was this deplorable rogation between Church and State that first gave rise to her heuristic atheism. Her mother enjoined upon her to never forget what Catholicism stood for. Hansberry's sufficient conviction in the potentiality of Man would solidify her humanism.

As she grew in years, revolution became more widespread in the world. Many had tired from the shackles of colonialism. The so-called Mau Mau insurgency began in Kenya against British tyranny in the 1940s. That insurrection may have served as an inspiration to *Les Blancs*. Hansberry hoped, as did other prominent Pan Africanists of that time like Marcus Garvey, George Padmore, Edward Wilmot Blyden, Henry Sylvester-Williams, W.E.B Du Bois, Paul Robeson, C.L.R James and Malcolm X, that an independent Africa would be enclitic towards the Civil Rights Movement in the diaspora. Imperialists, however, seldom relinquish power willfully. Their imputations are inverted into the conduits and organs of the territories they had incubated for centuries. These essences remain, generations after the ceremonial lowering and raising of flags, and the florescent explosion of Roman candles. After independence, many figureheads of a new dawn betrayed their revolutionary ideals. The promise of a new era rapidly dissipated. As Hansberry herself pointed out: *Rebellion seldom knows what it wants to do once it has finished rebelling.* These figureheads and their cadre became rich and powerful. They sought to remain in power until their deaths. The figureheads that kept to their ideals, Thomas Sankara, Pierre Ngendandumwe, Amilcar Cabral, Kwame Nkrumah, Patrice Lumumba and Abubakar Balewa among others, were either removed from power or martyred.

African soil remains the nacre of the earth. It is neither *Paradise Lost* nor is it *Paradise Regained*. When I was a kid, a friend of my father told me that God dropped His wallet in the Congo. I did not quite understand his point at the time. I soon learnt what he meant. The world's largest quantities of diamonds, cobalt ore, carbon and copper lie under Congolese soil. Approximately 50% of all the forests in Africa lie within the borders of this immiserated and beleaguered country. The long-proposed Grand Inga Dam, the largest of its kind in the world if finally constructed, could provide hydro-electric power for the entire African continent. But mighty Congo has never been free from the gluttony of imperial post-independence. The Belgians found God's wallet. They were hardly going to hand it back. Cold War lunacy cut the throat of the newly formed government in Kinshasa. Blood poured into Lake Tanganyika. A *broigus* between factions spiraled further slaughter, rape and mutilations. The native viverrids, who presumed to have the levers of power, allowed American hyenas and Belgian gaurs to moil in an international treasure fest amidst the rotting carcasses of dead natives. Patriots like Patrice Lumumba were executed by a recreant firing squad. His remains were dismembered and dissolved in sulfuric acid by the *shaitan* of the night. Mighty Congo broke into an internecine civil war, of which we find few parallels in the latter 20th century. Elsewhere, many African nations were overwhelmed by their respective vale of troubles. The aspiration that Africa could support her diaspora against homegrown systemic racism rapidly dissipated. She became asphyxiated by the rapaciousness of her ruling class. Many heads of state became infected with *Big Man Syndrome*, a lifelong ailment, whose antidotes include coup d'état's, exile and assassination. Neopatrimonialism became the state religion in these parts. It is practiced more heartily than Christianity and Islam.

Today, Europe have not foreclosed on Africa. France and the United States flex their *kratos* muscles by air and land, sea and outer space. More than a dozen francophone nations surrender four-fifths of their banking reserves to Paris. Other currency obligations and colonial encroachments are by the diktat of the French government, whether they be socialist or conservative. China exerts soft power expositions through its *Belt and Road Initiative*. Her appetites and exigencies are cloaked in a devoir robe. Her commodious ambitions are camouflaged in her benevolent quenching of Africa's dire thirst and infinite need for infrastructure. These Pan Twardowski pacts have their diminishing returns in parentheses and caveats. These Yuan bills are blinding like the Sun. It would be interesting to note at what mark doth China's soft power ossify? When will the awakened dragon breathe fire? We can keep an open mind, if you will for the sake of prejudice, and not mind the banality of trade between nation states. Or we can turn to history to elucidate ourselves further on past appetites and exigencies of foreign powers cloaked in devoir robes. While it is often reactionary to blame foreign roguery on the perverse saturations occurring over swathes of the African continent, kleptocracies oft-return to the old hierarchical colonial powers and the emerging heliacal 21st century ones to partake in their domestic spoils. It is an oft-repeated sequel of the *Belladonna Of Sadness*, of the ironclad claw. I am not unopposed to partnerships of African states with their European or Asia counterparts which are of mutual benefit to both parties. Plenty good things have emerged from Europe and Asia. And as Tshembe says in *Les Blancs*: *Europe – in spite of all crimes – has been a great and glorious star. Other stars shone before it – and will again after it. The heavens, as you (Madame Nielson) taught me, are broad and can afford a galaxy.*

In *Les Blancs*, liberation could only rise from a field of fire and a sea of blood. Traitors like Abioseh would irremediably perish. The settlers, no matter their politics, were not demarcated souls. Neither were they Snow White. These mercenaries, mastodons, moonrakers and meatheads drunk their fill with unbridled avarice. They reclined untrammeled on the lush grass. They bathed in the warm waters in this *heart of darkness*. They made themselves landlords by force of might. Their hosts were reduced to serfs and made subjects to a foreign, immanent usurper sat on an alien throne. Madame Nielsen, looked upon as a prepossessing matriarch by Tshembe and others because of her imperial preening, had stayed in this African everglade for forty years. She had partaken of her many privileges. Everybody addressed her *Madame* as an accretion. She remained an unshriven, venal handmaiden of empire. She possessed the vague mindedness of E.M Forster's Mrs. Moore from *A Passage To India*. Her description of the early seeds of the revolution demonstrates her aloofness to the people's right to self-determination and self-rule: *Some cold wind blew in over our people here and chilled their hearts to us. It's the times, you know. I'm afraid he'll never understand it - the Reverend. And what hurt most was Abioseh was the first to change. Old Abioseh, the husband, the husband of Aquah, my friend - a truly remarkable man. First Abioseh - and after him the village - then the tribe.* She is like Queen Gertrude, steadfast to both her former brother-in-law and husband Claudius and her vexatious son, Hamlet. By neither mourning nor showing guilt over the murder of the king, her former husband, she creates irretrievable damage to Hamlet. One could infer that, in Madame Neilsen's case, Claudius is the Reverend. Both Tshembe and Hamlet are more forgiving than I. I would not be so magnanimous. Neither would I have hesitated. By her maintenance of the status quo, she *is* part of the problem. Tshembe leaves it to the final scene to ask why did the Reverend permit his mother to die, whom she had previously described as her *dearest friend I have had in Africa*. And she replies (without answering the question): *Because, my child, no man can be more than the man he is. He was a white man in Darkest Africa — not God, but doing God's work — and to him it was clear; the child was the product of an evil act, a sin against God's order, the natural separation of the races.* Except that he had not been doing God's work. He *played* God. He did not tremble with biblical angst for the dead mother or her orphan child. He only exhibited biblical coldness. Neither was their biblical condemnation and justice charged against the rapist. Colonel Rice was above God's Law, never mind his diabolical works.

Only after her Reverend was butchered did Madame Nielsen encourage Tshembe to join the uprising. She refused to speak in her husband's name after receiving the news (and despite Charlie Morris' protestations) that Kumalo had treacherously been arrested and the country teetered on a powder keg. Perhaps she had subscribed to the adage often attributed to Stalin that one death was a tragedy and a million deaths a statistic. After the death of her tragedy, she could now forebode the nameless, faceless quantity. *Well, now. The darkness will do for this hour, will it not?* she tells herself. It was the fifty-ninth minute of the eleventh hour. When Tshembe finds her, he is still dreamy Hamlet: *I want to go home (to London)*, he tells her. *It seems your mountains have become mine.* He could no longer think of himself as Kwi. Only a man. Madame Neilson extols him to become a warrior. When Abioseh appears and tries to justify his betrayal of Ntali, she, more or less, says nothing to him. *I know he* (Reverend Nielsen) *would have approved of what I did*, he says. *There was no other way to handle the Terror. Madame, don't you agree? Well, it will be over for good now. If men choose violence, they will be met by violence. Am I right, Madame?* He was right. In the denouement of *Les Blancs*, justice was duly served. Tshembe slays Abioseh for his simpatico with the oppressor, and then closes his eyes. Ngedi destroys the Mission with a grenade. The insurgents move in on Major Rice's troop positions. Madame Nielsen is felled by an unintended bullet. Tshembe emits an animal-like cry of grief. And thus the play ends. And upon reading *Les Blancs* for the first time, my prehensions on racial, political and social matters with regards to their nuanced fault lines were considerably enhanced. These prehensions are still evolving. Truth is often said to be stranger than fiction. Fiction has opened many doorways to truth.

Lorraine Vivian Hansberry was inspired into becoming a playwright after watching a dramatized performance of Sean O'Casey's play *Juno and the Paycock*, a pensive, permafrost account of the languid

Boyle family. She was already finetuned to the biorhythmic skirmishes of everyman with her *sighted eyes and feeling heart*. Her prudent
and forensic narratives sequent human striations that sire immortal
storytelling. These accounts illuminate characters whose exchanges
and ecumenisms are expansive and rich. Their conundrums reverberate the world over. They redound in my mind's eye, twenty-five
years on from having first read them. Hansberry had arrived at an
enlightened carrefour that, *in order to create the universal, you must pay
very great attention to the specific*. In W.E.B Dubois' celebrated book *The
Souls Of Black Folk*, he wrote ... *the Negro is a sort of seventh son, born with
a veil, and gifted with a second sight in this American world...* Hansberry
extrapolated this proclivity of *a seventh son gifted with a second sight*
in her plays, and most particularly, in her *magnum opus: A Raisin In
The Sun*. The aural melody of the Younger Family was ameliorated
from her own tentative beginnings in tentative America. Her father
Carl Augustus Hansberry had worked tirelessly to adhere to the
liberalities of the *American Dream*. He was a real estate broker and
a member of the Chicago Republican Party. He was a supporter
of the two leading African-American civil rights groups of the
time, the *N.A.A.C.P* and the *Urban League*. And he was the founder
of the *Lake Street Bank*, one of the first banks established primarily
for the financial provisions of African Americans in the city of
Chicago. As a result of his efforts, he was better heeled than most
and very well-connected. Shakespearean dramatist Paul Robeson,
Olympian gold medalist Jesse Owens, jazz musician Duke Elling-
ton (among others) all passed through his front door and talked
politics. Incidentally, his older brother William Leo Hansberry
taught anthropology to Nnamdi Azikiwe, the first President of
Nigeria, and to Kwame Nkrumah, the first President of Ghana,
whilst they were both students in America.

    Carl Augustus campaigned for a seat in the United States Con-
gress. He was ultimately unsuccessful. During the Great Depression,
he purchased a home in the Washington Park subdivision Southside
of Chicago at 6140 S Rhodes Avenue. He encountered vehement

opposition from the American-Caucasian community. They insisted on permanent separation from their African-American counterparts. Whilst he warred with tailor-suited, reprobate racists in the courtroom, his wife Nannie Louise Perry kept the mewing, foaming mob at bay from her children with her German Luger pistol. A block of cement, hurled through a window of the Hansberry home, narrowly missed the infant Lorraine. The Supreme Court of Illinois ruled in favor of *restrictive covenants*, an edict that made it unlawful for American-Caucasians to sell property to African-Americans. An appeal was lodged with the United States Supreme Court. A landmark decision *Hansberry v Lee* unanimously reversed the lower courts' ruling on a technicality that invoked the Fourteenth Amendment of the United States Constitution. The judges, however, failed to countenance the problem of restrictive covenants nationwide. The Hansberry matter was treated as an anomalous case. The canker sores of racism took their toll on Carl Augustus. He decided to emigrate. He died in Mexico of a cerebral hemorrhage in the midst of moving his family there. He was but fifty years old.

I had often thought of that narcoleptic soundbite: *The American Dream*. The late American comic George Carlin noted rather sardonically that *you would have to be asleep to believe in it*. I had also thought of the narcoleptic Great British equivalent, the romanticized notion that if you worked hard and played cricket, you would succeed, whatever your sport. You could make that argument if you believed Great Britain was free from partiality and bias, bellicism and bigotry, class and race, and that unintended prejudice could not (and would not) lead to unintended consequences. If one were of African, Asian or Caribbean heritage, it was not uncommon to be given the calcified injunction that apply twice the gumption and reserve as your Caucasian correlative and then success, plus all its trimmings, would be yours. Outliers have either abandoned or hadn't subscribed to this idiom because of the unkind legerdemain served. I've listened to *white* working-class lads raising Cain and gnashing their teeth at the scorn and infractions exhibited by the illiberal elite coalition that exhorts its dictation. An incomparable struggle to the one I am accentuating in this essay but nevertheless, a salient one. *The struggle is real*. In this season, actors have delegitimized the cry of *Black Lives Matter* by cawing *All Lives Matter* which, if all lives did matter in the first instance, we would not have a race problem. By definition. We would not have tectonic disparities in society that conspicuously phlebotomize along color lines institutionally and culturally, especially in the areas of law, education, employment and economy if indeed we believed we all bled red regardless, and that was all that mattered. At the very least, irrespective of the politics of this issue, the subject of race is a disputatious matter whenever I have heard it argued in the public square. *All animals are equal but some animals are more equal than others.* At least Napoleon, the porcine prince of *Animal Farm* unmasked the creeping pretense to any perceived equality on Manor Farm. It is worth noting that, by the end of George Orwell's novella, the other farm animals could not distinguish between the physical comportments and behavioral practices of their former masters (the farmers) and their current rulers (the pigs) when both parties gathered for a celebratory dinner to commemorate their new alliance. The pigs that had professed that *four legs good, two legs bad* changed that dictum to *four legs good, two legs better* once they themselves had learnt to walk on their hind legs. I digress but it is worth the digression when we consider the power play dynamic of the oppressed mind when it assumes power. The pigs, wittingly or no, had embraced the cardinal habits of their former oppressors.

Upon reading T.E Lawrence's *Seven Pillars Of Wisdom*, I was invigorated by a surrealist text that felt more apt than adhering to the narcoleptic, tribal hubris' of the dream come true: *All men dream: but not equally. Those who dream by night in the dusty recesses of their minds wake in the day to find it was vanity: but the dreamers of the day are dangerous men, for they may act their dreams with open eyes, to make it possible.* I have subscribed to both text and texture of this passage. *Seven Pillars Of Wisdom* is an imponderable tome, impenetrable in places like the

Nefud Desert. It demanded the digestive metabolism of a boa constrictor. *Je rêve donc je suit - I dream. Therefore, I am*, to paraphrase French philosopher René Descartes. American poet and playwright Langston Hughes (from whom Hansberry borrowed a phrase that titled her most famous work) posited an analogous question in his poem *A Dream Deferred: What happens to a dream deferred?* He asks. *Does it dry up like **a raisin in the sun**? Or fester like a sore — and then run? Does it stink like rotten meat? Or crust and sugar over — like a syrupy sweet? Maybe it just sags like a heavy load. Or does it explode?*

We waft in choppy waters, punctuated by bitted tides. *The struggle is real.* Let us consider the lilies of the playing fields that toil and spin: few are arrayed with the gold of Solomon. Thieves have long pillaged his mines. And it is they, and not the girls that Beyoncé Knowles championed in her declarative feminist anthem, who *run the world.* And if one were to live but a generation from slavery, one may have justifiable reason to initiate their cause and graft to life, liberty and the pursuit of happiness as fervently as Carl Augustus Hansberry did. His youngest child Lorraine was moved to learn, in the needle's eye of time, of the arbitrariness of a system rigged against her for no other cause, save *she was Black and female.* The entrails of America would regurgitate inveterate crimes that continue to beset the interiorities of an entire group of people. Before her twentieth birthday, Hansberry had countenanced the following: the murders of Harriette and Harry Moore, of the *N.A.A.C.P,* by the Ku Klux Klan. The couple were bombed in their own home. They died within days of each other. They were the first martyrs of the Civil Rights era. There was the blinding of U.S serviceman Isaac Woodard, hours after being honorably discharged from the American Armed Forces. After an innocuous exchange with the bus driver over his use of a restroom at a service stop, he was set upon by law enforcement officers who blinded him. No one was ever convicted for this heinous crime. He spent the remainder of his life without sight. There was the eighty-three-day charging, conviction and execution of fourteen-year-old George Stinney by the state of South Carolina in 1944 for the murder of two American-Caucasian girls. Stinney's conviction was overturned in 2014 by a South Carolina judge, on the grounds of the egregious violations of his Sixth Amendment rights. Another American soldier, Booker T. Spicely was shot dead (in the heart and liver) by a bus driver for refusing to vacate his seat, and this was in the decade before Lillie Mae Bradford, Sarah Louise Keys, Irene Morgan, Aurelia Browder, Claudette Colvin, Susie McDonald, Mary Louise Smith and Rosa Parks chose not to vacate theirs.

In Hansberry's *A Raisin In The Sun*, the *American Dream* undergoes intense scrutiny. Among its subplots, I stumbled upon Joseph Asagai, a Yoruba student, who teaches Beneatha Younger about the way of the Yoruba, and the pangs of self-determinism. He calls her *Alaiyo* (One For Whom Bread Is Not Enough). His worldview contrasts with Beneatha's older brother Walter and the other African American males in the play if we can, for a moment, bramble the mulligan stew of their masculinity. It was as if the African American males in this play had been baptized in the River Acheron at birth. Walter and Joseph's prerogatives are marked of a different bine. Joseph is studying in the West so that he can prepare for the thankless task of nation building in the new Nigeria. He is not shackled to the tumult of America. He is in America for her advantages. Walter must contend with the claustrophobia and excrescences of *black* manhood *in* America. The United States is the only home he knows. He is thirty-five years. He is prepossessed by an immutable paralysis that marked his entire existence. There are no signs of this abating. He is married with a child. He has a blind alley job as a limousine driver. His stipend is paltry. He yearns to invest in a liquor store, of all things: and with Bobo and Willy, of all people. He requires a substantial portion of his late father's insurance check to fund this ambition. Lena Younger is the implacable matriarch and cornerstone of the Younger family. She objects to the liquor business on religious grounds. Nevertheless, she is empathetic to Walter's plight. After she pays a deposit on a new home for the family, she hands him the rest of the money on the condition that he puts aside some money for Beneatha's education. But Walter hands the entire money to Bobo, who entrusts Willy to secure the investment on the liquor store. Willy flees with the cash. Walter's business aspirations are crushed. Beneatha is understandably livid. She is considerably more able than her brother. Yet her educational aspirations are lost to him recklessly because he is firstborn, and their mother desires that he exerts his birthright and that his manliness be soothed, even if it be at the expense and inexertion of her autonomy and womanhood. Meanwhile, George Murchison, Beneatha's boyfriend, is assimilated, educated and affluent. He sneers at Walter's lamentations, his lassitude, his lack of learning. Beneatha finds this disconcerting. She discards him. Joseph's thought process is comparatively radical. He rebukes Beneatha for bemoaning the loss of her inheritance. He is critical that she straightens her hair. Nevertheless, she is left considering his marriage proposal and a new beginning in the new Nigeria. While the Youngers prepare to move into their new home in Claybourne Park, their prospective new neighbors offer to buy them out so that they can keep their neighborhood *white*. Walter speaks for his family by rejecting the buyout offer. He had contemplated accepting it. The play ends with the Youngers immobilizing their exodus from their old neighborhood. Whether Claybourne Park becomes their Promised Land is uncertain, but this play is a *mirabile dictu* that resonates. It is devoid of the hubris of the American Dream. It is testament of the American character.

The success of *A Raisin In The Sun* propelled Hansberry into the stratosphere. She became the first African-American dramatist winner of the *New York Drama Critics' Award*. She was only twenty-nine years old. She was the hottest writer in the city. The play made its Broadway debut on March 11, 1959, at the Ethel Barrymore Theater. One of the foremost American journalists of that era Mike Wallace proclaimed that Hansberry was *exceptional for her race*. These liberal expiations were readily construed as praise, even among the erudite and urbane. It is still not uncommon to hear stupefied condescension among tyro, cosmopolitan nabobs, never mind starchy, conservative nabobs in cerebral quarters. I should hasten to add that, though I was not alive to have seen the original stage play, I've watched the 1961 film version countless times. Sidney Poitier (Walter Younger), Claudia McNeil (Lena Younger), Ruby Dee (Ruth Younger), Louis Gossett Jr. (George Murchison) and Diana Sands (Beneatha Younger) reprised their stage characters for the cinema screens. Though the film centered on the lamentations and maturations of Poitier's Walter, Claudia McNeil produced a fulgurating performance as Walter's mother. Her spellbinding dramatization is one of the best I've seen on cinema. Hansberry placed the transcendent philosophy of unconditional love into her mouth after Beneatha bemoaned the loss of her inheritance. She chides her daughter thus: *Child, when do you think is the time to love somebody the most? When they done good and made things easy for everybody? Well then, you ain't through learning — because that ain't the time at all. It's when he's at his lowest and can't believe in hisself 'cause the world done whipped him so! When you starts measuring somebody, measure him right, child, measure him right. Make sure you done taken into account what hills and valleys he come through before he got to wherever he is.*

McNeil's own life was afflicted by personal tragedy. Her husband was killed in World War II. She lost both her sons in the Korean War. This brilliant woman, who was fluent in Yiddish, was only nominated for a Golden Globe Award for a depiction on celluloid that deserved a win among the industry's most sacred prices. The character of Beneatha Young, played by Diana Sands, was chiseled from a younger origination of her creator Hansberry. She even supplements the precepts of Hansberry's atheism. *It's all a matter of ideas,* she tells her mother Lena, *and God is just one idea I don't accept. It's not important. I am not going out and commit crimes or be immoral because I don't believe in God. I don't even think about it. It's just that I get so tired of Him getting credit for all the things the human race achieves through its own stubborn effort. There simply is no God! There is only Man, and it's he who makes miracles!* Tragically, Sands died a month short of her fortieth birthday from leiomyosarcoma, a rare form of cancer. I should also hasten to mention a recent reincarnation of *A Raisin In The Sun* starring Phylicia Rashad, Sean Combs and Sanaa Lathan, where the emotivism, pulsation and tenacity was homologous of its 1961 predecessor. Combs played a fitful, durable Walter Younger, ploughing forlornly through a predisposed America, not unlike the *angry young man* role played by the Indian acting phenomenon Amitabh Bachchan in the irrefutable classic *Deewaar*. Bachchan's Vijay ploughed forlornly through a predisposed India until his heartrending demise in his mother's arms, in the consecrated grounds of a *Mandir*. Yet the Youngers and the Vermas from *Deewaar* could have cited Claudius' admonition to Hamlet when cautioning Walter and Vijay before he found his senses. All three characters were firstborn of their mothers, as I am the firstborn of mine: *We pray to you, throw to earth this unprevailing woe, and think of us, as of a father. For let the world take note. You are the most immediate to our throne.*

In the Year of Our Lord, Nineteen Hundred and Fifty-Nine, when Hansberry began writing *The Drinking Gourd*, presidential candidate John Fitzgerald Kennedy, author of *The New Frontier* and the beloved of so many African Americans, did not consider civil rights a priority. He preferred not to offend the Jim Crow South. Few politicians are practitioners of moral conviction. Events, as it was with these whirligigs, forced his helming hand. America, in the penumbra of the Civil Rights Movement, approached the centennial anniversary of her Civil War. NBC producer Dore Schary commissioned a five-part series to mark the occasion. *The Drinking Gourd*, the second play in Hansberry's *Les Blancs* collection, was written with that mainspring in mind. The play was never shown on television. It was deemed too perverse for Middle America. I had already read Alex Haley's derivative (but less plaintive) tome *Roots: The Saga Of An American Family* before I even knew of *The Drinking Gourd*. *Roots*, the ground-breaking novel published in 1976, was primarily about Kunta Kinte, the young Mandinka warrior from *Kamby Bolongo*, and his descendants fettered to the so-called New World, unfettered from the soil of their ancestors. *Roots* was twee (yet epic) in comparison to the more compendious *The Drinking Gourd*. Another consequential book, of a similar vein given to me by my earnest mother, was *The Autobiography of Miss. Jane Pitmann*, written by the recently departed Ernest J. Gaines. The protagonist of the story, Jane Pitmann, lived for more than a century. She had gone from slavery to sharecropping, all the while seeking her rightful share of American citizenry whilst the marrow of American history loomed large in the backwater. Hearkening to those days, I remember reading *Adventures of Huckleberry Finn* by Mark Twain, an uninhibited tale that was, of course, about young Huck Finn, but also featured the story of fugitive-slave Jim who sought a pathway to emancipation along the shimmering Mississippi River. *Uncle Tom's Cabin* by Harriet Beecher Stowe featured Uncle Tom, probably the most misrepresented character I have read thus far in literature. His character, and its corruption, is worthy of an essay all unto itself. And there was Toni Morrison's *Beloved*, based on Sethe, who slays her infant Beloved rather than permit her spend a lifetime in slavery, having escaped her slaver. An indefatigable spirit, believed to be Beloved, haunts her home thereafter. The concurrences of these books are unsettling and unconscionable upon first reading. But perusals of this nature aren't supposed to be a passive pastime, scrutinized in some comfort zone perfumed in frankincense, whilst sipping a ten-pound triple latte served with pumpkin spice from Starbucks. After a reading break which would regularly consist of an ice-cold ginger beer no less, I'd often face east. I thanked God I was born in the late twentieth century, decades after the terror of two apoplectic world wars, in this verdant Jerusalem. Had I been born three centuries earlier, in the land of my fathers, and opted for a stroll alongside the Atlantic Ocean *easy like Sunday morning*, I maybe bound, chained and sent seabound to the so-called New World, to live and die as a slave; that was if I hadn't perished first in the noisome cargo hold of some merchant ship during that phantasmagoric voyage and have my carcass cast into the sea, feasted on by exophthalmic creatures of the Deep, five fathoms down.

The Drinking Gourd examines the granularities of a slaver society. The play derives its name from an old spiritual folk song *Follow The Drinking Gourd*. A mythical abolitionist named Old Peg Leg Joe was said to have led souls conditioned into servility through the Underground Railroad. Ambiguous verses extrapolate cryptic directions for the would-be fugitive. It suggests the time of year for flight. Its superintendence instructs the runaway to follow Polaris, the North Star, through north-eastern Mississippi and into Tennessee, by way of Tombigbee River at the end of Woodall Mountain and *a neighboring lower hill*, according to the folklorist H.B Park's interpretation of the song. On the other side of the mountain runs the Tennessee River. *'Nuther riva on the other side. Follers the drinkin' gou'd*. Then the Tennessee River conjoins with the Ohio one. *Wha the little riva meets the grea' big un*. The verse concludes that *the ole man waits* (most probably not Old Peg Leg Joe himself, but some Moses, Oskar Schindler, Harriet Tubman-type apostle). He'd carry the runaway over the Illinois state border, and into *freedomland. Foller the drinkin' gou'd*. The fugitive's journey could take an entire year. The escapee had to make-do with wild fruit, fowl and river water. And whatever provisions he could procure by theft.

Hansberry's acuity for such a story sprung from her *wrinkled as a prune* grandmother, who was born a slave. Her hardy recollections were unlike the cosseted aesthetics and overarching fictions of *Gone With The Wind*, one of cinema's colossal epics. Hansberry's mother would point out the hills overlooking Kentucky where her own father would hide from his slaver. His mother would leave food for him among the slopes in the moonlight. There are no handbags nor gladrags in *The Drinking Gourd*. There is neither bathos or melodrama, accompanied by a solemn orchestral score laden with stringed instruments. The Africans were coffled across counties from slave market to plantation, plantation to plantation. Like beasts of burden. Whilst they ploughed, sowed and toiled,

America was birthed from the bowels of the Enlightenment of Europe. She took her place among the world's leading nations, clad in robes of piety. Because, as Hansberry wrote *It is difficult for the American mind to adjust to the realization that the Rhetts' and Scarletts' were as much monsters as the keepers of Buchenwald. They just dressed more attractively, and their accents were softer.*

The Drinking Gourd converged on four encrustations of the American antebellum: the slaver, the slaves, the poor Caucasian southerner (pejoratively described as *white trash*) and the overseer. At the start of the play, Hansberry's narrator, an American-Caucasian male, dressed in nineteenth century military fatigues, illustrates those flinty days with an expedient brush: *There is no education to pay for... Some of the harshest laws in the slave codes are designed to keep slaves from being educated. Maiming, mutilation or death is the penalty for those who teach, even for white men. No wages, no maximum work hours or minimum wage. No trade unions.* The narrator reminds his audience that *please do not forget that this is the nineteenth century. It is a time when we still allow little children — white children — to labor twelve and thirteen hours in the factories and mines of America. We do not yet believe that women are equal citizens who should have the right to vote. It is a time when we still punish the insane for their madness...*

The first encrustation is in the person of slaver, Hiram Sweet. He is particularly proud of his uncultured roots. He constantly makes references to them. He is less of a brute than his slaver counterparts. His slaves labor nine-and-a-half hours a day. He favors his captive Rissa. She was one of four captives from which he built his plantation. With America on the cusp of a civil war, he foresees the end of these slave camps. His crops are failing. And so is his health. Though the cost of maintaining a slave *amounts to seven dollars and fifty cents* per annum, the plantation is barely churning a profit. His eldest son Everett is at odds with him over its management. His sawbone Bullett sides with his firstborn. Bullett and Everett are men of prime beef education. Everett is ashamed of his father's boorish beginnings. Over dinner, the three men debate the impending civil war. Hiram reckons the Southerners would lose. Everett is fanatically opposed to the vile North. He suggests *the blacks* be armed in the war against them. His father and the sawbone react with stilled horror. Such ideas are inconceivable. The thought process was that if *blacks* festered a bloodlust for killing *whites*, it would be akin to opening the Seven Gates of Hell. This was the single point of order that Sweet Senior and his sawbone agreed upon in the entire play. Everett accuses his father of neglecting the plantation to ruin. He is hopeful new legislation in America will reopen the slave trade. President Thomas Jefferson had overseen a federal edict that forbid the importation of human cargo from Africa as of January 1, 1808, but that was fifty years ago and some. Everett has designs to put the slaves under the yoke of wolfish overseers (parasites, as Hiram calls them) so that the plantation can sublimate *ten bales to the hand*. Hiram is satisfied with half that much. But his health is worsening. Bullett advises he quit field work and indulge in reading and afternoon naps, and to change the produce of his plantation to cotton. Hiram is equally dismissive of Bullett, hailing him as a blue-blood from *a long line of lace-hankied, Bordeaux wine-sniffers*.

Rissa uses her favor with Hiram to protect her son Hannibal. She lurks in the shadows till dinner is finished. She approaches him *sittin there now, white as cotton, sweatin' like you see the Horseman comin*. They reminisce about the good old days. Rissa is the last of his four original slaves. Ezra and Zekial had long escaped. Leo was dead. Rissa pleads that her Hannibal be made a house slave, which she felt was better than a field one. Hiram agrees to her request, much to the annoyance of his wife Maria. But he brazenly asserts his authority as if he were God Almighty Himself. ... *I am the master of this plantation and every soul on it. I am the master of those fields out there and I am the master of this house as well... When the Maker wants me, let him come for me in the place where He should know better than all I can be found.*

Hannibal is the indomitable, ignoble hero of this play. This deadpan radical was raised on a plantation with *more ears than leaves*. I could barely imagine his life of living death, this eternal realm of taphophobia. His slave master is the similitude of Father, Son and

Holy Ghost. His slave master is analogous to Satan, Anti-Christ and False Prophet. Asmodeus is his overseer. The Ifrits drive him in the fields irrespective of the smiting wind, the torrential rain, the scorching sun. And the jackal Coffin serves as the supererogatory snitch. Hannibal is nineteen years old. He yearns for liberty, his right by nature. His small acts of rebellion provide an inlet of dignity. He purposely damages tools. He toils slowly. He is absent for hours at a time. He believes *every slave ought to run off 'fore he die*. Most pertinently, he learns to read on pain of death. Rissa uses her favor with Hiram to protect him, and so he is seldom scolded or lashed. Her older son Isaiah had escaped the plantation after his wife was sold to another slaver.

The prohibition of literacy was a diabolical, egregious conceit, the capacity for literacy an unsung Promethean gratuity. These values have depreciated in our times with the contraction of abecedarian reading. Impoverished forms of communication such as text speak have diminished language. Prohibitive impositions on books and the promotion of depreciatory learning are, by no means, incidental. It remains a systemic contrivance, predicated upon fear, asseverated upon keeping people uninitiated and ignorant. This monstrosity manifested itself when I, as a child, first watched the *Roots* mini-series with my family. Kizzy Kinte, daughter of Kunta Kinte and Belle Reynolds, was made literate by the plantation slaver's assumed daughter, an adenoidal smurf named Missy Anne. Belle assailed Kizzy violently when she proudly scribbled her name. She forbade her forever from writing another letter or reading another word. (In the book *Roots*, Belle herself was literate. The film declines to mention this). After her slaver discovered Kizzy's literacy, she was sold forthwith. Her new slaver Tom Lea raped her on her first night on his plantation. She begot his son George, who became a cockfighter in his youth. Many years later, Kizzy returned to seek out her parents in Spotsylvania County, Virginia. Mother Belle had been sold to another slaver. Father Kunta was dead. She found his tombstone marked TOBY, his slave name. She erased TOBY with a recalcitrant pen. She wrote KUNTA KINTE in its stead. The significance of affirming one's name, never mind one's story, by use of a rapier pen was not lost on me, aged nine. Reading was an activity my parents enjoined upon me the moment I became sentient to my surroundings. I felt its power. I sought to master both reading and writing. We, who are of a deep-rooted tradition of learning and letters, write simply because we must, simply. I deemed it natural and befitting that Hannibal of *The Drinking Gourd* should take pride and pleasure in literacy. His tutor is Tom, Hiram's ten-year-old son. He is taught the banjo as payment. When Hannibal recites verses from the Book of Jeremiah to Mother Rissa, she responds less reactively than Mother Belle, first with joy and then trepidation. He is unimpressed when she tells him she has secured work for him in the Big House. Hiram had beaten him previously. Rissa doesn't rate him bad. *I know marsters in my time what come from hell* she says. *All marsters come from hell,* he answers... *I am the only kind of slave I could stand to be — a bad one.*

Hiram, though a rustic and analphabetic fellow, understood that the institution of slavery was comatose in the American Republic of the nineteenth century. The genesis of its moribundity is worth dawdling a few lines on. It is ahistorical blancmange to suggest that the death of slavery in America was primarily down to abolitionists advocating the emancipation of their brethren. To follow the logic on this (like the recent arguments over Brexit), we need only ask the question the wise Roman Lucius Cassius uttered at the scene of the crime. *Cui bono?* he asked. Who benefits? Who profited from the abolition of slavery? The answer lies *in the economy, stupid.* We *follow the* money! The abolition of slavery in the United States was borne primarily from economics, yet its decline is mythologized in the same spirit as its justification. *The Curse of Ham* and pseudoscience drivel like phrenology were among its diabolical conceits. Whilst the unanimity of the *monster sacre* were an existential problem for politicians like Thomas Jefferson and Abraham Lincoln, the economic factor is often downplayed.

In the nineteen century, Agrarian America was expanding from sea to shining sea. She was energized by her aesthetic belief in her manifest destiny. The Industrial Revolution had taken afoot upon her north-eastern shores. The new economy was dependent on trade. Skilled laborers, not work horses, were required to operate new machines that enabled rapid manufacturing of goods and produce. Luddites in the South were disinclined to train slaves with the new skills required for the new economy. They were content with their rudimentary way of life. For America in general, slave insurrections and desertions bore a dreaded toll upon both society and economy. People could ill afford to sleep easy at midnight, let alone daybreak, whilst the Horrors of St. Domingo, Sam Sharpe's Christmas revolt, Nat Turner's rebellion in Virginia and John Brown's raid on Harper's Ferry still knelled with habitual foreboding.

I honor abolitionists like Olaudah Equiano of the *Sons of Africa*, Mary Wollstonecraft of *A Vindication Of The Rights Of Woman*, Mary Birkett of *A Poem On The African Slave Trade*, the great martyr John Brown, Frederick Douglass who requires no introduction, Sojourner Truth of *Ain't I A Woman* and Ignatius Sancho who wrote that *the grand object of English navigators — indeed of all Christian navigators — is money, money, money*. The common misconception that abolitionists, steeled by their Christian faith, were able to sanctify the covetous, infernal appetites of imperialists, also steeled by their Christian faith, romanticizes the notion that, were it not for the *amazing grace* of ethical gentlemen, slavery would have tarried a while. No doubt ethical men such as Thomas Clarkson and William Wilberforce helped produce the Acts of Parliament that led to the outlawing of slavery in the British Empire. But the enterprise and commerce of this Gilded Age that eventually gave the United States pre-eminence over Great Britain hastened its pathway. Slavers were commiserated with compensatory bags of cash. Slaves remained tethered to former plantations. Contrary to erroneous belief, President Abraham Lincoln did not wage a Civil War against the South to free the slaves. *My paramount object in this struggle is to save the Union*, he wrote in a letter to Horace Greeley, editor of *The Tribune* dated August 22, 1862, *and is not either to save or to destroy slavery. If I could save the Union without freeing any slave I would do it, and if I could save it by freeing all the slaves I would do it; and if I could save it by freeing some and leaving others alone, I would also do that.* Just like President Jack Kennedy after him, Old Abe was a hard-nosed pragmatist. *It is ungodly. It is ungodly. No doubt it is ungodly*, he is reported to have said of slavery, in a conversation with abolitionist A.J Grover. *But it is the law of the land, and we must obey it as we find it.* Lincoln considered the free African a *troublesome presence* in America. He is notably credited as the originator of the Thirteenth Amendment of the American Constitution, which abolished slavery in the United States. However, the precept of this abrogation was birthed by the *Women's National Loyal League* led by Susan B. Anthony and Elizabeth Cady Stanton. After the amendment was passed, the organization folded. These conscientious ladies themselves have been abrogated from American lore.

Hiram Sweet, of Hansberry's *The Drinking Gourd*, looked upon the demise of slavery as a moral consequence, not an economic contrivance. Keeping slaves was a matter of status. Eventually, he became indisposed and confined to bed. His wife Maria enjoined Everett to take charge of the farm. *Every night, if necessary, you must sit with pencil and pad and let him (your father) tell you everything he wishes. And then — well, do as you please!* Everett hires Zeb as his overseer. He is tasked to grow cotton on a salary of two thousand dollars per annum. Zeb is a dirt poor, corn harvest farmer, but aspires to be a landowner with slaves for property. *It's a hard life if you ain't got slaves*, he mumbles. He has a wife and two children. He was poised to move west and seek his fortune in unrefined territory. When Everett makes his offer, he postpones his migration. Zeb's father was a farmer who drove no slaves, but Zeb deemed him *an old fool who died, eatin' dirt.* The local preacher, who happened to visit Zeb on the day Everett made his offer, admired the old fool. *He was honest and he worked hard. Didn't call anybody master and caused none to call him master.* The preacher not only abhors slavery but he despises the treatment of poor Caucasians, who are manipulated by nabobs like Everett on the back of their self-loathing and ignorance. But Zeb isn't bothered. *I'm a white man, Preacher. And I'm goin to drive slaves for Everett Sweet and he's goin to pay me for it and this time next year, Zeb Dudley aims to own himself some slaves and be a man!*

Zeb immediately puts Everett's will to work. The slaves are driven like mules. Their feet are matted by dust. Their boughs yield to the whip. Coffin promptly brings Hannibal's work-shy attitude to the attention of the new driver, and he is lashed in the fields before the other slaves as an admonition. *You carry trouble in your eyes like a flag boy*, Zeb tells him. Everett is displeased when he hears of this incident. He tells Zeb that he'd rather have someone else be made an example of rather than the son of his father's favorite. When Zeb objects, he is contemptuously reminded of his place. After Coffin informs them both of Hannibal's disappearance, they set off in search of him. They find him in the company of young Tom. Hannibal has written a story titled *The Drinking Gourd*. They discover he is literate. *The ability to read in a slave is a disease*, Everett remarks bitterly. Hannibal defiantly boasts of his knowledge. *As long as he can see, he can read*, Everett observes bitterly. He orders Zeb to destroy Hannibal's sight.

Hiram is apoplectic when he learns Hannibal has been blinded. He orders Zeb from his property. Zeb protests that he only followed instructions. Everett contemptuously orders him to leave. In the midst of this row, sawbones Bullett walks into the room jubilantly with a newspaper. He announces the start of the American Civil War. The Sweet family rejoice, except for their patriarch. *Don't you know that whoever that idiot was who fired on Sumter set the slaves free?* he fumes. *Well, get out the liquor, gentleman. It's all over. A way of life is all over. The end is here and we might as well drink to what it was!* In spite of his ill-health, he drags himself to Rissa's cabin. He finds her tending her son. He advocates his futility and powerlessness. She challenges his irrationality squarely, for he had once boasted that he was *the master of this plantation and every soul on it... master of those fields out there...*

master of this house as well. She does not fear her eyes maybe gouged too as a result of her impertinence. *I don't 'spect blindness would matter to me. I done seen all there was worth seein in this world — and it didn't 'mount to much.* Hiram leaves a dejected figure. He collapses a few feet from Rissa's door. He cries for help. She doesn't stir to aid him. One by one, the cabin lights go out. These silent reposes constitute acts of *resistante* that are inconspicuous to slavers: The crude spitting into goblets of wine and bowls of soup; Speaking ill of their slaver in his absence; gossiping heartily about the tribulations of the slaver household; quietly praying for their damnation. Hiram dies alone in the bitter soil. He is buried beneath his land. As the English poet Alfred Tennyson once wrote: *Man comes and tills the fields. And lies beneath...* The play concludes with Everett dressed in a Confederates Union uniform. He is set to slay or get slain in the Civil War. Maria Sweet is dressed in mourning black. She has already bid farewell to her husband. Now she says goodbye to her firstborn. Zeb has returned to drive the slaves in the cotton fields. And Rissa has stolen Hiram's old shotgun, a mainstay in the House of Sweet. She takes it into the forest for Sarah, who is with the unsighted Hannibal and young Joshua. They steal away to freedom on a fair wind through the forest. The slaves sing *Steal Away To Jesus* on the plantation. And this is where the story ends.

I had re-examined *The Drinkin Gourd* for the purpose of this essay. Hannibal's impressible desire for liberty was a natural want for any *sighted eye and feeling heart*. A distinguished Persian of the Abbasid age stated that if *kings really knew the pleasure of reading, they would forfeit their kingdoms to partake in it.* Reading is the sweetest privilege and elicits the deepest pleasure. In *Roots*, Kunta Kinte's natural inclination to affirm his Mandinka identity and attain his freedom meant he had to forfeit his name and then his foot. Where roots run deep, no succedaneum is demanded. However, this philosophy of self-determinism and self-defining is readily contorted by both villains and victims of an abject existence, spawned of self-loathing and servility. In *The Drinking Gourd*, this stultifying homunculus is revisited in the person of Coffin. Stoolpigeons like Korah, Dathan, Quisling, Benedict Arnold, Judas and Brutus appertain every plantation, ghetto, township, occupied territory. *Anyone can rat*, observed Winston Churchill nearly a century ago. *But it takes a certain amount of ingenuity to re-rat!*

The final play in Hansberry's three-piece collection is titled *What Use Are Flowers?* She originally titled the piece *Who Knows Where* – a line borrowed from Bertolt Brecht's *Mother Courage*. There are fictive similarities with William Golding's *Lord of The Flies*. However, the stimulus for writing her dystopian play was Samuel Beckett's *Waiting For Godot*. Her central character was a whiskery hermit. He had removed himself from society because he *could no longer stand the dominion of time in the lives of men and the things that they did with it and to it, and indeed, that they let it do to them*. Absorbing that school of thought was timely consumption in the year, 1994. I had deprived myself from human company, *medias res*. I liaised only with the Kinteh ménage and a lone friend Imran, who called upon me on occasion. Why mingle among my peers when all they did mostly was deceive and contrive, mock and intrigue against myself, themselves and each other?

The hermit's name is Professor Charles Lewis Lawson, a former English teacher. He had returned from his self-imposed exile in the wilderness to investigate man's progress (or lack of) before he dies. He can no longer recount his years. He presumes his age is either seventy-eight or eighty. He discovers a handful of feral children devoid of speech. He tries to engage them. They do not answer him. He does not regret his splendid isolation. *But you must not for one second take that to mean that I regret my hermitage or do in any whatsoever return repentant to the society of men. I return in contempt and... curiosity. Not love! Not once, not once at all in those years did I long for human company. Not once!* I understand the hermit's reasons to reengage on the grounds he stated. And why he had no cause to return repentant, for he had done no wrong. It is only after the children fell upon him and ate the raw flesh he carried with him did he realize how the final remnants of a once-cultivated civilization had recrudesced to a Neolithic Age in a matter of a few years. *What have they done?* he screams in absolute horror. *They*, meaning humankind.

He bestows the children names. He teaches them speech. He shows them how to make pots and baskets. He educates them of their utility. The boys are barbered. Lily, the lone female, has her hair left draping towards her back. He teaches the humanities and lessons in life such as the meaning of surprise. *A surprise is something that you don't know is coming and, in life, most surprises are quite unpleasant.* On the subject of flowers, he says *in the old days, certain perfectly tasteless individuals insisted on making wine out of them. But that was not a use. That was a violation. The uses of flowers are infinite...* Here, I part company with the teetotal professor! He teaches symphonies. Charlie, the natural leader of the pack, learns to play *Greensleeves* and *Beethoven's Ninth, The Choral* from his primitive flute. The Hermit renders time teaching him common courtesies like socializing and ensuring the protection and wellbeing of Lily, the prospective new Eve. Only her womb could bring forth the next generation of humans. The hermit and Charlie are disturbed by a fight caused by a boy rendered jealous by another boy's superiority in making pots. The hermit attempts to stop the fight. He is bundled over. His anger against mankind is rekindled upon the children. *I renounce you again! You and your passions and all your seed! May you perish forever from this earth.* The children each bring forth a flower by way of an apology. He rebuffs them. They appeal for a reengagement through his recreational pursuits; flowers, music and Beethoven. The hermit is unforgiving. *You are human. Therefore, you are repulsive. All of you. But you* (Charlie) *in particular.* When he is alone with Charlie, he explains his death is near. *When it happens, you will all stand for a long time with your mouths hanging open with wonder... It is in the nature of man to take life for granted. Only the absence of life will seem to you the miracle, the greatest miracle — and by the time you understand that it should be the other way around — well, it will be too late. It won't matter then.* The hermit spends his last breath cursing the woman who rescued the adolescents from the fate that afflicted mankind. *Foolish, foolish woman! That silly sentimental female. It's all finished with you, the lot of you.* These lambs are potentially doomed. What had been the point of saving them from the inevitable? They could never rekindle Copernicus. Shakespeare was gone. Einstein would not be revived. *Pretending that I could hand to you the residue, badly learned and hardly retained, of five thousand years of glory.* He laments with his last breath. *Our little adventure among the stars is over! Finis! The brief and stupid episode will end now. The universe will have power!* His last words: *Charlie! The use of flowers were infinite. . .*

After I first read this terse play, I wondered over the ambulatory prospects of these orphans. Despite the hermit's belated efforts, I surmised it was highly probable they'd return to their former state. People oft returned to their impulses, or what they classified as their First Principles, in the final analysis. It's easier to scuffle and scowl than apply reason and rationale. I wondered about the boys' looming adolescence, how they may eventually quarrel, fight and even kill out of their cardinal appetite for the ingenue Lily. We had already glimpsed the intrinsic envy that consumed a boy over a mere pot. The raptures of the body in the wilderness, where neither law nor society existed, could potentially extinguish the patina of their callow propriety. It was not implausible to think that others, apart from these foundlings, had survived the apocalypse. Perhaps there were fissile colonies of human folk belaboring a relinquished city, sheltering inside an army barracks or traipsing across a savannah in fear of wild snakes. I pondered how acquired knowledge obtained over five millennia, passed from generation to civilization, could be vanquished suddenly, like a once-lit candle in the dark. I imagined losing forever the *Tolkappiyam*, the *Epic Of Gilgamesh*, the *Egyptian Book Of The Dead*, the *Book Of Kells*, the *Rigveda*, the *Kebra Nagast* and the *Fetha Nagast*. Imagine the unborn deprived of the *Iliad* and the *Odyssey*, Shakespeare and Milton, the *Mahabharata* and the *Ramayana*, the *Koran*, the *Bible* and the *Pentateuch*. Whether one is tendentiously disposed to the divinity of some of these aforementioned texts is not the point. Their precocious erudition and received ideas are inextricably sown into the human spirit and sinew. I can recall *H G Wells'* novella

The Time Machine, where the Time Traveler's peregrination takes him 800,000 years into the future, when the sun is verging on entropy. He discovers a fragile but beautiful people, known as the *Eloi*, who are ignorant of literacy and history, work and danger. They speak in an impoverished language containing some five hundred words. They are well nourished by eating fruit. They absorb Vitamin D from the sun by reclining in the grass. They fear moonless nights. They are livestock for the *Morlocks*, a barbarous, cannibalistic tribe that dwell underfoot. When the Time Traveler visits the library, he finds books undisturbed for centuries. They crumble in the palm of his hand. It is conceivable that the abandonment of literature and the liberal arts could happen in our world in later times. It may not require an annihilation of the human race to render it so.

I wondered at the ill that caused mankind's destruction in *What Use Is Flowers?* Was this the will of a celestial mastermind, to unleash some ungodly Ragnarök as foretold by doomsday prophets and soothsayers? Had there been a latent burst of egotistic nationalist drivel from the charring jaws of strongmen standing erect on their podiums, provoking a rapid exchange of intercontinental ballistic missiles, ensuring mutually assured destruction as far as the whole planet was concerned? This was a real prospect in Hansberry's day. She lived during a time of international tumult: the age of Hitler, Stalin, Mao, Truman, Tojo and Mussolini. These aforementioned Minotaurs authored the vilest war in human history. Today, some of us are rendered frit by bullfrogs, contrarious proto-nationalists like Trump, Putin, Netanyahu, Bolsonaro, Lukashenko and Orbán. I'm not suggesting, for one moment, that the bullfrogs are in league, or in the same league, with the Minotaurs. There exists palpable, political and methodical dissonance between the two groups. These aforenamed latter-day politicians exhibit the great contentions of our narcoleptic age with their extraneous babble. But they are side issues to the real issue. The American philosopher and linguist Noam Chomsky, in his essay *On Resistance*, spoke of the *real terror of our age*, shards of wisdom like the percipient hermit, *scholarly and reasonable men*, teeming with indignation and self-righteousness, who observe pestilence and war with *equanimity and detachment*. They are neither squeamish nor unmoved from their apathy. These retiring folks, according to Chomsky, are more terrifying than the occasional crypto-tyrant. Not from what they do but what they decline to do. Admittedly, I find myself falling headlong into such a category. *All cruelty springs from weakness*, observed Seneca in *Seneca's Morals*. In the hermit's case, he vanishes into an indissoluble vortex. He returns, casting blame and calumnies. He curses the woman who led the children to safety. But he ascribes no responsibility for himself for the demise of mankind. According to Chomsky's logic, the hermit is as guilty of the resulting depreciatory (if it indeed were a man-made catastrophe). As Plato correctly illustrated in *The Republic: the heaviest penalty for declining to rule is to be ruled by someone inferior to yourself*.

As an adult, Hansberry had lived through a microcosmic world war fought on the Korean peninsula. She observed the Soviet Union and the United States come perilously close to World War III over the Cuban Missile Crisis. Towards the end of her life, America plunged herself into yet an asinine firefight in Indochina to maintain the colonial status imposed by the French (before World War II), the Japanese aided by Vichy-France (during World War II) and then the French again (after World War II). Whilst President Truman had used his atomic card upon Japan, both Presidents Eisenhower and Kennedy considered revisiting the same apocalyptic utility over their respective crises in Indochina and Cuba. While the United States and the Soviet Union raced each other to see who could acquire the most apodictic weapons, Hansberry opposed nuclear weapons vehemently and in all its forms. Doomsday scenarios, whether they be caused by a hecatomb the sheer size of Tsar Bomba or emitted by some unmitigated pathogenic violence like the Black Death, could plausibly take the form of *What Use Of Flowers?* These are not absurd propositions. A surfeit of whiskey need not foretaste the imagination.

✳   ✳   ✳

Only thirty-four years were allotted to Lorraine Hansberry. She died in January 1965 at the height of the Civil Rights Movement, a month before the assassination of her friend Malcolm X. They shared the same birthday. He was five years older. Though in mortal danger himself, he risked attending her funeral. Malcolm is universally recognized as a radical. But she was no less a radical then the storied figureheads revered during that era of intellectual, political and social ferment. When I use the word *radical*, I do not subscribe to the *pas de deux* commonplace interpretation that ascribes radicals to the *holy simplicity* of the foolhardy fanatic. The word *radical* is derived from the Late Latin word *radicalis* and *radix*, meaning root. These harriers, hectors and hod carriers of foolhardy fanaticism, rendered glib by dogma and other grotesque salvific allusions, are a similitude of the simple old lady who applied brushwood at the feet of the Czech heretic Jan Hus, when the authorities struggled against the elements to set him on fire. There are many fanatics, *true believers*, precariously certain of themselves and their cause, like that *simple old lady*, in our midst. They subscribe to the *one true opinion* as if it were the one true god. They are as reactionary as a flock of pigeons, taking flight from one totem pole to the next; fumy, *spartoi*, pent-up noisemakers fluent in *post hoc ergo propter hoc* (after this, therefore because of this). The animal magnetism of passionate intensity serves as a hallmark of our tin-eared, public discourse in these narcoleptic, neurotic and Lenten-driven times.

The counterpart of these noisemakers is the static liberal, who has a predilection for the plight of oppressed and deracinated peoples but has neither the stomach nor the fortitude to uproot trees and redress usurpations, lest the blowback diminishes her privileges and disturbs her peace. The politically astute liberal is inured to placate the urgency of the natural rights of others. Their agenda is proselytized as an essential prerequisite of their support. Your agenda, meanwhile, is auxiliary. *Not now but not never.* Her lickspittle is palliated by her ambition. Her political opponent, incidentally, is depicted as the Big Bad Wolf. Whilst your home is built from straw, the liberal toady lives in a brick house. No other than Martin Luther King, the utilitarian apostle of nonviolence, wrote unsparingly about the static liberal when he penned his famous letter from his jail cell in Birmingham, Alabama: *First, I must confess that over the past few years, I have been gravely disappointed with the white moderate. I have almost reached the regrettable conclusion that the Negro's great stumbling block in his stride toward freedom is not the White Citizen's Counciler or the Ku Klux Klanner, but the white moderate, who is more devoted to "order" than to justice; who prefers a negative peace, which is the absence of tension to a positive peace, which is the presence of justice; who constantly says: "I agree with you in the goal you seek, but I cannot agree with your methods of direct action," who paternalistically believes he can set the timetable for another man's freedom; who lives by a mythical concept of time and who constantly advises the Negro to wait for a "more convenient season." Shallow understanding from people of good will is more frustrating than absolute misunderstanding from people of ill will. Lukewarm acceptance is much more bewildering than outright rejection.* Hansberry understood this dynamic long before it became a reality for King, though King's political arc evolved through the sixties, finally succumbing to the notion that he was integrating his people into *a burning house!* Hansberry consorted with radicalism at the conception of her political awakening.

During the so-called lockdown, I read two enamoring tomes that granted me further heat and light into Lorraine Hansberry's afflatus and thoughts. Steven R. Carter's *Hansberry's Drama: Commitment and Complexity* provides acumen and scrutiny into the expansiveness of her work. Imani Perry's *Looking For Lorraine: The Radiant And Radical Life of Lorraine Hansberry* is laden with a trove of discoveries on Hansberry that I had otherwise not been privy to. Private notes, musings, letters, correspondence, archives and unfinished plays were categorically presented in this fine work. And though Perry's tome was more hagiography than biography, it was an excitatory read on the life of one of the most nonpareil personalities of the Civil Rights era. But like A. Phillip Randolph, Bayard Rustin, Ralph Abernathy and, until quite recently, James Baldwin himself, these

Atlases bore the equivalent of the uncomprehending skies upon their taxing shoulders. For a long while, only the initiated could name them among the constellation of men and women that fought for the civil rights of African-Americans.

Hansberry was *Black* evidently and thus oppressed. She was a woman and thus twice oppressed, by her own admission. Her physical components were presupposed and so she was judged unaccordingly. She was thrice oppressed, by the stultifying smoke of chauvinism, for her lesbianism. At the age of twenty-nine, she complied a vivisected list of what she loved and hated. Her homosexuality appeared in both columns. Her heterosexual marriage to Robert B. Nemiroff veiled her intimate relations with women. Under her pseudonym Emily Jones, she wrote private letters about her intramural skirmishes with herself about the things that mattered: commitment to family, same sex love, rendering unto gender what was gender. After her death, Nemiroff donated her private papers to the New York Public Library, where they were kept from the public until 2013. In Perry's noteworthy book, one can discover the curlicue of Hansberry's ambivalence to a maladaptive America. It read like a *confutatis maledictis*. In her youth, I learnt she worked for a leftist newspaper named *Freedom*, owned by the great thespian Paul Robeson; that she studied under the auspices of the legendary civil rights activist W.E.B Du Bois at the Jefferson School of Social Science; that she possessed a brilliant mind but secured mediocre grades at High School; that before she became as distinguished as her talent deserved, her struggles were familiar to many a writer. She worked six months in a fur shop stitching labels and four days as a typist at Wannamaker's Department Store. Her work experience included laboring as a production assistant for a theatrical firm and being employed as a recreational leader at a federation for the handicapped. She even grafted shifts as an occasional waitress at her in-law's restaurant, *Potpourri*. From her journal, she wrote *the thing that makes you exceptional, if you are at all, is inevitably that which must also makes you lonely.*

Her atheism contemned the prevailing, superannuated beliefs of the masses. Counterparts like James Baldwin and Bayard Rustin shared her skepticism. Her multiple identities precipitate the pedantry of bigots. She was discreet in her support for the *Daughters of Bilitis*, a pioneering lesbian civil rights organization headquartered in San Francisco, California. During the fulminant chauvinism of the 1950s, society perforated with hostility and hatred for the homosexual. These were the days of McCarthyism, Communism and virulent charges of Anti-Americanism. America was a new global superpower but lacked the self-assurance to accommodate heresy and subversion within her territory. The *Daughters of Bilitis* were neither heretical nor subversive, though no doubt there were those who believed they were, and more. In truth, they were a cornucopia of support and education to the lesbian community. They concealed themselves under the guise of an all-female poetry club. The character of *Bilitis* was plucked from the homophile pages of the French poet Pierre Louys, who placed her in the time of Sappho of Lesbos, a Hellenistic poet before the days of Aristotle and Plato. In their mission statement, they referred to themselves as *variants*. They sought to integrate into American life by osmosis. Their biennial meetings were marked by the FBI and politicians once their organization grew in number. Hansberry wrote letters to their magazine, *The Ladder*, in a tone of voice that could be described, to the modern ear, as inflections of intersectionality. In an issue dated May 1957, she wrote, using another pseudonym Emily Smith: *You (Daughters of Bilitis) are obviously serious people and I feel that women, without wishing to foster any strict separatist notions, homo or hetero, indeed have a need for their own publications and organizations. Our problems, our experiences, as women are profoundly unique as compared to the other half of the human race. Women, like other oppressed groups of one kind or another, have particularly had to pay a price for the intellectual impoverishment that the second-class status imposed on us for centuries created and sustained. Thus, I feel that The Ladder is a fine, elementary step in a rewarding direction.*

Throughout the Civil Rights era, men of faith and none preached Fire and Water from their podiums and pulpits. Theirs were broad positions emanating from a fissiparous movement, which proposed conflicting methodologies. Not all were integrationists. Some were separatists. Some advocated a return to Africa. The journeys proposed were stop-off points at Sinai, Nebo and Ararat, on route to Canaan, Goshen and Timbuktu. The landmark March on Washington in the year, 1963, was deemed the culmination of this call, that the African-American could be *free at last.* Malcolm X deemed the march the *Farce on Washington.* He declined to partake in it. Only two women, activist Daisy Bates and performer Josephine Baker, among the binders full of men, spoke from the rostrum that day. They made remarks rather than speeches. James Baldwin was not permitted to speak. He was considered a firebrand. But a lesser-known meeting, arguably of a more significant bearing, took place on the evening of May 24 (my mother's birthday), 1963. Frank words, not resplendent speeches, were exchanged in its stead and, arguably, was *The Fire Next Time* that forced President John F. Kennedy's helming hand. A detailed account of this event is recorded in Arthur Schlesinger's book titled *Robert Kennedy And His Times.* The Attorney General of the United States, Robert Kennedy, met the author, James Baldwin, at a Nobel prize event. Kennedy asked for a *quiet, off-the-record, unpublicized get-together of prominent negroes.* Hansberry was invited to partake in the discussion. Also present, among others, were Baldwin's brother David, performer Harry Belafonte, singer Lena Horne, actor Rip Torn and Clarence Benjamin Jones, attorney to Martin Luther King Jr. Kennedy began the meeting by trumpeting the Justice Department's work in support of the Civil Rights Movement. A young civil rights activist from the Congress of Racial Equality, Jerome Smith, was moved to speak. He told Kennedy of his recent arrest in Mississippi. Whilst the police beat him in the prisons, Kennedy's FBI panjandrums stood by as bystanders. Whilst he spoke, he stammered and became visibly upset. Kennedy was offended by his tone of voice. He turned his back on him.

Hansberry dolled upon Kennedy some shock treatment. *You've got a great many very, very accomplished people in this room, Mr. Attorney General. But the only man who should be listened to is that man over there.* (Smith). *That is the voice of twenty-two million people.*

Kennedy was particularly alarmed when Smith said he'd rather die than fight for America against her foreign enemies. Indeed, he and Hansberry openly spoke of the prospect of armed insurrection against *white people*. The disputatious meeting deteriorated further. *If you can't understand what this young man* (Smith) *is saying,* said Hansberry, *then we are without any hope at all because you and your brother* (President Kennedy) *are representatives of the best that a White America can offer. If you are insensitive to this, then there's no alternative, except our going in the streets... and chaos.* The meeting ended when she stormed from the room with the words *Goodbye, Mr. Attorney General.* The duplicitous New York Times reported on the meeting and dubbed Baldwin and Hansberry as *angry young Negroes.* Anger, that hackneyed, lazy pejorative! The Kennedys took a more concerted interest in the Civil Rights Movement thereafter, though they weren't worn of trying to fetter the activism of non-violent leaders like the Reverend King himself.

I hadn't planned an extensive essay on the life and times of Lorraine Hansberry. My pen had voluntarily summoned itself to arms by way of honoring *Les Blancs: The Collected Last Plays Of Lorraine Hansberry.* That tome had been a *coup de foudre.* But it was the irregular heartbeat of a woebegone year that made me reconsider the sum of her parts. I reread her plays for the first time in years. The avidity of the Hansberrian mind makes her difficult to categorize, for it was a mind in constant flux. Unlike the revered figures of our age who are long deceased, who are very much conducive to their time and space, whose false syllogisms we still dare to quote, Hansberry's work is juxtaposed and measured to the fretting questions that haunt our leaden skies in the year, 2020.

September 27, 2020.

THE PROBLEM OF YOUTH CRIME

QUITE RECENTLY, I MET my salt-of-the-earth friend and confidante Audrey at the Canada Water Library in south London. We live no less than five miles from each other. Yet we had not met in person for almost five years. She is the meritorious owner of *Oopsy Daisy Daycare Childminding Services.* As for myself, I scribble a bit, every now and again, with dawdling endeavor. Our friendship has endured those five years, thanks to WhatsApp and the iPhone. We had known each other a further twelve years before those five. Over coffee and some well-buttered scones, we disseminated our personal lives. We discussed the flux and indeterminacy of London. The prevailing zeitgeist meant we were predisposed into disheartenment. We examined the homomorphism of *urbe nostra.* We pondered at its disaffected calm. The working classes have been tethered by neoliberalism. They plod on with resilience. The toilers find their wages shrinking. Their bills do not recoil. The cost of living does not compute. *The center cannot hold.* Those that are supplemented by the State may have it worse. But then again, we live in an age where plenty will unapologetically argue that *they* have it worse. Some people empathize, even if they cannot quantify the suffering of others. The ruling classes patronize, whatever their political colors. Blue. Red. Yellow. They demonstrate this by the fruits of their policies, which reap schism and begets stress. I pay no attention to their fulminations on the podium. Political soundbites such as *we're all in it together* and that *we've never had it so good* are unabashed in their condescension.

Mandarins are readily on hand to palliate our chronic aches with *panem et circenses*, those stodgy nodes that are failsafe in the placating and procuring of the Mob. London is forever laden with merriment. Her timeworn condiments have rendered her renown global. A new cinecittá of skyscrapers contortions her skyline. The Roman satirist Juvenal noted, nineteen centuries ago, that once the multitude enjoyed a fair helping of *bread and circuses*, they abdicated their citizenry to entitled technocrats. They need not wear *steingrau* trousers and haughty smirks to impose their diminishments upon our public services and private lives. We are awoken by the nascence of Reality Television but not the nuance of our own realities. We slay Chronos recklessly on social media, as if granted the lifespan of Methuselah. We live vicariously through celebrity conceits and other tepid distractions. And then we sit back and wait for Kairos, Godot and the Messiah to goosestep from around the corner like The Three Muskerhounds to our Dogtanian. *I can hire one half of the working class to kill the other half*, a quote often attributed to the American robber baron Jay Gould, would be a mindset not misplaced in the minds of the haughty classes. They are mindful that the double bind of brass tacks we endure daily, and the avaricious quest for consumerism, will enumerate the slaughter. If I were a betting man, I would not wager against them.

To Audrey and I, London had made the *Bodhi* and soul debilitating. Neither of us are not heedless of the *London Street*. We bristle in her entrails. We live in her craw. Like the *Arab Street*, the London Street exhibits a fretted caw that cannot be replicated in tune by a single unit, from a soapbox or a pulpit. Bullhorn or no, the London Street speaks with a fissiparous argot that only sounds harmonic to a tinpot ear. We both find the stagnation of our nation's capital difficult to saddle or swallow. The eighteenth-century lexicographer Samuel Johnson wrote that *when a man is tired of London, he is tired of life*. That old Londonphile ought to rise from his grave and traipse through *The Great Wen* now! London is asphyxiating the lives of those that tire within her boundaries. You pay a premium to tread her waters. I have tired of London. It is wont of decay and declension. Inequality and poverty sear the city mist. Reported violent crime is rising. Affluence ineluctably soars around us, from Ealing Broadway to Epping Forest. Such is the schizophrenia of living here. Will London's influence wane because of Brexit or will she wax on regardless? How will the labor market fare in this upheaval? Food banks are now accepted as *part and parcel* of living in one of the richest cities on earth. Of course, London's reputation as a cosmopolitan, hyphenated city should be enhanced but not at the unfettered emendations to local communities. Friends and family are fleeing this redoubtable city, and the bottle-green Thames River. They settle outside the ouroboros of the M25 to avoid operating in a financial straitjacket. These folks are then required to commute at great expense back into London to tend to their jobs. Their money is not good enough to rent or buy in *urbe nostra*. The sloughing term *Affordable Housing* should be followed by a horselaugh. Meanwhile, both local and national governance are fixated into allowing privatization to seep into the once hallowed domain of Education, Housing and Health. The undertakers, that prey upon societal maladies, are poised to profit financially. They are not subject to the accountability required of elected officials. We suffer the sclerosis of disintegration. Like Gotham City, *this town needs an enema!*

Embarking to the continent is a tempting proposition, I say. We speak over the futures of our respective children. I am already looking at London through a rear-view mirror. I feel like Shakespeare's *Hamlet*, rendered uncertain by the night's visitation: *My fate cries out and makes each petty artery in this body as hardy as the Nemean Lion's nerve.* Audrey is contemplating folding her belongings into a knapsack and reaching for the escape hatch for The Gambia where, only a few weeks previous, she was exposed to an amazing cultural experience. But our coffee meet was not a council of despair. It was good to keep company with this dear old friend. I wish for London more than I express. I wish for a revitalized London that would invigorate many souls and allow some chill, instead of Pandemonium, where dwellings shrink in size and the streets are roiled by angst-ridden goons. In my lifetime, I've borne witness to an Icarian London, fastened from Thatcher steel, Blair metal and Cameron iron, generating more heat than light, flying perilously close to the sun. *As flies to wanton boys are we to the gods*, to quote Shakespeare's lamenting Earl of Gloucester from *King Lear. They kill us for their sport.*

Our conversation accentuated when we delved into the conundrum of the plight of the inner-city youth. Audrey and I did not go through our childhoods unscathed. We both know of people locked in prisons and buried in cemeteries, casualties of the bullshit of the streets. It should be said here that most youth do not turn to crime having suffered bad beginnings. But the focus is upon those that do, though their pathway to delinquency and carnage is criminally out of focus. The pretext for the random parturient entering the Underworld is enmeshed in a muddle. How many must obviate in angst because of the bitted cards handed them. Born into circumstances not of their making: born into vexatious and mean abodes. Rendered unwanted, unloved, unnurtured by bitter and vain procreators. Some endure physical and sexual violations at the hands of sick, depraved fucks that are their fathers and uncles, their mothers and aunts, and so-called friends of the family. Some kids witness their fathers inflicting violence on their mothers. His unabated fist pounding into her tender flesh are their *chimes at midnight, Master Shallow*. These kids are rendered withered and turbulent by their respective realities. They toil dreams of deliverance from their sad milieu. They attend more funerals than weddings. So when a child countenances her wretched state, her only thought is to escape it. The cognitive dissonance this incurs infects their reason. The German philosopher Friedrich Nietzsche wrote in his seminal work titled *Beyond Good And Evil* that *if you look long into an abyss, the abyss also gazes long into you.* These adolescents carry this deep void within when they venture onto the timorous circuitry of the streets.

Whether they be three or thirty in number, this disordered malignancy remains imbedded within. The streets become a rite of passage. They are prey to any Fagin, Morlock, Cain, Count Orlok or any other Minotaur who would avariciously feast upon their promise, and their souls. They can be initiated and emboldened, wooed with money and favor. Wads of the mighty greenback are shuffled beneath their noses, accompanied by boasts of their earning potential, and the usurpation of the child's mind is complete. These intractable artisans have their own parlance and their own code. And while they ride the surliness of the streets, they subscribe to that Hobbesian opine that life is *solitary, poor, nasty, brutish and short*. They are fatalistic, for all things appear futile. They self-harm. They harm others. They repeat the cycle. Ponder, if you will, the mental health of a child aspirated by such persistent traumas.

Audrey tells me that her sleep was disturbed at 5am that same morning after receiving a WhatsApp video from a friend. The clip lasted less than thirty seconds. It featured the final earthly moments of a teenage boy. He had sought refuge in a bedroom following a disturbance at a house party. Boys of a similar age climbed the stairs in search of him. One wielded a large knife. They soon discovered him. The child was reduced to pleading for his life. The video cuts, and then returns to reveal a ferocious amount of blood spilled on the carpet, and the youngster lifeless. Audrey could not return to sleep after viewing it. She had heard of a recent stabbing to death of a young boy at a house party. She could not be sure if the video was that same incident. Mindless slayings of youth by youth have ricocheted through the capital since. I found myself, on the train ride home from Audrey, envisaging the eighth verse of W.H Auden's *Shield of Achilles* in my mind's eye... *A ragged urchin, aimless and alone, loitered about that vacancy; a bird flew up to safety from his well-aimed stone: That girls are raped, that two boys knife a third were axioms to him, who'd never heard of any world where promises were kept, or one could weep because another wept.*

*   *   *

The pestilence of youth crime has persisted in this heteronormative hell. The tempests and tarnations associated with this pestilence exhibit more heads than the Hydra of Lerna. The decrement of society is all the rage. Some factors are worthy of scrutiny: the absence of dad has its conspicuous ill-effects. The *devouring* mother living vicariously through her children has its arduous returns. The Greek philosopher Aristotle had posited the theory that *nature abhors a vacuum*. The phony, the perverse and the preposterous will gleefully fill an empty heart. I know of a mother who fears the rage of her man-child. His listlessness was spun from a vacuum within his environmental space. She wonders how she can bridle his inexhaustible fury. She has no one, save him. *How sharper than a serpent's tooth it is to have a thankless child*, remarked Shakespeare's King Lear. I know of a young man who followed the masturbatory idiocies of his menfolk. Like his father and brothers who misdemeaned before him, he was raised in a disequilibrium of a *cold house*. And there is the case of another friend who never sleeps whilst her teenage son roams the night streets. Till he bolts the front door behind him would her eyelids rest with ease. These are anecdotal cases, of which I am privy to. They have their distinctions as well as their common factors. All are worthy of untiring scrutiny.

Many children are woefully and criminally miseducated, by their guardians and the State. Institutions have a condensed and presupposed view of the quotidian man and woman, sub-divided by ethnicity, sub-divided by gender, sub-divided by class, and so on. Some guardians have a condensed or predisposed view on the rights of children. These suppositions are a stereotype that many absorb into their psyche. This, in turn, infects their worldview. I would rather the individual adapts the principles of self-determinism than to seek validation from protean types and be treated like a willow in the wind. Sub-cultural mores have singed the souls of boys and girls, desensitizing any nurturing sentiment and compassion, and so we have these *Lord of the Flies* elements marauding in different postal areas, propelled by hubris and reprisal. These sub-cultural mores are far from serene. The banality of these so-called postcode wars are unsettling, especially when, presumably, nobody among these warring cohorts are landowners. To quote my debut novel *The Nepenthe Park Chronicles*, ... *these cards paid no taxes nor groomed no fields, yet they policed their postcodes like medieval landlords with pitchforks.* The cult of celebrity, the growth of consumerism, the psychopathic execrations being ping-ponged on social media and the exponential rise in mindless entertainment has riled an impetuous headwind that won't tarry. What sort of society marauds its people into becoming myriad consumers from the womb to the tomb? As for social media, may that medium be extirpated in our times!

Most people who suffer deficient beginnings do not trespass the law. They have productive lives. They raise stellar babies. Those who trespass the law quite often redeem themselves once they come to terms with the futility of the streets. Their experiences are cautionary tales. They counsel those that come after them. The impetuous wind spits in the faces of those who remain. For some, death will come, more unexpectedly than it otherwise should, foreshadowed by some asinine quarrel or petty grievance. Some will be like Abaddon, leading a band of locusts, taking life for pithy reasons. *It's a hell of a thing killing a man,* says Will Munny to *The Schofield Kid* in the 1992 revisionist western film *Unforgiven. You take away all he's got, and all he's ever gonna have!* If the youth is fortunate to escape the cemetery, the prison may be his abode. In the cooler, the courtyards and the canteen rooms, one still vacillates, and can be contortioned further into vulgar extremes. Young adults are ripe for the poultry logic of fascism and Islamofascism. They seek redemption and new meaning but layers of continued misguidance buries them alive in another grave.

Quality time is not devoted to, nor concentrated upon, the psychological pressures our narcissistic age inflicts on today's children. This is often excused to a retrenchment of resources. I put it down to the misapplication of will. John Bull readily finds resources to rain Tomahawks from his submarines at a cost of millions per launch when it embarks on military escapades with brother Uncle Sam and sister Marianne, the most recent ones being the Roman candles exhibition in the Libyan and Syrian skies. He produces billions of pounds to underwrite the losses of fat bankers, who played fast-and-loose with the British economy. There has been no shriving or contrition from the banks for their sweepstakes. Business continued as before while the government transferred the bill upon the heads and the shoulders of those who could not flee to Monte Carlo, the Bahamas or Cockroach City. If the government can bail out the banks, it can most certainly bail out souls. And what greater investment could there be in the promise of our babes, our infants, our unborn? Civilized societies have a duty to plowback upon those that are made gudgeons by globalization. We should excuse ourselves of this responsibility if we are not a civilized country.

The government's solution to the problem of youth crime, or to any societal problem, is to enforce palliative and reactionary measures. More bread and circuses are indicative of their soft power. More stop-and-searches and longer jail sentences reflect their hard power. Whenever a country faces a crux that unsettles the populace, and the government or other institutions advocate for more powers to tackle it, I am suspicious. The State and the police have already more powers they care to manage. They remain in a perpetual state of readiness for mission creep into our personal freedoms. And why should those freedoms (or what's left of them) be further infringed because of a few lopsided scoundrels? Better for the authorities to reign in hell than to serve in heaven is their thought process, I think. For at least in hell, or rather in a state of obfuscation, anxiety and fear, they are granted powers to drool over our Internet habits and keep our DNA for all time, and there is very little a Briton, or otherwise, can do about it.

Parliament, the police and the prevailing media squall over the retrenchment of public services like seagulls, flagrantly waving their political colors at the same time while waving away their own moral failings. Even if they were to fill the prisons of England and Wales with all the wrong 'uns on this island, they cannot wriggle free from Dostoevsky's instrumental observation that *the degree of civilization in a society can be judged by entering its prisons.* Middle England, through her Stradivarius sips of Earl Grey, are perplexed by the plebian classes. They pray they don't spy underclass goons loitering the cobblestone streets of Tunbridge Wells or the constituency of Northeast Somerset. Of course, if it's their own cubs smoking grass and having brawls in taverns after consuming gallons of barrels of beer, these are merely the shanghai hormones of cosmopolitan and rural youth. Reactionary measures are never an antidote to anything, let alone youth crime. And since the caprice of inner-city youth is all but criminalized by the State, it is no wonder, then, that the youth are of the opinion that the authorities are an adversarial, narky bunch. They have a niagara of empirical proof to support this. They also have generational proof of days gone by, of maltreatment by the police and injustice from the judiciary. This leaves scars upon the memory.

I was first subjected to an unwarranted stop and search at fifteen. I was a geeky kid with glasses as thick as double-glazed windows. I had left Prince House, an arcade/video shop in my hometown of Leyton. I was returning to school before the end of my lunch hour. Four policemen leapt from a van on Norlington Road, Leytonstone. They had followed me from the arcade place, they said. I had been behaving suspiciously. They proceeded to put their hands in my pockets without my permission. They found nothing. They asked my name, address and date of birth. They parted by warning that they hoped not to see me loitering the roads again if I knew what was good for me. I was stunned into numbness. *If I knew what was good for me?* I would be stopped and searched on two further occasions in my teens, and these experiences were no less sobering than the first. My brothers, friends and associates have endured more chastening stop-and-search ordeals. The police, granted, are required to police diligently, resourcefully. Some do, and they do it well. Some must be constantly reminded that their primary duties is serving their public. Therefore, their stop-and-search gambits should be policed also. Confiscated weapons can only be good for the public. As for Fagin, Morlock, Cain, Count Orlok or any other Minotaur, they are a scourge that society requires deliverance from. We should not permit them to hide behind our earnest concerns on policing. We ought to be forensic in our critique of the police but Cain must still answer for Abel.

I will propose, as a layman from the town of Leyton, prognostications that may aid the women and men of tomorrow, the babes and infants of today. Antidotes are nominally bitter. If they provide some convalescence to a wayward adolescent, why should not society adopt practical solutions rather than adhere to hackneyed methodologies? *The emancipation of the working class must be the work of the work class itself* was an international left-wing slogan of the 1960s. This is also true of this problem. For more than two decades, I've listened to deliberations on youth crime. *No raindrop ever believes itself to be the cause of the flood.* The arguments are ostensibly centered on what the other is *not doing*, permitting little introspection from the strands of conversationalists. Rather, we ought to audit how every segment of society is willfully aiding this continuous scourge. We must extirpate intended and unintended consequences. Public Health will require a massive injection of funding. Bespoke education, health and care plans must be constructed for every child vulnerable to the lure of the streets. I am under no illusion that hardened elements are deaf to any sort of counsel. They'd defy any form of authority on pain of death. The conundrum they face is not unlike the problem of Shakespeare's *Macbeth: I am in blood, stepp'd in so far that, should I wade no more; Returning were as tedious as go o'er.* It is a perverse tragedy of our times that a thirteen-year-old can mark his own oblivion. *He kills his own father but when he appears in court, he pleads for clemency because he's an orphan.* Such is his rationale. Some youths may pay heed to former hustlers who once walked the precarious road. Interventions by youth violence organizations would be crucial in these instances. One would hope these groups put aside their territorial claims that theirs is *the* authentic voice, and would, instead, concentrate their focus on the healing of troubled youth. Youth Offender Prisons must be subject to reformation and not privatization. It is obscene that repugnant companies are permitted to profit avariciously from societal ills.

I'd propose mediation centers for children and young adults trapped by the surliness of the street, where grassroots organizations, proficient with the stoicisms of the streets, are able to mediate between gangs, and act as a buffer between youths and the police. We de-clutter the glamor, but that can mostly be done by those who once walked those precarious steps. Child psychologists and Child Protection Officers have a prominent role to play. This area requires considerable financial investment from government. Mediation centers ought to be situated outside of major towns and cities. They must be equipped with educational, counseling, mental health and social facilities designated to reignite and revitalize the youth. Youths must be provided the resources to live in such centers till they can safely return to their neighborhoods. Once the glamorization is decluttered, that lifestyle become like ashes in the hands of its former proponents. The claim of earning £5,000 per day on road comes to naught. *We might as well say a cashier in Tesco is on £5K a day because that's what they handle,* as my friend Audrey put it. At regional drop-off hubs, knives and guns could be deposited safely, and then passed onto the authorities for destruction.

I'd propose a reformation of the National Curriculum. The word *education,* from its Latin roots, means to *lead forth* and *raise up.* Too many children leave the schooling system, rudderless and unmoored, and ill-equipped to grapple with the real world. Is the system delineated for the overwhelming number of children to *lead forth and rise up?* Or is it designed to fail those that are failing? From the moment a child enters the school system and is abound with rudimentary curiosities, qualitative effort must be concentrated, on par with Maths, English and Science, on preparatory life skills such axiology, logic, civics, reason, conflict resolution, learning by rote, pluralism and critical thinking. Such subjects would require a triumvirate of parent/guardians, specialist teachers and local grassroots organizations. The Dalai Lama was asked what was the most important discipline to study? His answer: *Logic*. Pedagogical breechings need not be abandoned. Youths should be permitted to pursue a vocational education that is in synthesis with their ambitions and interests if they find the curriculum disagreeable or rigid. PRU's (Pupil Referral Unit) should be disbanded. No child should ever be excluded from school. Consider the implications this raises if they are. Consider the imputations this brings.

I propose that the government embark on a revolutionary social program on the scale of Franklin D. Roosevelt's *The New Deal* that would bequeath a wellspring of opportunities for all Britons. A new Social Contract; a new Covenant; a new Frontier; a national investment bank bequeathing and renewing the promise and potential of every generation - call it what you will. As Jean-Jacques Rousseau's *The Social Contract* says... *The social pact, far from destroying natural equality, substitutes, on the contrary, a moral and lawful equality for whatever physical inequality that nature may have imposed on mankind; so that however unequal in strength and intelligence, men become equal by covenant and by right.* Those who thoroughly object to a salubrious system for the working classes may not demonstrate the same type of objection when it comes to dropping bombs on Aleppo or Aden, whatever the financial and human cost. There maybe profit in warfare, but the greater profit lies in renewing the promise of this nation. Perhaps there are those who believe the system is not broken, and therefore requires little or no tinkering. Some might say the system is willfully discriminatory. We may not know this for certain. The interpretation of facts are placed above the facts themselves. We must judge things by their fruits. The haughty classes may denounce my third point as *socialism*, an ideology they have no qualms practicing among themselves, even if they possess capitalist tendencies. I am not a socialist, a communist, a conservative or a libertarian in the slightest.

I desire we live on a salubrious playing field that befits all those that play fair. It would be churlish to suggest that the current system has not brought degrees of success to many. Many, however, remain hamstrung by it. We ought to be bold and ask: *How can we make our society better? How can we work towards a salubrious society? How can we work towards a meritocracy? How can we invest better in meaningful resources that grant dignity to human beings?* Even the most stable of families require healthy support systems. The so-called Royal Family, in spite of its bloated wealth and avoirdupois power, is not an exception to this rule. Poor families are not bequeathed with healthy support systems, hence the preponderance of off-kilter kids fed on chicken burgers and chips and raised by the social media and computer games. While the State and private industries continue to profit and seek greater powers from societal fluxes, the problem of youth crime will remain inexorable.

May 01, 2018.

FLASHBACKS OF A FOOL

F OR MOST OF MY portentous third decade, I worked as a temp in central London. I loitered on reception desks, in post rooms, call centers, and in office caches below ground level, for a sawbuck an hour, sometimes less. As the old Soviet adage goes; *So long as the boss pretends to pay us, we'll pretend to work.* I pretended well, and so did they. If you were to take a cursory glance at my résumé, it would confirm to you how I promiscuous I was, workwise. There were countervailing factors as to why my employment record was peripatetic and, at times, patchy. I cannot justify these reasons today. But I do not regret them.

My saturnine disposition preferred that I remain in my reservoir of nurture, uninterrupted in monastic mode, devouring immortal prose and gelato. I would have been content with this arrangement till it was time to cross the Styx River, shrouded and stiff. Where there are murmurations, there are catty feuds. Where there are no people, there are no problems. Though no man's an island, it is both sensible and beneficial that he be part of a fertile and thriving archipelago. I loathed much of what emanated in the social sphere. For in these days of excess, puerility has become a raging pestilence, laying waste to malleable and impressionable minds, killing time and creating distractions at every turn. Vicarious living, voyeurism, facsimile celebritism and social media have become insurmountable foes. However, I resurfaced from my furlough, dovetailing between bullheads, brainiacs and in-betweeners on an etherized plain. I needed money to tread water in this beguiling city. So down these rabbit holes I went.

Slapdash administration jobs were an easy find. I'd navigate between a dozen agencies, morning, noon and before closing time. My modulated overtones transmitted my angst over the phone. I employed this metered alchemy to good effect. I'd consider anything, I said. More's the pity, they said. I took shifts at very short notice. I drove my yeasty plough through the office spaces of Wigmore Street, Old Compton Road, Whitfield Street and Camp Paekakariki, to name but a few places. I'd grind earnestly in local and national government departments: Public Protection at Redbridge Council; Environmental Health at Newham Council; The Solicitor General's Office in St. James' Park. I'd like to think that I was more than a potted plant at the reception desks of EMI Music, Sony Pictures and TFL (Transport for London), where I transferred a near infinite amount of phone calls to their destinations daily.

I underwent a CRB check and gravitated to working in residentiary homes, caring for the elderly and the disabled in Edgware and Welwyn Garden City, and being attentive to toddlers in nursery schools in Maida Vale and Chalk Farm. My timesheets were signed off by simulacrums of fictional figures that were manifest in the everyday man and woman I encountered: Loki, Medusa, Nurse Ratched, Mrs. Danvers, Cruella De Vil, Darth Vador, Miss Havisham, Mr. Tamnus, Norma Desmond, Eshu and Foghorn Leghorn. *Truth is stranger than fiction*, wrote Mark Twain, *but it is because fiction is obliged to stick to possibilities. Truth isn't.* By the Sacred Cats of Nefertiti, the creator of Huckleberry Finn was not wrong.

Much of my daily iterations were Sisyphean. My unharnessed mind was not subject to the encumbrances of my petered body and so I was never bored. Roving devilments and moonshot ambitions kept my mind alive whilst I filed and faxed, as if I was an extra in

Dante's First Circle. There were other auxiliary staff who, like me, demonstrated their resilience in Limbo. These folks sprung from the Zambezi, the Mackenzie, the Murray, the Orange River, the Tiber, and from the banks of the Caspian Sea. Others were from the Thames, as I was, the Tyne and the Mersey. Sylvester, of Securicor Guarding, was a straight 'A' student and lived a straight edge lifestyle. Ananda, at EMI Music, signed me up to the vices of the email and the Internet. Kishmeister was a cognoscenti when it came to hip-hop, jazz and grime music. He aided me with the editing of my debut novel and gave me good counsel about writing and sundry. Audrey, at the EMMA Awards, became my sister-friend. We've been tight for twenty years. I was at PR21 for ten months. I worked with Bijal, Bobby and Nasrin. They possessed wit and generosity, charisma and love. They continue to be gracious to me after sixteen years. These were the good guys. The Magnificent Seven.

I met delightful human beings at all these places. I enjoyed long rapturous lunches with some of them. We pared religious and political theories by using Occam's Razor, carving age-old philosophies from their sinews and strands, and examining their foundational claims to great aplomb. There were many raconteurs among us, and we were as mad as a box of frogs. Witless sturgeons were barred, so as not to afflict us with the catarrhs of the heart. The inkwells of innovation flowed as a result, prompting an Epiphanius-like surge in my writing. But not all rabbit holes were alike. Some warrens were laws unto themselves.

In the more turgid burrows, many members of staff suffered from *Entfremdung*. They were expended by a parenthetical culture that was negligent of their career development. They required permission to take toilet breaks. *Comfort breaks* were regulated to precision. Employee rights were gradually abrogated by use of their employer's casuistry. These gauleiters cared more for their image and their corporate drolleries, and they did not seem to mind the flow of dispersed bodies floating downstream out of their organization. In some of these places, the estrangement between people becomes palpable after a few hours. Confidence was decimated. I've witnessed men and women weeping after enduring fingernails-along-the-chalkboard screeds from browbeating bastards with absurd job titles. They bore the tip of the spear against their collective aortas because that paycheck was their sole lifeblood. To seek redress from within the system risked contrivance from these gauleiters. Few had the means and the fortitude to withstand well-disposed dastardly vestiges, combined with the other strife of everyday life.

Would a mouse consider herself wise to arrange a meeting with the cat about what fears keep her up at night? Some, indeed, were intolerant to an inerrant culture. They left without a fuss. Some endured the slow depredation of their èlan. Some sunk into depression and took time from work. Some staff, however, did take the piss and felt it necessary to stick it to *The Man* by playing cat-and-mouse with the Sickness Policy. At one particular joint, there existed hatred and enmity between two rival colleagues. I was told no good word was even spoken from one to the other for several years. And whenever a sentence was spun, it was an opprobrious one and a full-scale battle would commence. Instances where the proverbial shots were fired were not uncommon. I was never there long enough to see how these onerous wars played out; though I was able to elicit feedback from those I maintained contact with. I, myself, was only as good as my last shift. If I wasn't good enough, I was not invited back.

I forwent a type of metallurgy in the workplace, pivoting between rocks and hard places, chided by wily and worldly ciphers, who took me for some sort of Clark Kent hick. I lacked the *l'esprit de l'escalier*. I was often caught flat-footed in my first job at TGI Fridays, Piccadilly Circus. The supervisor reviled and mocked me with vituperative remarks, behind my back and to my face. I learnt to traffic in mockery. It is implausible in the mindset of the haughty to suffer derision. It causes grievous distress to their pockmarked hearts and pavlovian pride. This particular donut was ranked one of the top bartenders in the world at the time. In spite of his admirable *talents*, he was pretty fucked up if he felt that the best default position for his fragile soul was to be mean-spirited to those under his supervision. And I was to meet many like the bull-headed bartender over the years. They came packaged in all genders and sizes, all colors and denominations. These folks, men and women, would have made plausible pantomime villains if they ever were to grace a stage, but they preferred to keep their ornery performances behind portcullises and within satanic mills, in the dark — like the light-hating, cave dwelling rats and bats that they were.

It was also notable to watch the finagling fence-sitters batting for both sides. They purported sympathy and solidarity with the problems of their colleagues but then acted as a rakish instrument that played an oleaginous tune for the big kahuna. You felt safer trusting nobody. It was a bit like that scene in *The Wizard of Oz* when Dorothy and her friends are trapped by the Wicked Witch and her hypertense guards as she attempts to flee the castle. When Dorothy unwittingly melts the witch, with a bucket of water no less, it is those same hypertense guards that hail Dorothy on bended knee for slaying their master and hand her the prize of her mission, the broomstick. In the workplace, one could be best pals with Dorothy and the Wicked Witch at the same time, and see no contradiction!

Temping was my first foray into the adult world. It schooled me with the practical nature of humankind. It dispelled myths I had been raised to believe as truths, which had made a fool of me once too often. Meritocracy, and all that garbage about working twice or three times as hard, was as much a myth as the Tooth Fairy and Wishing Wells. Class, race, sex, and nepotism are as quintessential as the classical elements in both the private and public sectors. One must be blind, dismissive or ignorant not to recognize or understand the iniquities at play here. I became a union steward so that I could be of help to workers, who suffered grave injustice at work, whose employment rights are infringed with impunity. Nothing rages me like injustice.

October 31, 2019.

SOUTHALL, THE GREAT

F ROM MY FARAWAY YOUTH, I can recall watching a First Division
League game between Everton and Leeds United on ITV's *The
Match*, on a Sunday afternoon sometime in February 1992. This was
the final season of the century old First Division. The dreamscape
of the Premier League was all but on the dissipating horizon. In
those days, Howard Wilkinson's Leeds United were locked in a
league title steeplechase with Alex Ferguson's Manchester United.
Within a few months, they prevailed. They became champions of
England. Contrarily, Everton wallowed unremarkably, paddling fair
to middling, playing milquetoast football. The Toffees possessed
only a few of the ensemble that enabled them to rule English
football for an ephemeral spell. Detractors would have you believe
their reign in England was a Lady Jane Grey moment. Arch-rivals
Liverpool had long thriven, like a Tudor rose. Everton were twice
league champions during the halcyon mid-1980s. They partook in
three successive FA Cup finals. They enjoyed European Cup Winners
Cup success. They contested four consecutive Charity Shield curtain-
raisers. Their frequent exertions at the national gladiatorial arena
made Wembley Stadium almost a second home. Goodison South, if
you will! All this contributed to an unbelievably happy childhood.
Further potential European glory had been denied arguably Everton's

most successful ever squad. The human tragedy at Heysel Stadium culminated in the deaths of thirty-nine people. English clubs were barred from European competition for five years. Everton, twice champions of England, were twice prohibited entry into European football's premier competition. When one considers the winners of the European Cup, in Everton's absence, were Steaua Bucharest and PSV Eindhoven respectively, Tyche had been inexplicably unkind to Everton. Like the Knights of the Round table, their champion players soon departed in search of the Holy Grail. Harquebusiers like Trevor Steven and Gary Stevens ended up at Ibrox Stadium, Glasgow. Superlative goal machine Gary Lineker sought and found success in Barcelona. King Arthur himself took a managerial post at Atletico Bilbao. He did return to Camelot, though his kingdom would not return to the kindled luster of his First Coming.

Everton's Welsh International goalkeeper Neville Southall was one of the last remaining stadtholders. Like King Canute, he could not command the high tides to do his will. The will to win games, and secure honors. Those plain drifts of water roiled and chopped before the rubicund faces aboard the good ship Goodison as the 1980s became the 1990s. The tintless water bled red as Arsenal, Liverpool and Manchester United won pearls buried oceans deep. Blackburn Rovers and Newcastle United were hunting those same treasures, high and low. Southall, meanwhile, had been a colossal part of Everton's own *Wonder Years*. In his prime, he was reckoned by punters and pundits alike to be the world's best goalkeeper. Those of us who believed so had marveled at the supernal grammar of his keeping. In his fast-paced memoir *The Binman's Chronicles,* he tells how Manchester United manager Alex Ferguson contacted him and asked if he wished to become a Red Devil. United were on the cusp of being a great power again. They required a figurehead in goal. Southall thought the call a prank from former Everton legend Andy Gray. He ungraciously told Ferguson to *fuck off*. One wonders whether he'd have mounted his Sleipnir-like steed for Old Trafford had an official transfer offer been submitted to Everton HQ.

Ferguson's future trophy bonanzas would make Manchester United the new Imperial Rome.

Five years removed from their last league title of 1987, Everton's prestige had waned considerably. They were going nowhere fast in 1992. Leeds United, barely promoted two seasons ago from the old Second Division, were challenging for the glories that once came naturally to Everton. The match preview, presented by the nonpareil Elton Welsby, provisionally focused on Leeds United's new semi-morose, incroyable, Gallic lodestar Eric Cantona. He had recently signed from Nimes. He was poised to make his full English debut at a tangibly eroding Goodison Park. *The place whereon thou standest (O Eric) is holy ground.* (Exodus 3: Verse 5). He arrived in England somewhat in exile from his native France. A concatenation of incidents led to his premature decision to retire from professional football, aged twenty-five. But then, *abyssus abyssum invocat* occurred. And so Goodison Park, home of so many firsts, witnessed this imposing, seigneurial princeling leading the Leeds forward line. One wondered why there was no *sabrage* to mark the occasion. Cantona might have welcomed it.

Approximately ten minutes into the game, Cantona laid first sight on the Everton goal. The ball ricocheted favorably into his lap. Having beaten the offside trap, he galloped into the Everton half like a fleet-footed pronghorn. The Everton backline scampered wildly in pursuit. The dependable warhorse Dave Watson was never going to catch him. Neither was the tough-tackling Martin Keown. I looked on with mechanical curiosity. Southall guarded the entrance of the Everton den as if he were Cerberus of the Underworld. I had already witnessed, over the years, his blunderbuss one-on-one duels against Ian Rush, Mark Hughes, John Barnes, Peter Beardsley, Alan McInally, Brian McClair, Mark Falco. Their rassles were never forgone conclusions. The aforementioned players knew this themselves when facing the most obdurate of goalkeepers. Now it was the future Manchester United musket Cantona's turn. He bore upon the Gwladys Street End, albeit from a slight angle from his left on the pitch. Southall moved forward incrementally. If the Frenchman aimed his strike for the near post, he would induce a routine save from the goalkeeper. Through the middle, and Southall would deprehend his effort with his hulky frame. His narrowing (and increasingly remaining) option was to take aim within the far post. And thus he fired – and missed by two yards. No save was rendered! Southall's acute positioning meant that, not only was Cantona not going to force him into making a save, but he was to make the marksman miss the target completely. It was an exceptional piece of goalkeeping.

I overheard two boys in the playground, Sam Harvey and Albert Freeman, discuss the Cantona-Southall faceoff when I arrived at school the next day. Like myself, we were intrigued by the inveterate underpinnings that made a good goalkeeper. I didn't intervene in their discussion. But I remember being pleased at their precepting on what I had also noticed about that mind game duel: the earnest importance of getting into the head of an opponent and forcing his hand to do your bidding. It was not unusual to hear classmates and friends apply meticulous thought to an incident from ITV's *The Match* or the BBC's *Match of the Day*. We debated the wisdom and folly of professional footballers on the pitch. Passages of play were oft re-enacted on the concrete surface. Some among us believed we were an embodiment of Ian Rush, Ian Wright and David Rocastle on the playground. Some self-commentated on their own performances as they dribbled past their peers. I was content between two makeshift goalposts created from rucksacks and school jumpers. I was known as *Ali Southall* and Ali *The Cat*, for my feline-like saves. I could never quite emulate the great man himself. I certainly tried. My efforts helped propel me into the school B team. I could not lodge the A team goalkeeper, Ovgu Ahmet, in spite of my pretensions.

England's Barclays First Division was saturated with reliable goalkeepers. They were mainly ineffaceable characters. They were secure with their handling. They were prone to the odd frippery. Some were blood and thunder types. The sort that would cut through a player to claim the ball. The type that would not permit both ball and man to bypass him together. The kind that caught the ball as a first resort. He seldom flapped his palms at it or pushed it to one side, as is the fashion these days. If he couldn't claim the ball with any certainty, he fisted it to safety with a great deal of emphasis. It was near criminal to concede a goal through the near post. That area was always prioritized. At school, you were ruthlessly mocked if nutmegged (when an attacking player rolled the ball between the keeper's legs on route to scoring). I had long observed the performative art of goalkeeping. I found that too many goalkeepers nowadays tend to react hastily as opposed to waiting a tad longer for the striker to make a harried decision. Like Southall a la Cantona. The longer the Mexican standoff, the greater pressure weighs on the forward. In a one-on-one duel, he *must* score. If the goalkeeper concedes, then he can simply shrug at the inevitability of the effort. For penalties, most goalkeepers tend to hazard a guess and take off, rather than respond once the ball was struck. I subscribed to the latter principle. It then becomes incumbent upon the penalty-taker to beat the goalkeeper with precision and power rather than opt for a Panenka, should he feel petulant. The baller is favorite to score a penalty. The law of averages favors him. But a good goalkeeper can attempt to read the disposition of the aspirant. He can steal subtle inches of the goal line before launching a feline glide towards the ball's direction.

The modern goalkeeper must be adept with both feet. He must make space for himself so that he receives the ball safely from his defenders. Teams prefer to build their attack from the backline. He must make acute, crisp passes to his teammates. He must pass the ball sixty yards up the field into the path of a player, as opposed to punting it into no man's land. Like the current custodian of the Everton goal, Jordan Pickford. Footballs are considerably lighter than its leather-laced forerunner. They are prone to change course on a squally day. Goalkeepers of old weren't protected as much by referees as it is almost customary today. Yet you can expect them to make a guest appearance in the opposition's penalty area when, in the final minutes of the game, a desperate goal is fiercely desired. Goalkeepers such as Rogerio Ceni, Jose Luis Chilavert, and Peter Schmeichel have scored notable goals that would have warmed the cockles of any striker.

Before the 1990 FIFA World Cup, a defender could pass the ball to his goalkeeper who'd retrieve it with his hands. He'd embrace the ball into his bosom. He'd bounce it several times into the turf. Then he'd roll it back to his defender. They'd repeat this action twice or thrice before the goalkeeper thundered the ball up the pitch, thereby killing some time on the clock. This was a common timewasting tactic and so FIFA penalized this practice on pain of a freekick to the opposing team where the offense took place. Before this habit was prohibited, Southall himself fell foul of an infamous referee's decision in a Littlewoods League Cup quarterfinal match between Nottingham Forest and Everton in November 1989. He handled the ball for all of thirteen seconds in the eighty-fifth minute of the game. The score was set at 0-0. The referee deemed this timewasting. He awarded Nottingham Forest an indirect freekick in the Everton penalty area. From the resulting freekick, Forest scored. Lee Chapman. They went on to win the game 1-0. And the tournament thereafter. Everton crashed out of a competition that they have never won in their illustrious history.

By the Rings of Saturn, I became an Evertonian, unbidden, when I watched the Toffeemen defeat Southampton 1-0 in an FA Cup semi-final game at Arsenal's old Highbury Stadium, in the spring of 1984. Striker Adrian Heath scored with three minutes of extra-time remaining. I am often asked, why Everton? *Were you born up there?* I have friends who are supporters of Liverpool and Manchester United from Lagos and Lisbon, never mind London, who aren't subjected to this question. Everton Football Club are one of the guvnors in English football, though they slumbered for fourteen years when I jumped on their bandwagon. *Nil satis nisi optimum* was to receive an awakening. A month later, Everton defeated Watford 2-0 in the FA Cup final. Miracles, thereafter, were abound. A blue tide rose from along the River Mersey. England and Europe were in thrall of this particular Liver Bird. Footballs were sucked into the back of the opposition's net by the Gwladys Street End of Goodison Park. Striker Andy Gray would throw his weatherworn head to within a foot of the muddy turf to steer the ball home. Ball technician Kevin Sheedy's left foot operated like an inscrutable wand, weaving wonderous magic before the multitude. Gary Lineker's forty goal wonder sprees during the 1985-86 season was some fairy-tale of the Vanishing Hero. He scored a hattrick at hallowed Hillsborough. Three more followed at Glorious Goodison. Why he was then bundled on a plane bound for Barcelona after barely ten months at Everton still rankles me four decades on but that is a subject for another essay. Midfielder Peter Reid was like Sai Baba of Shirdi. Such was his ability to cover every blade of glass, it appeared as if there were two of him on the pitch. It was said of Trevor Steven that were he to run *through a puddle, it wouldn't make a ripple.* Graeme Sharp was like the Celtic Sun God, Belenus, rising majestically above a cabal of defenders to thunder the ball into the net with his forehead. Captain Kevin Ratcliffe was as fleetfooted as the Greek god Hermes. And Southall, during this period and a latter one known as *The Dogs Of War*, continued to confound mortals by plucking goal bound efforts with lithe agility that belied his haunch limbs.

Southall was nimble on the floor. He spun like a cyclone in the ether. He possessed expeditious reflexes. His finetuned bearings made it difficult for said marksmen, whether they be in full flight or striking from distance. Many of his saves have been committed to memory. Nottingham Forest's Scott Gemmill had his effort miraculously tipped over the cross bar by Southall in a 1991 league game at Goodison Park. *What a save by Southall!* cheered ITV's voice of football the late Brian Moore, who commentated the match. *We've seen him make top saves over the years but that was simply out of the top drawer.* Tottenham Hotspur's Mark Falcao was spectacularly denied a certain goal at

White Hart Lane in the 1984-85 season when Southall's recoil under his crossbar defied all sequitur. The Daily Mail's Jeff Powell described that piece of goalkeeping *as the most astonishing save since Gordon Banks left Pele dumbfounded in Mexico*. Of the second game of the 1988-89 season against Coventry City at Highfield Road which Everton won 1-0, Southall was like a djinn, brilliantly saving a thunderbolt penalty from their stalwart Brian Kilcline, stupendously denying a certain goal from their forward Gary Bannister, turning a 30-yard rocket from Greg Downs around the goalpost. I can recall a match between Derby County and Everton in the 1989-90 season where a series of stupendous saves from Southall was met with applause from his counterpart, England great Peter Shilton. After a World Cup qualifier between the then European champions, Netherlands, and Southall's native Wales, a headline crooned the following headline: *Holland vs Southall*. The Dutch forward line was led by Marco Van Basten, considered by football purists as one of the greatest strikers that ever lived. The Dutch possessed panache and pugilists abound in Ronald Koeman, Frank Rijkaard, Ruud Gullit and Jan Wouters. The Dutch players cannonaded Southall's goal like an invading horde. They threw the proverbial *gootsteen* at the Welsh defense. They found him almost impenetrable until the final minutes. Gullit headed into an open goal after his first effort had been parried by Southall unto the crossbar. The Netherlands was victorious. 1-0.

In Ian Rush, Liverpool possessed the 1980s most prolific striker in England. I dreaded his wolfish relish for goals against Everton. He hounded defenders into error and then terror. Their discombobulated clowning often led to his clinical finishing without prejudice. The ball drew itself to him as if he were a neodymium magnet. He tucked goals home with either foot. By his indefatigable work rate and unembellished goals, he invoked the fear of Spring-heeled Jack. When it was announced that Rush would be playing against Everton, my inauspicious soul vacated my despairing body. Nobody scored more than he in matches between Everton and Liverpool. He was a shark beneath the Everton blue. He scored twice in both the all-Merseyside FA Cup finals of 1986 and 1989, ensuring that I'd be mocked remorselessly at school the following Monday by Red Rush groupies whilst we filed in line on the school playground.

I only ever saw Neville Southall play twice. Everton came to my hometown to play Leyton Orient in the fall of 1989 to contest a Littlewoods League Cup fixture. There was no point asking if I could go. My parents would have forbidden it. My father believed *the funny old game* was a waste of a man's money and time. In fact, he was in concord with Michel de Montaigne, French philosopher and master essayist: *Mistrust a man who takes games too seriously. It means he doesn't take life seriously.* But a visit by Everton to a mile from whence I slept had to be taken seriously. (Unbeknownst to me at the time, it would be another seven years before I saw Southall play again, when Everton visited Arsenal at Highbury and registered a 2-1 win). So I conjured a narrative about a midweek school event that required my participation. My parents brought the story. My friend Matt purchased the tickets among the home crowd. We were warned of a racist element among some Everton fans. A banana skin had been thrown at the Liverpool dynamo John Barnes by a numbskull at Goodison only one year previous. We were advised to be mindful. But I had always felt safe in Leyton. E10 was hearth and home. We sauntered along Leyton High Road. My joy was inexpressible. As we stood in the Main Stand, Orient fans screeched like fishwives. Their team gave a good account of themselves. They began caterwauling when the tenor of the game favored their superior opposition. Southall produced his usual stock of quality saves. He was a scruff in the Everton goal. My friend Mazhar has since described him as *an unmade bed!* An Orient player, whose name I've long forgotten, was through on goal with only Cerberus to beat. I knew the effort would be saved before the ball was struck. Mike Newell and Kevin Sheedy both scored. Everton won the game 2-0. I went home elated. Though by the time I reached home, my fib had been untangled. My father was furious. I covered one falsehood with another. I said I had played an away football match for the school team. I was given a clump. I went to bed happy.

The 1990s was a trepidatious time for Everton. It marked the most ominous period of the Grand Old Club's recent history. The first game of the 1990-91 season against Leeds United served as a precursor. Per usual, I listened earnestly to BBC Radio 909MW for updates. Everton were already 0-2 down by halftime. At the interval, Southall emerged onto the pitch. He plonked himself against a goalpost. It was as if he were the Prophet Jeremiah, foreseeing swirling ill-tidings yet to come: Wimbledon 1994, Coventry 1998. Mediocrity had stunk the place out. Of the so-called Big Five clubs of England, Everton had unwittingly fostered a myopic, provincial outlook. Three of the Five, Arsenal, Liverpool and Manchester United enjoyed trophy success and a groundswell of global commercial activity. The fourth, Tottenham Hotspur, wallowed in the ordinariness that can be attributed to Everton. But they were an arresting London club. They were media darlings. They still could attract enthralling players of pedigree and renown like Lineker (what were Everton thinking?), Klinsmann, Sheringham, Gascoigne and Ginola. Newly promoted clubs Leeds United, Chelsea, Newcastle United and Blackburn Rovers were led by men of ambition. They desired what the biggest clubs in England desired. They invested substantively in a bonanza of ballers: the Ruud Gullit's, Gianfranco Zola's, Les Ferdinand's, the David Ginola's, the Alan Shearer's. Manchester United produced an infusion of talent from their factory whilst cherry-picking everybody else's best players, save for Liverpool's. Everton floated aimlessly like a raft along the Mersey River. And Southall sat upon the drift on that day in August 1990, before the Goodison crowd. But King Canute he was not. The tides had turned against the Toffeemen.

Southall wrote in *The Binman's Chronicles* that, by coming onto the pitch during the halftime interval against Leeds United, he merely wanted to clear his head. Everton had endured a painful first half. He undertook the same action at a game the previous season to zero fanfare. But the rumor mill had already whirled. Speculation was abound that he was agitating for an exit from a palpably sinking ship. He had already submitted three transfer requests in the past year. Everton had rejected all three. He believed the club hadn't afforded him the respect he'd earned. He was, after all, the best goalkeeper in the world. *Yet some of the people in the director's box treated me as if I was still a binman,* he wrote. *They thought I was stupid and wasn't worth listening to. They liked the fact that I played for Everton but as a person did not respect me.* The club was forced to act for what they perceived was insubordination. They fined him two weeks wages.

Nevertheless, he stayed another seven or so years. He became a crucial component of the Dogs of War team of the mid-nineties that won the FA Cup in 1995. The slump, however, was terminal. I was aghast by some of the results. Everton were battered 5-1 by Norwich City at Goodison Park. A Sheffield Wednesday team destroyed Everton by the same score-line. New mangers arrived but they could not halt the decline. After Joe Royle's resignation as Everton manager, Southall was on a shortlist of two to succeed him – the other being the dependable stalwart Dave Watson. Everton chairman Peter Johnson, in a conversation with Alan Myers (press secretary at Everton), mooted the idea of Southall being the frontrunner. He presumed goalkeepers had lesser responsibilities. Southall emerged from his car suddenly. He greeted Myers with *Hello Alan, you fat cunt!* And Johnson narrowed his shortlist to one.

Southall's final game for Everton was his 751st. The result was a 0-2 loss at Goodison Park against Tottenham Hotspur in November 1997. Another mercurial Frenchman, David Ginola, starred that day. During the furore of the second half, he advanced with the ball into Everton territory, like the huntsman Orion walking on water. Upon arriving in the opposition's penalty area, he unleashed a second goal that nailed Everton to the foot of the Premier League table. Everton's *dégringolade* was complete. The Grand Old Lady Goodison resembled an old panopticon. The natives gnashed their teeth at the chairman Johnson. They protested the monstrous decline of a football institution fast becoming a mausoleum preoccupied with ghosts of a bygone, zesty era. The past had been glorious. The future looked tenuous. Did they provide a plan, a blueprint, a project to return Everton to its proper place? The hell they didn't! Southall was the last remaining player from the last league title winning side. And after the Tottenham Hotspur game, he was summoned before old but grand King Arthur. According to *The Binman Chronicles, I was told that I couldn't train with the first team, the kids or the reserves, that I was finished...* It was unfair for Southall to be banished in this manner. The Everton's 1997-98 squad harbored some of their worst players in living memory. Nobody in the squad matched his seventeen years of service. His trophy count was incomparable. And though he was far from his peak, only a few goalkeepers were consistently more impactful in matches. Norwegian goalkeeper Thomas Myhre had newly signed from Viking Stavanger, and he was to become the new custodian of the Everton goal. Thus, Southall's Everton career ended, on this dour exit through the side door.

Before his meteoric ascent, Southall had been a hod carrier and a binman. After Everton, he played in the lower leagues with the likes of Stoke City, Bradford City and Torquay United until he retired from the game. Nowadays, the unassuming legend can be found applying his unconventional wisdom working within marginalized communities that have borne the effrontery of wider society. In areas where successive governments are found wanting, he uses his social media platform as a reservoir of awareness in addiction, mental health, trans rights and poverty. He rallies against racism, homophobia and transphobia. He is positive proof that humility, engagement and understanding are incalculable values. His triumphs at Everton Football Club and with Welsh International football are long carved into the annals of their respective but proud histories. Being a lantern in the dark, as a resource and a recourse to those made destitute by prevailing bigotry, attests to the true greatness of the man. For that, there is no substitute.

October 28, 2019

THE AGONY AND ECSTASY
OF PENMANSHIP

I DON'T THINK IT would be an exaggeration for me to claim that I was born with a protuberant pen clasped in my right hand. But I make no boast here, dear reader, so please do not interpret it as such. I intend to make several plaintive admissions. Allow me first to state for the record that my penmanship is a mercurial gift for which I am grateful. It is a bestowal that I have cultivated and weaponized to inscribe my peculiar font upon the page, particularly in this age of disillusionment and adversity. The page is a stage to a penman. As a child, I composed fables. I liked stories and storytelling. I loved language and lexicons. Storytelling took me on a flighty path, to the lands of witches and djinns, giants and gnomes, and then further afield to magical realms and outer space. Whenever my world became staid, disassociation from it was bliss. I'd lose myself in writing heaven, pluck whatever was real and whatever was imagined from the ether, submerge into the elixir of a world that was solely mine, and breathed life into those dry bones. My stories were unanimously applauded by those who read them. Then again, most people would praise a child for effort alone.

I experienced the acute pain of learning in school, with its plodding, structural monotony. *It's not enough to keep the mind alive, is it?* to paraphrase British satirist, Peter Cook. Throw in the near disastrous ingredients of a few bad peers, and some mediocre teaching, and therein is this toxic brew that could force a sane mind to flee into a tundra of indifference, if he were to drink the brew without relish. Thankfully, I had an alternative learning space at home. I gave that prominence. I was able to deconstruct whereon it was necessary and add flesh to the bones on what was minutely touched upon in the classroom. Study accelerated me into maturity. Learning can only be acquired through difficulty and sacrifice. The pleasure of a free mind initiates wanton bliss. *I am free, my mind is free*, wrote Bulleh Shah, an eighteenth-century Sufi philosopher. *Emancipate yourself from mental slavery*, crooned the Jamaican songwriter Bob Marley from *Redemption Song*, his immortal track. *None but ourselves can free our minds*. Because, after it is all said and done, The Koran says in Chapter 17, verse 14: *Read thy own book (of thy life's account). For thou art sufficient as a reckoner against thyself this day*.

The pain of writing only began after I had decided to make a career from it. Writing (and getting paid for it) is a harbinger towards a commodious life. I would not hesitate to unsheathe my pen from its scabbard and scribble upon any subject that moved me. *Blessed be the Lord, my rock. Who trains my hands for war and my fingers for battle!* (Psalms 144 verse 1). Such a freedom is an essential part of my existence, an inviolable discipline of which I have wholeheartedly subscribed to.

Most of my early submissions to publishing firms were met without response. Every purported rejection had an adverse effect on my serotonin. Occasionally, I would succumb to the ludicrous flights of fancy, that I would eventually be published to great fanfare, and that my works would be widely read. Morpheus appeared to me whilst I was asleep. He'd shower me with glory in a carbon copy universe. On frequent occasion, an impersonal email would arrive with a message that was contrary to my dream. So I wore a rueful mask wherever I went, while a muted donnybrook waged within my bosom. I couldn't fathom the flame that burnt inside me. It was either an indignant fire of ambition or some *ignis fatuus* borne from hubris. Whatever it was, it caused great anguish. To make matters worse, unsolicited do-gooders subjected me to their constant brain farts, suggesting ways of increasing my chances at getting published. *Write a book in the spirit of Paolo Coelho's The Alchemist... Write a novel about a galactical mice invasion of Britain ...How about if I present to you a synopsis of my life story and you can write a book about it?* The antitheist journalist and author Christopher Hitchens once said that *everyone has a book inside them which is exactly where I think it should, in most cases, remain.* And every time I found myself looking down the barrel of these lame proposals, I took some solace from his truism.

I was asked to take comfort in the fact that a plethora of successful authors suffered rejection before reaching critical acclaim. That maybe so. My mind, however, stumbled upon the unknown genial poets and playwrights whose works remain lost and unread. I found this analogous to that old philosophical thought experiment: that if a tree falls in a forest and nobody is present to hear it fall, does it still make a sound? If nobody has read these lost masterpieces, how could we have ever known for certain that these works *were* masterpieces? How many lost poems and plays have been sucked into the egregious black holes of time? Would my own work be destined for oblivion? Or were my writings simply not good enough? I am an outsider, knocking on the doors of the petite bourgeoisie who are deaf to my experience. And as Nikos Kazantzakis' *Zorba The Greek* said: *You can knock on a deaf man's door forever.*

The chances of a 21st century author ever losing their works forever are extremely slim, thanks to innovations like the memory stick. A greater dread for the simple writer is having her work embraced by the masses having departed this mortal coil. For how could that be consoling? Would one not prefer to be vindicated in one's own lifetime? Permit me, therefore, to summarize the careers of four writers (and there are more, believe me) who died before the glorious manifestation of their efforts. They never were to revel in the undraped knowledge that their works had assuredly been rendered immortal after a physical lifetime of literary alienation and rejection; the readers of the distant future had decreed it so.

Edgar Allan Poe is one of the most famous writers of American literature today. He composed a profusion of terse but brilliant fables. However, he lived an impecunious life. He suffered grave misfortunes, resulting in his mysterious death aged forty. His writings were posthumously revitalized. They are a must read for today's literary student. I was enamored to Poe's literary work as a kid. His writings were unharnessed. He delved vividly into the macabre. Three of his stories immediately come to mind. *The Pit and the Pendulum* is a short fable of a chronicler's depiction of torture and torment in a prison cell during the Spanish Inquisition. The grievous penalties he fortuitously avoids are a pit, that he narrowly avoids not falling into, and a pendulum slowly descending upon him with the dreaded intention of cutting him in half. We are not told whether he is innocent or not. His judges had condemned him to death at the beginning of the story. His angst at his imminent demise, in a constricted jail cell occupied by rats, looms over the breadth of each page. He is rescued at the end when the town of Toledo (where he is imprisoned) is captured by the French Army.

The System of Doctor Tarr and Professor Fether is another peculiar tale of the lunatics literally taking over the asylum. It is told through the mouthpiece of an exploratory narrator who seeks revolutionary procedures that provide better treatment for the mentally ill. The doctors and nurses are rendered as patients against their will. They are tarred and feathered as part of the regimen. The story contains that oft-repeated, infamous line: *Believe nothing that you hear and only half that you see*, in answer to the narrator's incessant querying of prescriptive techniques. I read many of Poe's stories before sleep as an adolescent. They allowed me no respite by accompanying me into the chthonic realm, inviting upon me nightmares of the worst kind.

The Imp of the Perverse is a brooding but succinct narration about a man who commits murder upon his fellow with the aid of a candle that released a poisonous vapor into his room. The man inherits the dead fellow's possessions. He delights he got away with the crime. His conscience cannot put such a depravity to bed. He grapples with his own annihilation when all that is required of him is his silence. He becomes beguiled by his own capture. He implicates himself by screaming allusions to the murder in a public street. After his arrest, he is haunted into confession by an *invisible fiend*. He is finally condemned ... *to the hangman and to hell.*

A few months later, after rereading this story, I found myself in somnambulistic motion alongside the febrile traffic of the M4. I was contemplating suicide. I was nineteen years old. I wept bitterly as if I were a child aged nine. I was exhausted and made sick by living. As I scraped my tardy trainers through the prairie towards the roadside, I, among other things, tried to recreate that arcane sensation that Poe spoke of in *The Imp of the Perverse*, of being on a precipice, and then falling ... *And this fall*, wrote Poe, -- *this rushing annihilation -- for the very reason that it involves that one most ghastly and loathsome of all the most ghastly and loathsome images of death and suffering which have ever presented themselves to our imagination -- for this very cause do we now the most vividly desire it. And because our reason violently deters us from the brink, therefore do we the most impetuously approach it.* I could almost anticipate the precipitating buzz that would follow, after hurling my loathsome self before some seething bonnet speeding headlong at seventy miles an hour. It would be all over in a minute or less: I am felled by vehicles that just cannot get out of my way. My body falls into subsidence. My organs are ruptured. My bones are smashed. My face is besmirched by blood, snot, mucus and tears. The shadow of *morte* consumes my cells to naught before finally laying siege to my hippocampus. My life heights and my life lows flicker before me. My eyeballs roll back into oblivion. The Roman poet Catullus called death, *nox est perpetua una dormeinda*: *(one perpetual night to be slept without awakening)*. *Death is nothing to us*, according to Epicurus. *When we exist, death is not. When death exists, we are not.* Welsh poet Dylan Thomas meanwhile declared that *death shall have no dominion.* The thought of how my death would affect my mother prevented me from taking the plunge from this fastidious world. It was she that had given me life. I loved her too much to even prick her finger, never mind having her identify my detritus remains in a cold morgue. If my death weren't to exist for me, it would certainly upend her world till her final day. And in the afterlife, I'd be taken to Dante's *Wood of the Suicides*, where I'd be transformed into a withered, thorny tree and subject to the torment of Harpies. So I welched from leaping. The imp was silenced from his goading. I sat among the grass, before the phosphorescent full moon. My weeping gradually subsided. I kept on living. But, dear reader, I digress once more... Perhaps, in a future offering, I may return to what led me to this precipice. Perhaps I may not.

But back to the luckless Edgar, who himself arrived at Death's door in a state of delirium through the streets of Baltimore. He died days later in an infirmary. His death certificate is lost forever. The cause of his death, though often speculated, is not really known. Rufus Wilmot Griswold, his sworn nemesis, somehow became his literary executor and set out to ruin his reputation by publishing his memoir. His feeble publication contained forgeries that depicted Poe as depraved and insane. Griswold's attempts at ruining Poe, however, became dust. A few years later, he would lie under it. The nineteenth-century French poet Charles Baudelaire was an early translator of Poe's work from English into French. As a result, his penmanship became immensely popular in France and then Europe. But Poe had been long dead. He would know nothing of his fame.

Today, Zora Neale Hurston's literary exertions stand at the centerpiece of American literature, and the Harlem Renaissance. Her writings crystallized her personal struggles as an African-American woman living in the Deep South amidst the pestilence of racism. She was largely ignored in her lifetime. She was buried in an unmarked grave. Commercial interest in her work only came about in the decade after her death. *The New Negro: An Interpretation* is an anthology of essays and other compositions featuring some of the greatest African American writers of the early twentieth century: Langston Hughes, W. E. B Du Bois, Rudolph Fisher, E. Franklin Frazier among others and, of course, Hurston herself. Her sole contribution was a short story titled *Spunk*. The title character is cavorting with married Lena in plain sight. The local residents gossip. They goad her timid husband Joe into action. Unfortunately, he is killed in the resulting fracas with Spunk, who is considerably Herculean than he. Lena marries Spunk but matters worsen as he loses his mind. He is killed in a freak accident at work, convinced that the spirit of Joe pushed him onto the saw which he handled better than anybody. The story ends with the neighbors gossiping as to who will be Lena's new man. The story is rich with thrift and ambience, and the dialect of the Deep South.

Hurston's best-known work *Their Eyes Were Watching God* is a sturdy novel that defies the epoch it was written. The book is inexplicitly about racism, though its simmering presence is palpable. It was not unusual for African-American authors to articulate this most hardy of foes that constricted every sinew of their being. Hurston refused confinement. She defied categories. For she wrote about the life and times of Janie Crawford, spawned by rape and raised by her grandmother Nanny after being abandoned by her mother. Janie would not be defined by her humble beginnings, her subsequent strife, her three marriages, or the slaying of her third husband – the love of her life – in self-defense. The story ends with her acquittal. She becomes a woman of independent means.

Emily Dickinson, the third of my four chosen writers, lived in splendid isolation for much of her life. She seldom left home. She published no more than a dozen poems in her lifetime. Her poetry was just as stark and macabre as that of Poe's. She constantly explored issues surrounding death and immortality. Her writing was in concert with her eternal witness, or her daemon (as the ancient Greeks called it), for she required little outward experience. Therein lies one's best work, if one can parley the ecstasy and agony of penmanship that finespun the aorta. *Because I Could Not Stop For Death* is one of the many extraordinarily bewitching poems she composed in her solitude. *Because I Could Not Stop For Death*, she wrote. *He kindly stopped for me. The carriage held but ourselves, And Immortality...*

Death is a coachman who is abrupt in his intervention in this mortal coil, for who has the wherewithal to herald a ride for which there is no turning back? He appears agreeable in the first instant. She puts away her anxieties for the sake of civility. She becomes nostalgic when she hears the playing noises of children from the outside. As the sojourn to the grave progresses - *We passed the Setting Sun - Or rather, He passed us* - Death becomes obscure, sequestered, and she arrives at her final resting place. ... *We paused before a House that seemed a swelling of the ground — The Roof was scarcely visible — The Cornice — in the Ground — Since then — 'tis Centuries — and yet feels shorter than the Day I first surmised the Horses' Heads Were toward Eternity —*

I can recall my horripilation when I first read *Because I could not stop for Death*. It was at that age again, nineteen, when the aspirated tone of her couplets induced a concord with my fragile constitution. Dickinson's beguiling poem was perhaps the closest glance I could get to the other side of Death's door without sticking my head through the gap. One cannot not read her work seriously and wander away unreflective. Universally, she is today recognized as one of the greatest poets to have ever lived in all of America.

One of my lifetime long literary heroes, and the final of the four, Franz Kafka, also an unknown unknown, died in a sanatorium aged forty. I have yet to read a book that rivals the doughty opening line of a Kafka novel. In his classic work *Metamorphosis*, he begins thus: *One morning, when Gregor Samsa woke from his troubled dreams, he found himself transformed in his bed into a horrible vermin*. In another translation, he has metamorphosed into a *monstrous insect*. When I first read that chilling line, it was as if I'd been punched in the solar plexus. In *The Trial*, he begins thus: *Someone must have been telling lies about Josef K. He knew he had done nothing wrong but, one morning, he was arrested.* Throughout the book, we never learn of Josef K's crime. Neither does he. He attends court and attains legal representation. He is stonewalled by an annulled bureaucracy that is exhaustively endless and tires him out. At the end of the book, two men escort him to a quarry, where is executed... *like a dog.* Over the decades and centuries, millions have been slaughtered worse than cattle without just cause as to why they should no longer exist. As to why it is necessary for them to die at that moment. Must one simply die because he is a Tutsi or a Jew? Because she is gay or has a darker hue of skin? The horrors endured by our fellow brethren in their final breath are an inordinate tragedy. So long as Man believes his immutable traits grants him supremacy over others, and he possesses the means to murder those he considers lesser, his savagery will rear itself, from generation to generation. Forever.

Upon his death, Kafka requested his friend, Max Brod, to consume his entire literary catalog to the flame. We would not have known of Kafka or his fictions had Brod carried his final will. Kafka sought no fame whilst he lived. His writings lay unfinished upon his death. His works like *The Metamorphosis* and *The Trial* are among the classics of 20th century literature. *Josef K.* is among the most memorable characters I have read. Indeed, it would be great to be vindicated in one's lifetime. I have yet to meet an author who disagrees with me on this point. Perhaps, in all likelihood, Kafka may have held a different opinion.

Alas! I have no discipline as a writer. Neither have I yet to experience the writing romanticisms that have allegedly befallen other authors. Alcohol and cigars do not boost the moxie of my pen. Neither does it weaken it. All I have ever felt is angst, even upon the publication of my debut novel *The Nepenthe Park Chronicles*. I have no routine, ritual or schedule. I simply write by night. On alternate nights, always in sophrosyne. Insomnia, I hear you say? Nay, sleep is for the weak!

Sometimes, I manage three hundred words in one sitting. At best, I conjure up to a thousand. I do not suffer from Blank Page Syndrome. I steer clear from subjects I consider pabulum. The world is filled with whippets laden by pubertal and piteous interests. I can ill afford to fritter away my time when I have so little of it left.

I am only interested in what is equitable and what is authentic. I now write for my sole pleasure. That elicits the greatest reward. *Curving back within myself, I create again and again.* So says the Bhagavad Gita in chapter 9, verse 8. Still I persist, with enthusiasm and resourcefulness, the twin engines of my endeavor. Whatever works I leave behind will rightfully serve as my epitaph.

July 16, 2017.